The Exceptional Child

A Primer

Second Edition

Lita Linzer Schwartz

The Pennsylvania State University
Ogontz Campus

Wadsworth Publishing Company, Inc.
Belmont, California

Wadsworth Series in Special Education

Series Editor: Eli M. Bower
University of California, Berkeley

Deafness and Learning: A Psychosocial Approach
Hans G. Furth
The Catholic University of America

The Exceptional Child: A Primer, 2nd Ed.
Lita Linzer Schwartz
The Pennsylvania State University, Ogontz Campus

Visual Handicaps and Learning: A Developmental Approach
Natalie Barraga
The University of Texas at Austin

Education Editor: Roger Peterson

Front cover photo, part opening photos, Chapter 13 photo: Elizabeth Crews

© 1979 by Wadsworth Publishing Company, Inc.

© 1975 by Wadsworth Publishing Company, Inc., Belmont, California 94002.

Printed in the United States of America

1 2 3 4 5 6 7 8 9 10—83 82 81 80 79

Library of Congress Cataloging in Publication Data

Schwartz, Lita Linzer.
  The exceptional child.

  (Wadsworth series in special education)
  Bibliography: p.
  Includes index.
  1. Exceptional children. I. Title.
HQ773.S327 1979   371.9   78-21489
ISBN 0-534-00633-7

For my Mother, who taught me to care

Foreword to the Second Edition

A teacher asked me if increasing educational services to handicapped students was a result of new knowledge and skills. While legislation at federal and state levels has done much to promote programs for the handicapped, I was somewhat at a loss to point to breakthroughs in research or practice that made all this activity more effective or efficient for students. New and old concepts abound—mainstreaming, least restrictive environments, individual educational plans, resource specialists, and others soon to appear or disappear.

With the possible exception of the completely deaf and severely disturbed and retarded child, almost all special education children can now find places in regular schools—provided of course that the school can manage the extra services that these children require. This means knowing the special needs of children and what all school personnel can do about educating such children. The author has provided and updated such knowledge. Readers will find the material clear, honest, and comprehensive. For those interested in knowing and working with exceptional children, this is an excellent beginning.

Eli M. Bower
University of California, Berkeley

Foreword to the First Edition

One of the few advantages of aging is the opportunity to see things in perspective. The "figure" and "ground" related to the education of exceptional children have in the last twenty-five years undergone significant shifts. In the late 1940s the "ground," public education and public support, were only beginning to accept handicapped children as part of the picture. The "figure" in those years was dim, not clearly understood or identified. Some of the larger school districts and communities had some programs for children with retarded mental development and children with sensory and motor problems. Some of the larger states had special schools for the blind and for the deaf. For the most part, however, many of the handicapped children received little educational or supportive services in schools or communities.

In mid-century, aided by significant shifts in attitude brought on in large part by the formation of national parent groups of handicapped children, the "ground" gave way slightly and began to accept the realities and needs of handicapped children. During this period, the major educational resource was the special classroom, small self-contained groups, with specially trained teachers and situated somewhere in a regular school. As a consultant for a state department of education in this field, I met with and assisted school officials, training institutions, public officials, parents, and interested others while developing exemplary classes for retarded children. At that time, many school districts were educating all kinds and degrees of handicapped children in separate schools. Some parents of handicapped children were frightened at the prospect of their children going to the same school as their nonhandicapped peers. In one case I still vividly recall, a district solicited our help in replacing its special school with special classes in regular schools. The superintendent called to let me know that I faced an angry, up-in-arms parent group who bitterly opposed the change. None of us could guarantee that all the real and imagined fears for their children could be avoided. We discussed the risks in changing the nature and philosophy of the program as well as the risks in not changing. "Our children must learn to live with others and others have to learn to live with them. It may hurt but it may hurt more if we don't do it.'' So said one of the more persuasive parents. They agreed to try it.

Such changes were not without heartaches and failures. On the whole, such special classes flourished and in many places became models of what elementary education could be. Teachers were trained in the use of special curricula, given ample support in equipment and resource staff. In a short time, administrators, other teachers, and the community could point with pride and a sense of regenerated virtue at their successful special classes for handicapped children. The picture was not that rosy but better than expected.

With state and local support, special classes grew in numbers and in services to more kinds of handicapped children, especially seriously handicapped children. In a sense the success of the special class programs encouraged some to apply such approaches to all difficult or defeated children. So children from various cultural backgrounds—including ethnic groups, ghettos, and extreme rural areas—were temporarily sheltered in the calmer waters of special classes; and many of these children should not have been in the classes.

Beginning in the middle 1960s and early 1970s, the figure-ground began to shift markedly as schools found themselves seriously mandated with the education of large numbers of alienated and unreachable children. Labels and concepts were hedged and attempts made to serve children meaningfully and realistically under misleading banners.

The current figure-ground for handicapped children is mainstreaming—a term which suggests "we're all in it together.'' Wherever possible handicapped children will be with their peers and adjustments will be made to meet the different rates of learning or other learning problems.

This book will serve as an introduction to the changing and present figure-grounds in the past, present, and future of handicapped children in our society. It can whet your interest and appetite to learn more about the groups of children who may need extra help in their growth and development. I recall someone saying that education in a democracy does not mean the same education for all but a different education for each. It is this ''difference'' in the pursuit of equity and excellence which is celebrated in the following pages.

Eli M. Bower

Preface to the Second Edition

The need for all school personnel to be informed about exceptional children's needs and abilities has been accelerated by the passage of the Education for All Handicapped Children Act of 1975. Thus, the value of an introductory volume such as this one, that provides both information and resource sources, is greatly increased. Passage of the act also means, however, that there is a need to bring the material in the book up to date.

Although the format of the first edition has been retained, there are several changes in this revision:

1. Explanation of "mainstreaming" and "IEPs" (including sample IEPs)
2. Etiology of exceptionality where appropriate
3. Material on the "battered child"
4. Material on the preschool exceptional child
5. Updating of resource materials (including Canadian references)
6. Changing patterns of teacher education
7. Addition of a glossary
8. A more balanced use of female and male pronouns

Several colleagues who have used the first edition were kind enough to comment on its virtues and deficiencies. In addition, Lottie Rosen (Merritt College, Oakland), Peggy D. Forsyth (University of New Hampshire), and Charlotte A. Shroyer (University of Maryland) reviewed the draft of the revision and offered valuable and realistic comments. This new edition reflects as many of the much-appreciated suggestions as possible. Special thanks are due to Michael Rothstein for sharing his gifts and expertise.

The support and assistance of Roger S. Peterson, Education Editor at Wadsworth, is gratefully acknowledged. As always, the patience and understanding of Melvin, Arthur, Joshua, and Frederic with the author in their midst is much appreciated.

Lita Linzer Schwartz

Preface to the First Edition

Too often, we who work with children that differ from the so-called "average" tend to pay more attention to the disabilities of these children than to their abilities. The purpose of this book is to assist educators and other adults to enhance the abilities of "different" or exceptional children.

This primer is not intended to replace more comprehensive texts on the psychology and education of exceptional children. The emphasis here is on the awareness of the scope and nature of the challenges, what is being and remains to be done to meet the challenges, and the educational, rehabilitative, and legal resources available to persons working with the exceptional child—for parents, classroom teachers, school administrators, social workers, paraprofessionals, and other personnel.

Information has been gathered from a wide variety of sources: federal and state legislation, publications of the Council for Exceptional Children and similar groups, observations, conversations, professional meetings, and both professional and nonprofessional publications. Extensive references offer the reader an opportunity to familiarize himself with the many aspects of work with exceptional children. These range from self-care to mobility, special teaching techniques to parental attitudes, preschool programs to vocational preparation. Kaslow's article, Appendix A, demonstrates an application of the creative arts approach to special education. Also included in the Appendixes are lists of resource agencies, particularly useful directories, films, and special groups dealing with different exceptions.

Children with problems have been a reality to me and a personal concern since I first met them in my own childhood. Sensitivity to their special needs was developed early through exposure to my mother's work with orthopedically handicapped children and has grown through my work with emotionally disturbed and learning-disadvantaged youngsters, my acquaintance with adults who have a gift for emphasizing these children's abilities, and my interaction with families that included children with one or more of the handicaps included here. Once the diagnosis is made by the professionals and accepted by the parents, the universal question is "What do we do now?" I hope this primer succeeds both in providing some answers and leading the reader to his or her own answers to that question.

Several people have shared their experiences, resources, and expertise with me as this book moved from idea to reality. My thanks to Patricia J. Elliott, Judy Featherman, Harry Freedman, Eve Levitan, and Louise B. Sandler for their help. I am particularly indebted to my colleague, Sunnie R. Spiegel, who provided much appreciated time and effort as a sounding board for ideas and a reader of every chapter. Thanks is due, too, to Betsy Olsen, for her skill in typing the manuscript.

Dick Greenberg, editor at Wadsworth Publishing, has been most supportive of this effort from our first meeting. No author could ask for more.

To my husband, Melvin, and our sons, Arthur, Joshua, and Frederic, who once again have survived book-cluttered rooms and a preoccupied wife and mother, my affectionate gratitude for their patience and forbearance.

Lita Linzer Schwartz

Contents

One: **Setting a Foundation**   1

    Chapter 1. Educating the Exceptional Child: An Introduction   2

    Chapter 2. Personality Development and Exceptional Children   7

Two: **The Intellectually Different**   13

    Chapter 3. Gifted and Creative Children   15

    Chapter 4. Mentally Retarded Children   23

    Chapter 5. Children with Learning Disabilities   31

Three: **The Physically Different**   39

    Chapter 6. Orthopedically Handicapped Children   41

    Chapter 7. Hearing-Impaired Children   49

    Chapter 8. Visually Impaired Children   57

    Chapter 9. Multiply Handicapped Children   65

Four: **Oral Communication Difficulties**   71

    Chapter 10. Speech-Impaired Children   72

    Chapter 11. Language-Handicapped Children   77

Five: **The Culturally Different**   87

    Chapter 12. Learning-Disadvantaged Children   88

    Chapter 13. Cultural Minorities   97

Six: The Psychosocially Different   105

Chapter 14. Emotionally Troubled Children   106

Chapter 15. Socially Maladjusted Children   115

Seven: Afterviews   125

Chapter 16. Administration and Special Education   126

Chapter 17. Special Considerations   135

References

Appendices

A. "The Use of Creative Arts Therapy in Special Education," by Florence W. Kaslow   179

B. Visual Aids for Special Education   188

C. Agencies and Resource Centers   197

D. Individual Education Programs (Sample IEPs)   202

E. Literature and Exceptionality   216

F. Glossary   218

Index   219

One

Setting the Foundation

To set the stage for a discussion of exceptional children and their needs, it is appropriate to inquire about the size of the population involved, the diversity within that population, and the considerations that must be taken into account in working with this population. These inquiries are made and partially answered in the first chapter.

When discussing any children, it is also appropriate to refer to their various stages of development, or at least some of the theories about those stages. There are theories relevant to children's cognitive or intellectual learning, psychosexual development, motor development, and so on. These theories help teachers, parents, and others to pinpoint strengths and weaknesses for children for more effective and more individualized instruction. In the present context, however, it seemed wisest to focus initially on children's psychosocial development, that is, how they develop their personalities. When we first meet people, after all, it is their "personality," be it displayed in sunny or sour behaviors, that makes the first impression. The relationship between the normal progress of psychosocial development and the differences that make children exceptional is an important one, with much interaction between the two. This relationship is the basis for the discussion in Chapter 2.

Together, the two chapters establish a foundation for the presentations in the balance of the book. They provide perspective and orientation.

1

Educating the Exceptional Child: An Introduction

Most of us have directly experienced the "normal" or "average" classroom in which an entire class is taught a body of content in a fairly standardized manner. Recent innovations in education have made it possible for each pupil to progress at his or her own pace through individualized instruction. However, when the learner's pace and/or abilities are very different from the average range, individualized instruction alone may not meet the child's needs. According to the U.S. Office of Education, there are more than 7 million children who, because they differ from the average, are considered to be exceptional. As you can see from the data in Table 1-1, the majority of these children are not being served.

Educators have a longstanding goal of providing equal opportunity to learn for all students. "Special education," then, is an all-encompassing term describing attempts to modify classroom programs to allow nonaverage learners to achieve their full learning potential. Special education consists of anything from a small group session one hour per week to a full-time program in a special school.

State Responsibility

State laws vary in their specifications for programs for exceptional children. Generally, however, they affirm the "right to learn" for all children, describe the populations to be served under special education provisions, delineate administrative and financial responsibilities, and, in some cases, stipulate the number of children at varying age levels in specified types of classes. The laws are intended to protect the rights of exceptional children and their parents, while providing appropriate educational programs, and to protect the special teacher from unrealistic teaching situations: overcrowded classes, many types of exceptional children in a single class, and unspecified and unlimited teacher functions.

All states take responsibility for the exceptional child's right to education. Several states specify upper limits for class size, the specifications varying

Table 1-1.   Estimated Number of Handicapped Children Served and Unserved by Type of Handicap (USOE/BEH/ASB)

	1975–76 Served (Projected)	1975–76 Unserved	Total Handicapped Children Served and Unserved	Percent Served	Percent Unserved
Total age 0–19	4,310,000	3,577,000	7,887,000	55	45
Total age 6–19	3,860,000	2,840,000	6,700,000	58	42
Total age 0–5	450,000	737,000	1,187,000	38	62
Speech impaired	2,020,000	273,000	2,293,000	88	12
Mentally retarded	1,350,000	157,000	1,507,000	90	10
Learning disabilities	260,000	1,706,000	1,966,000	13	87
Emotionally disturbed	255,000	1,055,000	1,310,000	19	81
Crippled and other health impaired	255,000	73,000	328,000	78	22
Deaf	45,000	4,000	49,000	92	8
Hard of hearing	66,000	262,000	328,000	20	80
Visually handicapped	43,000	23,000	66,000	65	35
Deaf-blind and other multihandicapped	16,000	24,000	40,000	40	60

Source: National Advisory Committee on the Handicapped, 1977 Annual Report.

according to handicap and age level. Almost all states have special state schools for specific handicaps, such as deafness and blindness, in their education code. Others provide special schools within state institutions or public welfare programs. States may or may not provide funds for physical plant and equipment to local school districts for special education classes.

Under state laws the learners who need special handling may be grouped in a number of categories: intellectually different, physically different, psychosocially different, and those with difficulties in oral communication. Within these categories, laws may specify subcategories according to the modifications in program and setting required.

Each group of exceptional children calls for special teaching methods, variations in the teaching material, and, in many cases, modifications in the physical facilities of the classroom. The teachers who work with these students also need special preparation in their college years.

Mainstreaming

For many years, educators, parents, and others concerned with exceptional children have argued about the relative desirability of segregation or integration of exceptional children into regular classes. Since the passage of PL 94-142, the Education for All Handicapped Children Act, in 1975, the issue has taken on new dimensions. The act requires that a free public education be provided for all handicapped children, ages 3 through 21 years, in the least restrictive environment appropriate to the child's needs and abilities, at no cost to the child's

Case in Point

Because of the recent legislation mandating mainstreaming, it is urgent that those planning a new school plant or renovating an old one consider the needs of *all* children. Architects and special education personnel should collaborate in the planning stage, carefully considering each group's strengths, weaknesses, and goals and translating this knowledge into a compatible physical environment.

The McDonald Comprehensive Elementary School in Warminster, Pennsylvania, is one example of this type of preplanning. For the orthopedically handicapped, the designers have provided two classrooms and an adjacent therapy room, with ramps rather than stairs linking wings of the building, as well as a large swimming pool (used for other purposes as well) and specially adapted lunchroom tables. The trainable retarded have a suite of small rooms approximating the major rooms in a home so that they may learn self-help and household routines by actually performing relevant tasks. The gifted children benefit from a well-stocked library and instructional materials center. Each of these groups also has opportunities to interact with children in regular classes, some through integration in those classes, the lunchroom, assemblies, and so on.

parents or guardians. This does *not* mean that special education programs will be abandoned and all exceptional children thrown willy-nilly into regular classes. It *does* mean that exceptional children will be integrated into regular classes or "mainstreamed" to the degree appropriate for them. Their unique needs will be provided for through specially designed instruction, or special education, as before.

Appropriate schooling for each child is based on a multifaceted assessment of his or her academic, physical, and social abilities and needs. The results of the evaluation are the basis for designing the child's individualized education program (IEP). The written IEP spells out the nature of the personnel, resources, and environment that are expected to be most helpful to the child's progress. It also provides for revision of the IEP based on continuing evaluation of the child's progress toward prestated goals.

The IEP will allow a great many handicapped children to spend part or all of the school day in regular classes. This presents a variety of challenges. The regular classroom teacher has not usually been prepared to work with the handicapped, or even gifted and talented, children. The passage of PL 94-142 is therefore bringing about changes in preservice and in service teacher education to prepare teaching personnel for mainstreaming. We have already noted the need to modify the physical environment to accommodate handicapped children. (Note: This also applies to higher education institutions that receive federal funds, under Section 504 of the Vocational Rehabilitation Act of 1973). Another challenge to be faced is the acceptance of the exceptional child by his or her classmates. If the child receives appropriate academic instruction in the regular classroom but is ignored or taunted by classmates, then the placement is not satisfactory. These challenges will be considered further in Chapter 16.

For those children for whom mainstreaming on a full-time basis is inappropriate, special education teachers, resource rooms, and special schools will continue to be available. The principal concern of the new legislation is the child's welfare, not his or her adjustment to a predetermined slot in the school system.

Assessment

The Education for All Handicapped Children Act mandates that states seek out all of their handicapped children and assess both their needs and their abilities. Initial screening procedures may reveal areas in which children have problems, but these are too unreliable to be effective diagnostic tools. Educational diagnosis, using tests that are as unbiased as possible, indicates the skill levels at which the child is functioning in reading (or reading readiness), language, mathematics, and other academic areas. Medical, developmental, social, and emotional histories also contribute to the child's assessment. The total team evaluation is oriented to planning appropriate team instruction rather than to pinning a diagnostic label on the child. The resulting IEP is developed by the child's teacher and another qualified special education person, in consultation with the child's parents and, if at all possible, the child himself.

The law requires that "all IEPs include statements of the child's present level of educational performance, annual goals, short-term instructional objectives, the extent to which the child will participate in regular programs, the dates during which the IEP will be applicable, and the criteria and procedures that will be used in evaluating the program's effectiveness."[1] These specifications are unusual in that they call for continuing evaluation and accountability. Also, through forcing a written program, they make the actual teaching task somewhat easier.

The shifting view of educating exceptional children has also led to changes in preparing their teachers. Although teacher training in this book and in most states is oriented to specific certification, Pennsylvania, the District of Columbia, and a few other certifying state education departments now require that the teacher be a generalist in special education. There is some controversy about this policy. On the one hand, many exceptional children manifest more than one special condition (e.g., learning disabled with emotional problems), so that the teacher needs to be prepared in more than one area. On the other hand, critics of the

---

[1] "Implementing the IEP concept," *American Education*, 13, No. 7 (1977), p. 7.

policy question whether the generalist is sufficiently prepared to teach any of the exceptional children effectively. We will probably not have a definitive answer to this question until we have had several years of experience with both mainstreaming and generalist preparation.

Realities of Teaching

In any case, the emphasis in special education, as it should be in all education, is on the abilities, rather than the disabilities, of the exceptional child. The blind can play basketball, the deaf can respond to rhythm, and the retarded can function as useful members of society. To accomplish these things, the child needs first, parents who encourage a positive self-concept, and second, teachers who teach with patience, imagination, adaptability, and an ability to juggle the reality of the present with the goals of the future. The college coursework for future teachers may pose few problems, but the realities of weeks of helping children to learn with only occasional minute signs of progress may not be sufficient reinforcement for otherwise well-intentioned teachers. Warmth and a sincere concern for the growth of these children are not enough, although these qualities are essential starting points for a positive learning situation.

Teachers have a marvelous power in their hands, for they can significantly affect a child's life. Not only can they modify curriculum content as needed and control the mode of instruction, but they also set the climate of the learning environment. They can help or hurt the children entrusted to them—a statement especially true of teachers of exceptional children.

The most effective way for you to investigate the field of special education is to become involved with the children themselves, for there is no substitute for real-life experience. Ideally, by the time a prospective teacher reaches the student-teaching term, he or she should have had several such opportunities for direct classroom experience.

This primer is designed to introduce you to and familiarize you with the special needs of each group of exceptional children and the special talents required of their teachers. We shall be asking the following questions about each group:

1. What are the characteristics of the group?
2. What are realistic educational goals for the group?
3. What modifications in physical facilities and/or instructional materials are necessary?
4. What training is necessary for teachers of these children?

Twelve of the following chapters have a common format that specifically answers these four questions for each group of children.

2   Personality Development and Exceptional Children

Exceptional children, like other people, need to feel good about themselves. They grow in many of the same ways as other children, but, because of the ways in which they may differ from their peers, may have a more difficult time achieving a positive self-concept or feeling of self-esteem. This is a major concern to parents and educators. A child's personality depends in part on her view of herself. How does that self-concept develop? How do self-esteem and personality development relate to the exceptional child? In this chapter, I will turn primarily to the work of two men, Erik Erikson (1950) and Stanley Coopersmith (1967), to answer these questions. Together, their work has great meaning for all concerned with exceptional children.

Development of Self-Esteem

Coopersmith maintains that an individual's self-esteem stems from four factors, or antecedents: a feeling of competence, a feeling of one's significance to others, a sense of virtue (or "doing the right thing"), and an awareness of one's power. He suggests, however, that an individual is more likely to see himself in terms of perceived deficiencies, and thereby develop a negative sense of self-esteem, rather than in terms of areas of strength. Thus, a handicapped child may focus on his lack of competence in a certain skill and lose sight of his significance to those who love him. Or, he may employ "two bases that are mutually incompatible, thereby leading him to believe that he has failed to live up to one of them" (Coopersmith, pp. 262–263). Consider, for example, the creative child, who is frequently nonconformist in her thinking or behavior. Instead of being proud of her creative ability, she might focus on criticism she receives for not doing things the "right" way. Or, a culturally different child may focus on her lack of power over her environmental status despite the positive significance she has to members of her family. In both illustrations, the child may have an ideal self which is competent and powerful but her self-concept cannot match the ideal. The conflict, or dissonance, between these two views of oneself can be quite damaging, particularly to the exceptional child.

The factors leading to one's self-esteem develop during childhood and adolescence. Erikson has shown how the self-concept, which includes self-esteem, is the result of the resolution of conflicts that occur at different stages in these years.

Table 2-1.   Erikson's Stages of Development

Approximate Ages	Developmental Conflict
Birth-2 years	trust vs. distrust
2-4 years	autonomy vs. shame and doubt
4-7 years	initiative vs. guilt
7-12 years	industry vs. inferiority
Adolescence	identity vs. role diffusion

Infants begin to develop a self-concept through their nonverbal feelings, or percepts, about how others perceive them. From birth to 1½ to 2 years, the infant begins to develop a relationship with her parents and begins to sense their attitudes toward her through their actions and tones of voice. If her parents are dependable and warm, answering her needs when she cries, she develops a sense of trust in them and a sense that she is worthy of their attention. If, on the other hand, they are not dependable and warm, she may feel that other people are not worthy of her trust and that they do not care for her because she is somehow unworthy of their love. Emotionally disturbed children have usually grown up in such situations of distrust. To use Coopersmith's term, such infants perceive themselves as not having significance to others. (If you doubt that an infant can respond to a tone of voice or to nonverbal behavior, try a small experiment. You might prefer to do this with a pet rather than a baby. For example, tell a dog in firm, angry tones what a good dog he is, and watch his tail go down. Then, tell him how naughty he is in a warm voice, and watch his tail wag.) The orthopedically handicapped child quickly learns to distrust the adults who feel guilty or hostile toward her, and as she grows older, she may blame their behavior on her lack of physical competence. The hearing-impaired child may develop a sense of distrust because he cannot hear the responses of others and, through misinterpretation, feel that he is unworthy of their attention. He, too, assumes that his lack of competence is at the heart of people's reactions to him. In some cases, of course, parental neglect is a reality, but due to deficiencies in the parents rather than in the child. The very young child cannot make this distinction, however, and believes that he is somehow not worthy of care and attention.

Jean Piaget refers to this early period as the sensorimotor stage, when, he states, routine and increasing voluntary control over physical actions occurs. The establishment of routine is important in the first two years because the infant is learning to exercise increasing control over her physical actions. A routine lets the infant know that her adult caretakers consider her important and assures her that her care is not haphazard. Secondly, the ability to exercise control over one's actions at this stage is a source of feelings of competence. If the exceptional child lacks the ability to exercise this control because she is physically handicapped, she may focus on her inability to the detriment of self-concept. Routine care by her caretakers may be so constant, furthermore, that she has no opportunity to practice whatever abilities she may have. By the age of 2, the exceptional child's self-esteem can obviously be suffering from a case of "What's wrong with me? Why can't I do that?"

Later Development

Erikson states that the 2- to 4-year-old enters a second stage in which she experiences a conflict between a sense of autonomy and a sense of shame and doubt. This period is characterized by increased mobility, growing independence, and rapid language acquisition for the average child. It is also a time when the child becomes aware of other children, begins to interact with them, and begins to compare his accomplishments to theirs. A gifted child, for example, may do very well in expressing herself verbally and getting about on her own but feel frustrated because she has no power to exercise her growing desires for independence. Or a handicapped child may have difficulty moving around and be frustrated by his lack of competence. Thus, these children are feeling shame and doubt at their inability to act on their desire for independence. Needless to say, if parents stress children's abilities, the children develop greater self-esteem and feel less hampered by their deficiencies.

In the immediate preschool and primary years, ages 4 to 7, children are notoriously curious. If they exercise their initiative without reproach, they develop a sense of power and competence. On the other hand, if they are rebuked for asking questions or exploring their environment, they develop feelings of guilt and unworthiness. Children who are overprotected and not permitted to explore may start to believe that they lack the ability to climb, visit others, ride a tricycle, and so on. The conflict between initiative and guilt is particularly difficult to resolve for emotionally disturbed children. If adult reaction to their exploratory behavior is largely negative, they grow increasingly anxious and guilt-ridden to the point where they become extremely withdrawn and unwilling to venture out on their own. Or, some children respond to this conflict by acting impulsively without thinking and without feelings of guilt, leading ultimately to asocial behavior in later childhood and adolescence.

At the end of this third stage of development, most children enter school. Children who have not found others trustworthy in their early years and are doubtful of their abilities and ashamed of their behavior are often counted among the emotionally disturbed when they enter school. Children with learning disabilities, too, have probably come to believe that they can't trust their own perceptions or body. Their behavior may strongly resemble that of disturbed children, and schools must be careful in their diagnosis so as not to mislabel learning-disability children as disturbed children.

Once children do attend school, their differences become even more apparent than in the earlier years. (Not attending school at all, of course, due to disabilities, makes one even *more* different.) During the school years, there are more criteria against which to measure oneself, the most important being competence—academic, athletic, and so on. Erikson rightfully calls this the stage of industry versus inferiority. The normal child who achieves less than her best friend is either demoralized, accepting of the realistic difference in abilities, or challenged. For the exceptional child with handicaps, differences in ability are too often both demoralizing and frustrating, and not often enough accepted realistically or as a challenge to do well in some other endeavor. The retarded child should not have to wallow in misery because of his lack of intellectual achievement in comparison with average children, nor should the handicapped one be made to suffer because she can't play "catch" with her classmates at

---

Case in Point

At age five, Ned's parents were told that he should repeat kindergarten because he was "obviously unready" for first grade. Despite the teacher's vague reasons for this recommendation, he was promoted. In first grade, he was declared retarded because of his inability to read aloud clearly, lack of participation in class "show-and-tell" activities, and reluctance to play with his peers at recess. He also refused to draw, a common activity in the primary grades. The teacher commented on all these behaviors in front of the class, adding intense embarrassment to the frustrations Ned was already experiencing.

What were the facts? Due to prenatal injuries, Ned had a severe speech problem, an orthopedic problem which made him unable to run, and poor hand-eye coordination. An independent psychological evaluation revealed that, far from being retarded, Ned had an I.Q. in the 135 to 145 range.

Because of the negative behaviors of his early teachers, Ned viewed himself for several years as unacceptable to others. Fortunately, he *was* able to read well (silently) with good comprehension, and he was strongly self-motivated to learn despite his physical difficulties. Today he is a gifted college senior planning to become a research chemist, gregarious, and reasonably self-confident in social as well as academic areas.

But what would have happened if his parents had believed those early teachers? Or if his teachers had refused to accept the facts?

recess. Indeed, a major reason for special education programs has been to reduce such frustrations.

In approaching exceptional children, teachers learn to accept realistic limitations while encouraging the children to put forth effort in tasks in which they can be successful. Since learning disabilities in children are often not discovered until they enter school, teachers need to expend special effort to undo the damage to self-esteem that many such children have experienced as a result of constant failures.

The last of Erikson's stages that has relevance for exceptional children is probably the one for which he is best known—the "identity crisis" of adolescence. Erikson labels this conflict "identity vs. role diffusion." Again, this stage is difficult for normal as well as exceptional children, for they are seeking their own personalities, the "real me." The emotionally disturbed, with their long history of negative self-concept and low self-esteem, seem to have the greatest problem during this period. Their doubt of their significance to others affects their competence. The socially maladjusted, who have come to believe they lack "virtue," may try to raise their self-esteem and find an identity through the exercise of "power," as demonstrated in antisocial behavior. The retarded, although chronological adolescents, may not reach the search for identity for several years beyond their peers. They may, however, exhibit role diffusion because of having a child's mind in an adolescent body. The gifted children, on the other hand, may experience this conflict prematurely because of the opposite situation: an adolescent's mind in a child's body. Their independence, desire for power, and competence may overwhelm their parents at this stage, creating further conflict.

Exceptional children, therefore, face the same conflicts in growing up as do other children. However, as I have tried to show in this brief discussion of theory, there are additional complicating factors for exceptional children. Thus, parents and all school personnel need to build the children's sense of their own importance and help them increase their competence so that their conflicts can be resolved on the positive side of Erikson's ledger. This theme will be repeated many times in the following pages as we discuss specific groups of children. Emotional problems too often complicate, and sometimes overshadow, the primary problems of a child, making it all the more difficult for the child to achieve success in any area. Thus, the urgency of promoting emotional adjustment needs to be recognized by all those involved with exceptional children.

Two

The Intellectually Different

Children who are academically gifted, creative, retarded, or learning disabled all fall into the category discussed in this section. With the exception of some retarded children, these children don't look different from their classmates. However, they do often behave differently from the average child as a result of their abilities, interests, and experiences. And they do learn differently from the average child—in pace, depth of comprehension, and ability to apply what they have learned. For these reasons, the intellectually different call for special attention from teachers and parents.

Educators usually distinguish the intellectually different child on the basis of standardized tests, observations of the child's behavior and rate of development, and other less formal measures. Intelligence test scores (usually referred to as an intelligence quotient, or "I.Q." score) can show how a child compares to the average performance of children of the same age. The average I.Q. equals 100, but scores in the range, roughly, of 90 to 110 are also accepted as average. The statistical normal curve shown in the figure on the following page illustrates the distribution of intelligence generally found in the population. A single test score, particularly if derived from a group test of intelligence, should not be accepted as the sole indicator of "difference," however. The score indicates at what level the child is functioning that day on that test. A group test does not take into consideration whether the child's functioning was affected by ill health, a family disturbance, test anxiety, or test conditions.

Developmental norms, derived from thousands of psychological and pediatric observations over the years, are particularly useful with the child below school age. There are average age ranges for walking, talking, various other motor activities, interaction with family members and peers, self-care capabilities, and so on. According to child psychologists, for example, a child of 2 should walk and talk, assuming normal physical conditions. A physically able 3-year-old who does neither might be mentally retarded, or might have some other contributing problem. A 1-year-old who performs at the level of the average 2-year-old might be considered gifted.

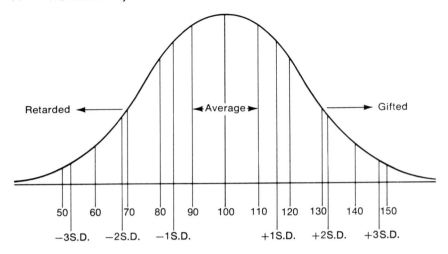

Retarded ◄──────── ◄Average► ────────► Gifted

50   60   70   80   90   100   110   120   130   140   150

−3S.D.   −2S.D.   −1S.D.   +1S.D.   +2S.D.   +3S.D.

Distribution of Intelligence Test Scores

Combined with careful testing, a case history of the child's development, relevant medical information, and performance records, parents' or teachers' informal observations in play and work situations can help to "fill out" the picture of the child's intellectual abilities and give us clues to how we can help the child learn to function in society.

3

Gifted and Creative Children

Group Characteristics

As soon as exceptional children are mentioned, people tend to think of deficits and handicaps. Gifted and creative children, however, make up the one group that is abundantly endowed but frequently overlooked when provision is made for special classes. The public too often assumes that intellectually gifted and creative children can go forward by their own efforts and without public support. However, this is no more true for this group of children than for any other group.

Intellectually gifted children usually score well above the average range on intelligence tests (usually I.Q. 130 and above) or on other academic measures. That is, they are as far above the "average" as the retarded are below. Their level of achievement is usually more than one grade level above the average of their peers, although some are underachievers for various reasons and may not even be identified as gifted. They may have an intellectual affinity for most subject areas, or, more often, their interests will lean toward a specific field, such as mathematics, physics, social sciences, or foreign languages.

The gifted child may also show his abilities in other ways: resourceful thinking abilities, generalizing ability, perceptive ability, perseverance, logical thinking, and curiosity. Gifted children can be, and often are, problems to their teachers because they outrace them in their areas of competence.

The creative child's gifts do not necessarily center on an academic field. She may shine in writing, art, music, problem-solving, spatial relations, science, mechanical arts, or leadership. Most studies indicate that the creative child is highly curious, persistent in her creative pursuits, and often nonconformist in behavior as well as above average in academic intelligence. Teachers may view the creative child's behavior as peculiar or troublesome because she refuses to conform to classroom standards of behavior or daydreams in class.

Identification of both the gifted and the creative must be made on the basis of more than routine intelligence or achievement tests. First of all, not all of these children test well, whether because of test anxiety, boredom, ability to see an unanticipated and therefore uncredited but superior answer, or some other reason. Secondly, most education-oriented tests are tied to a standard curriculum and may not tap the gifted student's area(s) of expertise or the creative child's divergent thinking abilities or specific talents.

What are alternative identification techniques? One is careful observation of the youth's vocabulary, discussion topics, peer relationships, elective activities, and extracurricular interests. Another possibility is to use creativity tests and tasks such as those developed by Guilford, Torrance, Parnes, and others. Yet a third alternative is to use a peer evalation technique that describes various nameless children in terms of behaviors (e.g., leadership, knowledge, problem-solving ability). Each youngster in the class then writes next to the paragraph the name of a classmate who most closely matches the description. This technique might be particularly effective with culturally different pupils who are gifted and/or creative but do not test well or meet the school's academic standards because of language or experience difficulties.

Case in Point

Picture a 12-year-old girl with braces playing a difficult violin concerto with a major symphony orchestra. See her in the classroom, where she earns high grades and is considered extremely gifted. Watch her as a pre-teenager concerned about buying a new bicycle and a small, "one-person" dog. This is Dylana Jenson, already a master violinist, but with the interests typical of her age as well.

According to the Associated Press story about Dylana, she practices four hours a day in the midst of a bubbling family. Her older brother (14) plays the cello and classical guitar, her younger brother (11) sculpts, writes plays and short stories, and gives mime plays, and her 13-year-old sister acts and studies ballet. The mother of these talented youngsters is a former teacher of musical history, and their father writes film scripts.

From "A Family of Gifts,"
The Philadelphia Inquirer, September 1, 1973.

Group Goals

Goals for gifted children should be basically the same as for all other children—that is, to provide them with as many opportunities to use their abilities as possible. Gifted children need as much encouragement as other children, for, despite the good fortune of their gifts, they can still find it painful to be different from their peers.

Despite prevalent stereotypes, gifted children are not automatically physical, emotional, or social misfits. However, they may find their talents give rise to rivalries and anxieties within their families. Thus, one goal should be easy accessibility to professional counseling for parents of the gifted. Such "preventive medicine" would tend to reduce undue psychological strain on the child before it becomes a real source of difficulty for her.

Some parents and teachers tend to push children with superior intelligence—aiming at sending such children to college at age 15 and expecting a Ph.D. at age 20. A more compassionate goal, however, is to encourage a gifted child to progress at his own pace, allowing the child to experience the joys and jolts of childhood and adolescence, while providing a wide variety of intellectual and interpersonal stimulation. The more challenges the child meets, the better prepared he will be to choose personal and vocational goals in keeping with his highest interests and abilities.

For the highly creative child, psychological freedom to create is another essential. Her snowman may have a red pepper for a nose instead of a carrot, or her sense of pitch may be outraged by an out-of-tune piano. "Tinkering" with an old car may be the first step to a career in modern technology. Thus, it is important that concerned adults provide opportunities for the child to explore and develop her special gift. The role of the teacher and parent should be that of catalyst, rather than judge or exploiter. Within this freedom, both the creative and the intellectually gifted child need to develop self-direction and self-discipline.

Both groups also need to be encouraged in the development of social and personal skills. Consideration of others' needs can coexist with independent thinking and action. Curiosity, determination, perseverance, and sincerity are other characteristics we hope to see manifested in the child's behavior as she matures. In the intellectual or creative realm, realistic critical thinking and an increase in the ability to make wise decisions are two important skills that the child can be helped to develop. It is important for both parents and teachers to remember that the ultimate overriding goal for the gifted and the creative is to help them become effective whole persons.

Modification of Education
and Facilities

A survey of state support for special education for the gifted (Laird, 1971) showed that of the thirty-seven states from which responses were received, only seventeen had laws providing special programs for this group. Only four of these seventeen states provided special equipment for gifted children's classes. Only three states—Florida, Kansas, and Louisiana—had special requirements of professional preparation and experience for teachers of the gifted. In Pennsylvania and North Carolina, measures for the handicapped have been extended to support programs for the gifted and talented as well (Reynolds and Birch, 1977).

There are a number of alternatives available in specializing education for the gifted and creative. Under the prevailing disenchantment with "skipping" such students, enrichment is the most frequently exercised option. Enrichment programs for gifted and creative children take the form of individual in-depth study separate from daily class assignments, or additional studies using different resource materals, seminar sessions with itinerant teachers, or intensive lessons in music or art, fieldwork projects, visits to museums or other places of special interest, or to meet with resource people in the community. Such activities should be planned in keeping with the age, achievement level, maturity, and special capabilities of the individual child. If necessary, enrichment programs can be planned for gifted and/or creative children from several schools. Support for such special projects can be obtained through Titles III and V of the Elementary and Secondary Education Act and the Education Amendments of 1974, Special Projects Act (Section 404).

Facilities at the elementary level for experimentation in the biological or physical sciences should be provided, with faculty available as resource rather than directive personnel. Similarly, science-math tables equipped with concrete materials can permit the gifted child to investigate concepts on her own. Film-making projects are another avenue of expression for the gifted child interested in the social sciences or the arts.

Parents and teachers can enhance the child's learning by encouraging her curiosity while freely admitting their own areas of ignorance and guiding the child to sources where she can discover the answers. It is essential, then, for gifted children to learn appropriate research and library skills. Special privileges for inter-library loans and other uses of library resources should be extended to gifted children so that they may pursue their interests. The librarian, in fact, may be among the first to recognize a child's abilities through observations of her choice of reading materials.

Biographies of several eminent people who were not viewed as gifted or creative, or perhaps even "average," during their school years indicate that their "blossoming" in late adolescence or early adulthood resulted from interaction with a significant adult. In Einstein's case, for example, it was an uncle who nurtured the interest in science and mathetmatics. In other cases, a parent or a nonrelative played the catalytic role (Pang, 1968; Uhler, 1977). What this would suggest to us is the use of adults in the community as mentors for youngsters gifted or talented in a specific field. There must be good rapport between adult and student as a basis for the student's development, so the adult must be selected with some care. The relationship, also based on mutual respect, should provide opportunities for meaningful gift-related tasks.

Flexible programming (allowing a fourth grader to attend sixth-grade math or reading, for example), in graded or nongraded schools, permits the intellectually gifted child to move ahead more rapidly in her areas of competence without skipping over weak areas. By eleventh or twelfth grade, such a student can take some college-level courses and earn advanced placement when entering college. Several institutions of higher education now permit unusually well-prepared and mature students to enter as freshmen at the end of eleventh grade, thus encouraging continued growth rather than stagnation at what would have been the child's twelfth-grade level.

Case in Point

Research workers on the Study of Mathematically and Scientifically Precocious Youth at Johns Hopkins University have used a variety of acceleration techniques for highly intellectually gifted children. A 13-year-old eighth-grader was admitted to Hopkins as a freshman in 1969, received a B.A. degree in quantitative studies and an M.S.E. in computer science in 1973 and enrolled in a doctorate program at Cornell that same year—not yet 18 years old. Several of the students tested skipped two to four grades, without personal or academic problems.

Other alternatives included leaving high school early in order to become full-time college freshmen or taking college courses on a part-time basis. One fourth-grader, age 10, for example, earned a B in college algebra and trigonometry at Johns Hopkins Evening College.

Julian C. Stanley, "Accelerating the educational progress of intellectually gifted youths," *Educational Psychologist*, 10, (1973), 133–146.

At one time it was common to promote intellectually gifted children to higher grades more compatible with their level of academic achievement. This approach is rarely taken today, however, except through advanced-placement programs or where there are no other alternatives, for research studies have shown that advanced grade placement places an added strain on the gifted child's social and emotional development, particularly during early adolescence. Early admission to school, perhaps as early as age 4, is often criticized for the same reason. Although intellectually gifted students do tend to be psychologically more mature than their age peers, they are not always ready for the social activities and group interests of older children.

Homogeneous grouping offers the possibility of learning challenges, but also evokes pressure from parents whose children are not included to admit them to the "gifted class" and possible inferiority feelings in those children who are not admitted. Heterogeneous homeroom assignment combined with one or more of the enrichment programs has therefore been generally better accepted in recent years.

Supporters of homogeneous grouping maintain that it is easier for the teacher and that it increases the student's enjoyment of learning. But when ability grouping means only that the teacher gives the same assignments to a gifted class—occupying it with ''busy-work'' to take up the time needed for a slower group to complete the same assignment—the gifted are allowed to be only industrious drudges. Critics suggest, too, that class selection is most often based on only one criterion so that differences within the class are reduced only slightly.

A more reasonable alternative seems to be the heterogeneous class that provides a variety of options to the gifted for meeting coursework goals. If the gifted child persists in avoiding the options that would challenge her abilities, the teacher should discuss the matter with the child and, if necessary, her parents and the school counselor.

Gifted children are particularly concerned with the meaningfulness and purposefulness of their assignments and consequent efforts. If they understand they are learning a basic skill and given an explanation of the long-range purpose for acquiring the skill, they are likely to be happier learners than if they must perform seemingly isolated daily tasks. Reinforcement of the skills may occur if the gifted child is encouraged to teach children who have less understanding or ability, although this practice should not be abused by the teacher. Indeed, the gifted child's creative abilities may be stimulated in attempting to teach the younger or less able child, as the former devises new approaches to the material to be learned.

For the child who has creative abilities in the arts, a few ''magnet'' high schools in the country stress art and/or music majors, with courses offered in composition, style, and other appropriate advanced content. Additionally, of course, parents can provide after-school music, art, drama, or other lessons. Scholarships are frequently available, too, for the talented, if parents cannot afford such lessons. Support for the magnet-school concept is available under the Emergency School Aid Act of 1973.

Children whose gifts lie in less academic areas usually have to wait until secondary school for appropriate enrichment activities, unless there is an institution locally available such as the Museum of Natural History (New York), the Franklin Institute (Philadelphia), or the Smithsonian Institution (Washington). At these and similar institutions, after-school and weekend classes in science and technology are often offered even for preschoolers. Large cities and multischool districts often have technical high schools where the mechanically gifted can learn special techniques and prepare for industrial careers. An industrial arts shop at the elementary level can provide some limited and basic opportunities in these areas for younger students.

In recent years, as educators have become generally more cognizant of the desirability of encouraging creativity, they have provided more opportunities for creative expression at the elementary level for all children. Students now receive instruction in such creative pursuits as haiku poetry writing, drawing or composing in response to music, and writing about imaginative themes (such as those presented in Harper & Row's "Making It Strange" series). Teachers are becoming increasingly aware of the importance of flexibility and psychological freedom for all children in their classes, but obviously this classroom atmosphere is vital for the creative child if he is not to be labeled a "misfit" or worse.

Additional tasks or activities for the gifted and/or creative might involve, for example, developing plays related to class studies. The able and interested students could write the dialogue, design and create the sets, and direct the production of the play. The tasks can be rotated to meet the varied talents of the students. Scientifically talented students, and interested creative ones, could work on community ecology or similar problems. Artistic and musically talented pupils can work on presenting an arts festival. Hobbies can be integrated with academic studies through research projects. Writing topics can include futurism, interpreting various cultural values and practices, "second-guessing" history, and similar mind-stretching themes. This might lead to assembling and producing a publication (newspaper, magazine, or booklet) that would utilize other talents of the gifted and creative.

If tied to their age group in grade placement and if not challenged to use their abilities, intellectually gifted children may become bored, mentally "dropping out" or exhibiting behavior problems. In short, they are often short-changed by short-sighted administrators and teachers. They may, in addition, have to contend with the hostility of narrow-minded professional staff who resent, or are jealous of, the talents of the gifted young. Boredom is the enemy of all learners but has particularly devastating effects on the gifted and creative attending regular classes on a full-time basis. Repetition, drill, and busy-work are undesirable for most children, although necessary for some, but they are especially to be avoided if the gifted and/or creative child is to use her gifts effectively and with joy.

Teacher Preparation

A teacher of the gifted or creative need not possess talents of the same magnitude as her students. However, a teacher of this group does need to be open-minded, adaptable, and resourceful. She must be able to guide without being authoritarian, to know where answers may be found if they are unknown, and to provide access to human and material resources in the community and in the school. A group leader at the Creative Problem-Solving Institute says that this means being "a guide by the side, not a sage on stage." The teacher outshone by a student must not become flustered. In fact, the ideal teacher of the gifted and creative should rejoice in the successes of her pupils, and perhaps learn from them, too. This requires a strong positive self-concept on the teacher's part.

The teacher of the gifted and creative needs to be ready to work differentially with his students. For those students who are self-motivated, the teacher should provide freedom for exploration and perhaps some guidance for coordinating multiple interests. For those who are not self-starters, the teacher must be more of a stimulant. He will find that gifted and talented youngsters vary in their self-confidence, desire to conform to authority, and willingness to function independently much as other students do.

There are programs in some colleges specifically designed to prepare teachers of the gifted. Harold Lyon, Director of Education for the Gifted and Talented in the U.S. Office of Education, found, however, that in the early 1970s there were only twelve American universities offering graduate programs to prospective teachers in the field (Lyon, 1974, p. 65). There are numerous special workshops, however, such as the summer National/State Leadership Training Institute for the Gifted and Talented in California. The curriculum of such a workshop typically includes courses on the psychology of the gifted child, educational adjustments for the gifted in the standard curriculum, and techniques for teaching and guiding these children. Certification requirements for teachers of the creative have not yet been established. However, an increasing number of colleges offer courses in the creative process that can help those who teach creative and gifted children.

4

Mentally Retarded Children

Group Characteristics

Of all the groups of exceptional children, perhaps the best publicized and most familiar to the general public is the large aggregation known as the mentally retarded. In educational and general performance terms, the retarded are defined as those who learn at a slower than average rate. They are divided, by I.Q. or performance scores, into three groups, with some differences among the states on the limits of each range: (1) the educable or mildly retarded, I.Q. 50–70 or 75, maximum mental age about 8 to 12 years; (2) the trainable or moderately retarded, I.Q. 25–50, maximum mental age roughly 3 to 7 years; and (3) the profound or severely retarded, I.Q. below 25, maximum mental age of 3 years. If you think of the performance level of children chronologically of these different ages, then you get a better idea of the potential maximum capabilities of the retarded when they are chronologically mature adults. (Note: In some settings, the division is mild retardation, I.Q. 68–52; moderate, I.Q. 51–36; severe, I.Q. 35–20, and profound, I.Q. 19 and below [Hobbs, 1976, p. 51].)

Retardation may result from genetic (endogenous) or external (exogenous) causes. Among the endogenous causes are a single dominant gene appearing in more than one generation of the family, a genetic mutation specific to a particular pregnancy, or the matching of two recessive genes at the time of conception. Where several children in the family are retarded, it is sometimes difficult to be certain whether the cause is a genetic one or the result of environmental deprivation. Exogenous causes of retardation may occur before, at, or after birth. German measles (rubella), use of drugs, and toxemia of pregnancy in the mother-to-be are examples of prenatal causes. At birth there may be anoxia (lack of oxygen) that results in retardation. In the postnatal environment, the child may lack opportunities for normal intellectual growth or have a severe emotional problem such as infantile autism that leads to retardation in intellectual development. Retardation may also result from some illnesses or injuries that affect brain functioning, or even from inadequate nutrition.

In recent years, the public has become more aware of the retarded, thanks in part to the openness of public figures in discussing their familial problems with retarded children. During the presidency of John F. Kennedy, commissions were formed and legislation passed to study and develop programs for the retarded. There is a President's Panel on Mental Retardation, and a number of laws providing funding and facilities for the programs involving retarded children and adults were passed by Congress in the 1960s and 1970s.

Much can be done to prevent mental retardation. Medical research almost daily provides new diagnostic techniques and new prenatal and postnatal methods that can reduce the incidence of retardation. Most familiar is the test for phenylketonuria (PKU) performed shortly after birth. If PKU is present, the infant's diet can be controlled, preventing retardation. However, there are more than 1½ million retarded children already with us. Facilities for educating the retarded have been expanded in recent years, both on a private and a public basis, in clinics, schools, and recreation programs. All of these are appropriately subsumed under education, because in each type of facility the retarded individual is taught in some way to perform more effectively.

Group Goals

Since children exhibit varying degrees of retardation, one cannot establish uniform educational goals for them. The profoundly retarded, for example, can be expected to learn certain minimal self-help practices by maturity, such as toileting, use of table flatware, dressing and undressing, and a limited use of language. Since they cannot function with full independence as adults, they are frequently placed in residential institutions for long-term care. They typically do not profit from traditional education, even at the nursery-school level, although some eventually learn to develop a routine.

The trainable mentally retarded learn more social and adaptive behavior than those in the most severely retarded group, and, at the higher levels, they may learn routine tasks and thereby contribute to their own welfare and to society. As adults, the trainable retarded will be able to work in a sheltered workshop, doing simple assembly-type work or other relatively unskilled tasks. For parents of the trainable retarded, however, one of the major concerns is whether to keep the child at home or not. If kept at home, what effects will there be on any siblings, and what will happen to the child if she outlives her parents? Although the trainable retarded child can learn to care for her immediate personal needs, it is unrealistic to expect complete functional and economic independence.

Goals for those in the educable retarded group are somewhat higher than for the other two groups of retarded children. In addition to a higher educational potential, the educable retarded tend to have more adequate physical development and better motor coordination than the less capable retarded. They can fill simple unskilled and semiskilled jobs as adults and may in some cases gain a considerable measure of economic and functional independence. A significant increase in employer cooperation with vocational counselors in the training and employment of the retarded has opened up many new opportunities for this group.

A study published in 1967 (Baller et al.) of 109 men and women who had been diagnosed as educationally mentally retarded in their school years and who were in their mid-fifties at the time of the study offers some cause for optimism and some clues to educational practices. Apart from the questions raised about the quality of the original classification, three common factors emerged for the 65 percent of the sample who were self-supporting:

1. They had more middle-class habits, speech, and dress, making them more acceptable to society at large.
2. They either worked for a large paternalistic business or had learned and continued to use a single marketable skill.
3. As children, some significant adult had given them a sense of their personal worth.

These factors suggest some specific ways in which parents, teachers, and counselors can help retarded children.

Modification of Education and Facilities

In Pennsylvania, the state Association for Retarded Children successfully brought suit to have all retarded children educated in the public schools beginning at age 6, maintaining that retarded children should not be forced to delay their entrance into public school nor should they be required to find private facilities. The State Supreme Court rulings on the Pennsylvania Assocation for Retarded Children suit clearly state that no school district may postpone, terminate, or in any way deny the right to a free public education or training program to any retarded child between the ages of 6 and 21 years. Further, the ruling holds that if public preschool programs for normal children less than 6 years old exist in a school district, then a public preschool program must be available also to the younger mentally retarded children in that district. The school district then has the alternatives of placing a child in a classroom situation, a publicly supported training program, or home-bound instruction. These provisions have been extended by the federal Education for All Handicapped Children Act, as noted earlier.

Too often, the provision of facilities and equipment for the retarded has a low priority on the school district's list of things to finance. Thus, mentally retarded children are frequently educated in old buildings with poor light, inadequate equipment, and dingy surroundings. The children need color to bring warmth to their lives, appropriate space for their learning experiences, and certainly good lighting. Heated floors are necessary for those at the trainable and custodial levels, since they spend much of their time on the floor.

Three good examples of physical planning I have observed in Pennsylvania schools come to mind. The first is a small wing in a public junior high school with separate instruction rooms for the trainable mentally retarded and the educable mentally retarded. These are roomy, well lit, with bathroom facilities, sinks, cooking areas, and good storage space. Both rooms are located close to the industrial arts, home economics, and physical education facilities (both regular and specially equipped), all of which the mentally retarded students use frequently. A second example is the wing for the trainable mentally retarded at a comprehensive elementary school. In addition to spacious, bright classrooms, there is an "apartment without walls" to help the children become more familiar with self-care skills and the rudiments of home maintenance. They learn to make beds, wash dishes, and recognize the function of each part of a home. A third example is a facility planned with classrooms for instruction, separate girls' and boys' training areas, arts and crafts room, kitchen, and multipurpose area. Outdoor recreation areas are included in all three settings.

Among the teaching techniques favored for mentally retarded children are the behavior modification or operant conditioning techniques, which have been used effectively to teach self-care habits and reading, as well as socialization skills. Behavior modification is based on the principle that reinforcement of a behavior will increase the probability that the behavior will occur again. For example, a teacher may give a child a piece of candy for accomplishing a task, or perhaps points to be accumulated and traded for a desired "prize." Such reinforcement can be given at the completion of a task or assignment, for attending to a task for a stipulated length of time, or for exhibiting other desired behaviors. If the task to be completed includes several steps, the teacher may reinforce each step along the way. For example, in teaching a child to print her name, one can reinforce her for printing the first letter, then for printing the first and second letters, and so on until she succeeds in printing her whole name.

Retarded children learn more limited tasks than average children and require more frequent reinforcement. B. F. Skinner has developed a linear program (small bits of information presented in clear, sequential steps) that has been adapted quite successfully for retarded children. Through such programs, which provide built-in reinforcement by making it easy for students to choose the correct answer, the children acquire "reading readiness," number skills, and other learning skills. High-interest, low-vocabulary readers are extremely valuable, too, for older retarded children. Segments of "Sesame Street" have also been especially designed to teach young retarded children and those who interact with them.

Because they learn slowly, retarded children need unusually patient and very dedicated teachers who can set up realistic goals with realistic expectations. The retarded should learn as much as they can, and the teacher therefore needs to provide a stimulating environment that will give them opportunities for attractive and desirable learning experiences. Practical arithmetic for daily use can be taught using almost any concrete object in the classroom, beginning perhaps with a simple count of the number of children or chairs or windows in the room. Social studies, too, can be presented in very concrete ways, with visits to the local fire station, talks with understanding policemen, and the development of basic manners and awareness of social conventions.

Audiovisual equipment can often help stimulate the children's interest. Some children can also be taught to operate audio tape players or to assist with the overhead projector, movie projector, and closed-circuit television.

A major task in the education of the retarded is socialization. That is, retarded children must learn minimal social amenities, as well as how to behave, so that other people will not resent their presence. In one elementary school, for example, a class of trainable mentally retarded was in the habit of leaving behind so much of their debris in the cafeteria that the "regular" students complained bitterly to the principal about having to clean up after them. This sort of negative feeling can be prevented by regular instruction in personal habits and social awareness.

Music, physical education, and art all fulfill important roles in the education of the retarded. Both the trainable and the educable retarded are capable of learning to sing or hum songs, to play simple instruments, and to follow directions set to music. Such activities are not only pleasurable but also offer the chance to increase coordination and gain a sense of rhythm. Physical education similarly strengthens coordination and is necessary to the children's physical well-being. The physical education program should be adapted for the trainable mentally retarded, for their coordination is often so poor that they cannot catch a ball thrown to them from a few feet away. Directions for exercises should be extremely simple and involve only three or four steps in a sequence. Arts and crafts offer children an opportunity for demonstrable achievement. Their activities can range from simple cut-and-paste tasks to woodworking, weaving, sewing and knitting, and other crafts. Finger-painting and crayoning also provide opportunities for self-expression. Arts and crafts can be especially satisfying to retarded children because they have something concrete to show for their efforts, as well as hobbies to turn to throughout their lives.

It is essential that the retarded child be taught to recognize commonly used public signs and signals. Red and green, for traffic lights, can be taught first as colors, then as signals in classroom activities, and finally as safety signals. The shape, if not the wording, of signs such as "Stop," "Caution," "Exit," and skull-and-crossbone poison symbols must take on meaning for the retarded individual for his own safety.

Among the teenaged trainable retarded, there are factors to consider with which teachers have had less experience. The physical changes of puberty mandate attention to personal hygiene. These youths are also aware, from family living and from watching television, of the activities of their age peers. They enjoy and respond to rock music, and welcome the opportunity to learn new dance steps. Swimming instruction with young adults and escorted day trips in community recreation programs not only expand their world but boost their

---

Case in Point

Retarded children need recreation and exposure to the larger world as much as other children. Local associations for retarded citizens frequently sponsor programs at a playground or neighborhood center. Trips to museums, zoos, and nearby cities, also group-sponsored, are adventures out of the ordinary for the educable retarded.

In Philadelphia, the Ronald Bruce Nipon Association has both day and weekend programs for retarded young adults. Through these programs, young people have made friends, acquired skills and jobs, and have traveled to Niagara Falls and England as a group. Their parents benefit, also, as they observe the greater independence of their retarded children and experience new freedom from worry and from their 24-hour duty as protectors.

---

self-image. It is important to them to be treated in accord with their chronological age rather than their mental age—at least some of the time.

For the educable mentally retarded, less rigorous academic learning activities can take place within regular classes—that is, through "mainstreaming." This approach is one way to achieve some integration and to increase participation and socialization with children of their own age. An alternative to complete integration is the assignment to regular "homerooms." In this setup, the retarded children leave the homeroom temporarily to work in the resource room or learning center, just as other children leave to attend speech clinic or special music sessions. This kind of partial integration creates a more positive psychological situation than totally segregated groups. However, nonretarded peers need to have their misconceptions about the retarded explored and corrected if such mainstreaming is to work well. Even watching the retarded enjoy "Sesame Street" or other television programs or films can reassure the "normal" that they have *something* in common.

One reorganization of special education that attempts this type of integration is the Madison Plan (see Blum, 1971) in which an integral factor is changing the regular classroom teacher's feelings of being imposed on when retarded children are placed in his class. Each of the four levels of the Madison Plan represents greater integration of the exceptional child into the regular class. A floorplan for this kind of education program (see Figure 4-1) illustrates the steps that prepare exceptional children for placement in the regular classroom.

Retarded adolescents need preparation for their postschool years. Those who are able to carry responsibility can participate in work-study programs, working in greenhouses, service stations, dry-cleaning shops, supermarkets, factories, and so on. Through these programs, they learn how to manage money, how to plan a budget, and how to plan for the future. Further, they need sex education so

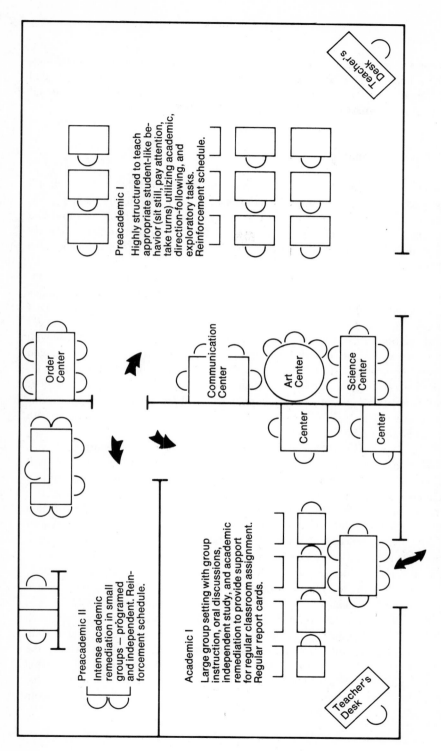

Figure 4-1. Two Typical Learning-Center Classrooms with Connecting Door
(Used by permission of Frank D. Taylor)

that they are not taken advantage of and can function appropriately should they marry. This kind of realistic preparation for adult life is crucial if retarded children are to be contributing members of society rather than overprotected and completely dependent older "children."

Teacher Preparation

Successful teachers of the retarded have patience for their students' slow-paced learning, as well as enthusiasm, energy, flexibility, and a good measure of self-esteem. In many ways, their personal traits should be those of a good nursery school or kindergarten teacher, for they will be working normally with children of elementary school age but preschool abilities. The teacher also needs intellectual commitment and capability.

Programs for teaching the retarded are common in colleges of education. Students who enter these programs take courses in special teaching techniques and materials, and they usually prepare for working with a specific age group—primary, intermediate, or secondary. Those who plan to work with younger retarded children focus on the study of early childhood development. Those who expect to work with retarded teenagers need course work in vocational and personal counseling, so that they can help their students prepare for adulthood. Experience throughout the undergraduate program in programs for the retarded, whether academic, vocational, or recreational, will provide realistic applications of course work as well as the opportunity to become increasingly familiar with the needs and problems of retarded children.

The Board of Directors of the National Association for Retarded Citizens (NARC) has adopted several standards for teacher certification that will undoubtedly affect preparatory programs. They recommend that teachers have a bachelor's degree that certifies competencies in: "(a) a basic body of knowledge of mental retardation; (b) methods and techniques for teaching mentally retarded persons; (c) curriculum for mentally retarded students; and (d) demonstration of teaching competence with mentally retarded students" (*Mental Retardation News*, 23, No. 1, 1974). They also recommend that standard minimal requirements be adopted throughout the country and that universal reciprocity (that is, recognition) of the teaching certificate be instituted. The NARC standards also urge teachers to specialize in one or more areas of teaching the retarded.

Not all of those contributing to the growth of the retarded have or need such extensive formal training. Paraprofessional personnel are being prepared in two-year programs at community colleges and other institutions. Under the direction of certified teachers, these trained aides work closely with individual retarded children on specific tasks and lend general assistance throughout the school day. Their presence means additional attention to individual children from the aide as well as the teacher.

5

Children with Learning Disabilities

Group Characteristics

Children with learning disabilities have average or above average intellectual potential, but they learn and achieve in very uneven patterns because of alleged damage to specific areas of the brain. They look like any other children, yet they constitute between 1 and 10 percent[1] of the public school population and are categorized by such terms as specifically learning disabled, minimal brain damage, minimal cerebral dysfunction, dyslexia, and so on. Most of these children are boys, although it is not clear why this should be so.

The multiplicity of diagnostic labels does little to help plan the child's program. The labels are not as interchangeable as some people think, nor do they really pinpoint the source or nature of the child's difficulty. Beginning with research in the 1940s, emphasis has been variously placed on brain damage, on perceptual-motor disturbances, reading problems, hyperactivity and, most recently, on difficulty in sustaining selective attention (Ross, 1976, pp. 12–15). In fact, what constitutes a learning disability is not known except as the child displays symptoms. Since the symptoms vary widely, it is impossible to ascribe the presence of learning disabilities to a single factor or to prescribe a single pattern of remediation.

Identification of the learning-disabled child should result from a team approach, for there are many possible causes for learning disabilities. Frequently, no attempt at identification is made until the child begins to show marked academic weaknesses and/or emotional problems at the second- or third-grade level. Their difficulty in handling educational tasks eventually marks them as "intellectually different."

Few learning-disabled youngsters show gross neurological defects in diagnostic examinations and many, in fact, have normal examination results. Developmental optometrists or ophthalmologists may, however, detect visual

---

[1]Estimates vary in the literature from 1 to 3 percent to 10 percent or more, depending upon the definition used.

perception difficulties, and hearing specialists may discover developmental lags in speech or defects in auditory acuity or perception through hearing tests. Psychoeducational tests also give clues to the nature of learning disabilities through comparison of I.Q. scores with achievement scores in reading, spelling, and arithmetic, or through study of the pattern of scores on subtests of the intelligence test.

Nina's case illustrates several points about learning disabilities. There is the gradual decrease in school functioning that finally alerts someone to the fact that there is a problem. There is uncertainty as to the source of the problem. There are difficulties in making a diagnosis, especially one specific enough to give direction to the remedial teachers. There are too few public schools available to help these children. Through all of this, there are great emotional strains on the child and the parents. Finally, with appropriate guidance, there can be a happy outcome for all concerned.

Many school districts now attempt group screening of kindergarten children for perceptual disabilities in order to minimize later problems. Because the validity of group-testing results is always open to some question, such results should be evaluated with caution. Overzealousness in the application of screening standards can be as unfair and potentially damaging as the failure to provide any diagnostic programs or remedial courses.

There *are* symptoms and signs to which kindergarten teachers can be alert. For example, if a child has difficulty focusing attention on one stimulus at a time (a phenomenon known as hyperdistractibility), she *may* have minimal brain damage. Similarly, a child who cannot shift attention from one stimulus to another can also be showing signs of minimal brain damage. The teacher should also be on the lookout for hyperactivity, impulsiveness, and emotional instability (that is, overreaction to minimal stimulation). Children with learning diabilities may exhibit motor dysfunctions as well, such as poor gross motor coordination, clumsiness, fine motor disturbances (for example, inability to draw a circle or copy simple patterns), eye-hand coordination difficulties, right-left discrimination problems, and so on.

In the perceptual and conceptual areas, the learning-disabled child may be unable to reproduce figures that are perceived, to distinguish figures from their background, or to perceive things as a whole. Or he may suffer from perseverative perception, continuing to see a circle, for example, when he is shown other shapes. He may be bound to the concrete and unable to cope with the abstract. These deficits can create problems in learning to read, or in learning other academic and developmental tasks and skills.

The learning problems may be receptive, in which case the child has difficulty sorting out and comprehending incoming stimuli of one or more sensory modalities. If the problem is expressive, the child comprehends quite well but cannot effectively transmit her response to the hand, foot, or speech mechanisms involved. The emotional problems of negativism, defective self-concept, low frustration tolerance, and hypersensitivity often are secondary

Case in Point

Nina, 9 years old, was becoming more difficult to live with at home. She had difficulty controlling her temper; she complained of early morning stomachaches and headaches; and she seldom showed her usually warm smile anymore. Her schoolwork, too, was slipping. Her parents didn't know which was cause and which effect.

A general physical checkup showed no illness brewing. Talks with her teacher yielded little, other than that Nina's classroom performance was erratic. Her teacher reported that sometimes she knew an answer and sometimes she didn't; the level of difficulty of the task didn't seem to matter. Tests by the school psychologist produced a similar erratic pattern. Neurological and ophthalmological examinations followed, and these test results pointed to minimal brain damage. Dismayed by this diagnosis, Nina's parents sought further information. Specific areas of dysfunction were delineated by psychiatrists (working out math problems on paper was one), and special school placement was recommended. By this time, Nina was academically a year or more behind her classmates and increasingly frustrated by her problems in school.

Because no public school program was available, Nina's parents enrolled her in a special private school that was ungraded and had a very low pupil-teacher ratio. Special techniques were used to remediate Nina's academic and coordination deficiencies, with frequent reinforcement for her successes. Family therapy, also part of the program, helped to reduce Nina's anger over frustrating experiences and her parents' tensions and anxiety.

After several years at the special school, Nina entered a small "regular" private boarding school as a transition to secondary education. (Again, no public, or even private, schools in the area had a program appropriate to Nina's needs.) Her new school, 300 miles from her home, could supply the combination of ungraded, low-pressure academic and "life-preparation" courses from which Nina could profit. In her four years at the school, she learned to be more comfortable in social interaction, and she developed self-confidence in nonacademic affairs. She graduated with children her own age, and two junior colleges accepted Nina as a student in programs preparing preschool teaching assistants, a field compatible with her interests and abilities.

Perhaps the most difficult problem for Nina and her parents over the years was to accept the reality of the situation. Constant reevaluation of abilities, deficiencies, and expectations led to the realization, at last, that Nina would function successfully as an adult, except in a few relatively unimportant areas, and could have a high degree of social and economic independence. At 24, she has a responsible job in a day-care center, lives and travels alone, goes out on dates, cooks, reads, and looks forward to a bright future.

symptoms that result from the difficulties which the learning disabled child has already experienced.

The Bureau of the Handicapped estimated that 1,966,000 children were learning disabled in 1975−76 and that 260,000 were receiving proper attention. We don't know how realistic these figures are, since testing and diagnostic techniques vary widely and are still imperfect. In recent years, it has become fashionable to label every child who exhibits one or more of the symptoms we have mentioned as learning disabled. Similarly, "difficult" or underachieving children are often considered in this category. Teachers and other diagnosticians should remember, however, that learning problems can also stem from mental retardation, slow maturation, learning disadvantages, and many other possible causes, including poor teaching at an earlier grade level.

Group Goals

The teacher's immediate goal for learning-disabled children is to teach them techniques to overcome their difficulties so that they may function more effectively in class and elsewhere. They need to be able to read with understanding; communicate effectively, if simply, in speech and writing; and do simple, practical arithmetic. The natural long-range goal, of course, is to prepare them for independent adulthood. Depending on the nature of the problem, however, there may be limits to what can be done in school placement, even with extensive therapy. Therefore, in addition to remediating as much as possible disabilities that are relevant to classroom activities, stress must be placed on developing the child's existing abilities and talents. Further, psychotherapy may alleviate the emotional difficulties besetting both child and parent, as well as enabling the child to interact more positively with her peers.

Modification of Education and Facilities

With the growing awareness of the number of learning-disabled children in the public schools, there has been a corresponding increase in the number of special classes for these children, usually at the elementary level. Large urban districts sometimes have several special classes in a single school building, or they may have centers in different sections of the city to which students from several schools are referred. In suburban and rural districts, it is often difficult for a single district to support the special class, so a few districts pool their resources and their students. These may be operated under the auspices of a federally established regional center or an administrative intermediate unit, with support from federal programs for the handicapped as well as state subsidies.

There are not, however, enough public classes for the learning disabled at either the elementary or more especially at the secondary level. Thus, numerous day and residential private schools have sprung up, most of which are very costly to parents. Tuition, transportation, psychotherapy, and sometimes boarding can cost from $5,000 to $10,000 per year per child. There is no real alternative, however, in areas where there are no special classes or special teachers for this group. Distasteful as sending a child to boarding school may be, it is a more desirable alternative than having a child who is continually frustrated in the public school and beset by emotional problems and low self-esteem. The financial cost is shared by the local school district, the state, and the federal government under current laws.

The teacher-to-pupil ratio is important in insuring learning-disabled children proper attention. In most special programs, a ratio of one teacher to ten children is most desirable. Larger class sections may have a teacher plus one or more aides who assist in demonstrating tasks, evaluating work, and other activities.

Teachers of children with learning disabilities usually focus on motor training, reducing environmental stimulation in the classroom (the opposite of what you do for the "normal" child), establishing a routine program schedule, and providing special auditory training, eye-hand exercises, speech therapy, or psychotherapy, depending on the nature of the disability. Many teaching techniques can be incorporated into music, art, and physical education programs so that recreation, learning, and therapy become integrated aspects of an overall school program.

To enable the child to move his body in an integrated way, the teacher can introduce such activities as walking through simple mazes in the classroom or in the play area, assuming body positions as directed by the teacher or a record ("Simon Says" is a good game for teaching body coordination), or learning to play Ping-Pong.

Auditory training activities include decoding verbal stimuli (through matching games in which the child identifies or duplicates sounds and noises), responding verbally in a meaningful way (through sentence-completion tasks providing verbal opposites, or interpreting jokes and proverbs), memorizing and recalling sequences of auditory information, and similar tasks. Visual discrimination, figure-ground differentiation, recall of prior visual experience, and other skills can also be taught through games and exercises. And teachers can encourage language development in the areas of discrimination, articulation, word-attack skills, reading comprehension, and composition through similar gamelike activities.

For some learning-disabled children, number concepts are the primary source of difficulty. The use of Cuisenaire rods and other concrete objects for counting and arithmetic operations can ultimately teach the child to deal with money, time, weights and measures, and other numerical relationships requiring the ability to reason arithmetically. The abilities to categorize, to remember learned information and apply it, to use common sense, and to understand time spans are also taught via tasks that move from the basic to the more advanced levels. Social skills, from peer interaction to the ability to assume personal and social responsibility, are important areas in which the learning-disabled student must also work.

Teachers can make use of many special materials in teaching learning-disabled children. Climbing apparatus, pegboards, mirrors, commercial work-study kits, and a wide range of audiovisual materials can all be effective teaching tools. Physical education should include body movement and dance and should encourage the child to accept her body.

Each learning-disabled child has specific disabilities and developmental lags. His program must be individually prescribed if he is to derive maximum benefit from it. Diagnostic evaluation of his specific strengths and weaknesses must precede the development of individually prescribed learning and behavioral objectives. Continuing evaluations will enable the teacher to modify these prescriptions. The results of formal and informal tests, including, for example, the *Gates-McKillop Reading Diagnostic Test*, the *Durrell Analysis of Reading Difficulties*, the *Key Math Diagnostic Arithmetic Test*, and phonics inventories, and an analysis of the child's cognitive style should be synthesized to formulate the learning objectives and to determine the means by which she will work toward attaining those objectives. Obviously each child must have a large measure of individual attention from her teachers for her most effective learning.

Learning cubicles similar to those found in language laboratories are currently in use in many schools. Not all specialists agree, however, that the cubicle is appropriate for every learning-disabled child. Such study cubicles (or a cleared desk in an average classroom) are designed with the idea of confining the child's environment and reducing stimulation so that she can focus on immediate tasks without distraction.

Teachers frequently follow behavior-modification principles in their class-room work. For example, children are assigned learning tasks (or contracts) that are limited in scope and appropriate to their abilities and needs. The child then receives reinforcement (from candy to recreation time) on completion of the assignment or contract. Teacher control of the learning situation involves paying close attention to the needs of the child and to the effectiveness of the reinforcers, since not all individuals will respond positively to the same reinforcers. The teacher must also engage in continual diagnosis and evaluation so that appropriate therapeutic activities and materials can be made available. Teachers can also benefit from interaction with available consultants so that they may stay in touch with current diagnostic and teaching techniques.

Most of the modifications and activities mentioned are introduced in self-contained classes for the learning disabled. However, it is also possible that the learning-disabled student needs these special aids only on a limited basis, perhaps for an hour or two a day. In such cases, under PL 94-142, the "least restricted environment" would combine the resource room teacher and activities and integration in regular classes, each on a part-time basis. The handling of integration would be specified in the student's IEP and would obviously vary with the individual's specific learning disabilities.

Teacher Preparation

Teachers are usually trained in a four- or five-year program that typically includes coursework in education and/or the psychology of exceptional children, diagnosis of learning disabilities, elementary-level methods, diagnostic and remedial reading, and a practicum with learning-disabled students. Other appropriate learning experiences for the teacher include working with the emotionally disturbed, learning guidance practices, and participating in vocational-rehabilitation counseling. State certification requirements vary so much for teachers of the learning disabled that they do not make a coherent pattern. Indeed, as recently as 1969, only twelve states had or planned to have certificates specifically labeled "Learning Disabilities" (Schwartz, 1969). The teacher should be prepared to work with parents and be involved in the continuing evaluation of therapy programs.

Three

The Physically Different

Physically different children have difficulties that stem from prenatal or perinatal damage, genetic factors, and postnatal injuries or accidents (ranging from meningitis to auto accidents and shootings). Professional experiences with the victims of traumatic war injuries have given impetus to the development of educational and vocational-rehabilitation techniques, as well as effective methods of physical therapy. These experiences have also taught educators and their professional colleagues much about the modification of the environment for the physically handicapped. Nevertheless, many administrators and regular classroom teachers are uneasy in the face of physical differences. They are uncertain and anxious in approaching the handicapped child or adult. The public, too, often reacts in ignorance, some believing that the physically handicapped are intellectually handicapped as well. Support from special-education specialists, particularly itinerant teachers, is necessary when the handicapped child is integrated into regular classes, a practice that is increasingly favored.

Extensive federal legislation has been passed for education of the handicapped. Under legislation passed in 1971, a National Advisory Committee on Handicapped Children was established to operate within the Office of Education. A Bureau for Education and Training of the Handicapped was established in 1970, as were regional resource centers that were to "develop and apply the best methods of appraising the special educational needs of handicapped children referred to them." These centers provide much valuable information to teachers working with exceptional children. At the state level, bureaus of vocational rehabilitation offer services and support to those working with 16- to 18-year-old handicapped children who have finished school. A large number of privately organized associations (for example, the Easter Seal Society, Lighthouse for the Blind, March of Dimes), with membership drawn from parents, teachers, and the general public, also contribute to the improvement of services to the physically handicapped.

This section focuses on children with orthopedic handicaps, children with sensory disorders, and children with multiple handicaps. In each group, the degree of the child's problem varies both with the extent of physical damage and the motivation of the individual child. That is to say, the label attached to the child's physical problem tells only part of her story.

Both the Vocational Rehabilitation Act of 1973 and the Education for All Handicapped Children Act of 1975 have special relevance to the physically handicapped. Provisions of the 1973 act require that educational institutions receiving federal funds make all classes physically accessible to the handicapped. In practice, this means removing or modifying architectural barriers, supplying sign-language translators to the deaf, and providing guides or other aids to the blind so that physically handicapped students can participate in classes from which they were previously excluded. The 1975 law increases the possibility of having an educational experience that conforms to the individual's abilities as well as disabilities.

6 Orthopedically Handicapped Children

Group Characteristics

According to the figures in Table 1-1, the estimated number of crippled and health-impaired children in this country in 1975–76 was 328,000. This category includes victims of poliomyelitis, muscular dystrophy, muscular atrophy, spina bifida, multiple sclerosis, Legg-Perthes disease, arthritis, congenital amputations, osteomyelitis, cerebral palsy, tuberculosis, serious posture defects, cardiac conditions, and orthopedic problems due to accidental injury.

Physical disabilities do not necessarily have concomitant mental or intellectual handicaps. Taking an acute rather than a chronic condition as an example, does the average student become intellectually impaired as a result of an accident that places her in a wheelchair or on crutches? Children with orthopedic or cardiac handicaps often have intellectual abilities in the normal ranges of other children. Thus, the school situation should provide them with every opportunity to work up to their physical and intellectual potentials.

Educational difficulties, apart from the physical ones allied to individual conditions, are then principally in the realm of psychosocial factors and personal adjustment. Many parents, for a variety of reasons, neglect this aspect of their child's development. It is important, however, that the child be included in the normal home routine, so that she need not succumb to the feeling that people do not want her around because of her ''peculiar'' appearance.

Children will have handicaps ranging from a missing or drastically shortened limb, paralysis, tremors, limps, low energy level, clubfoot, thinness, or curvature of the spine, as a few examples. School-aged children, particularly, are self-conscious about their differences from other people and may be extremely reluctant to appear in public. Parental attitudes toward the child and her problems are crucial in encouraging or discouraging the child's adaptation to her handicap.

Extensive hospitalization may lead the child to feel rejected by her parents as well as society. Happily, modern medical techniques are reducing the length of hospital stays, and better counseling by the hospital staff is alleviating the impact of such separations on both the child and parents. As with other disabilities, much of the new awareness is the result of work with injured military personnel.

Group Goals

Goals for the orthopedically handicapped child are much the same as for "normal" children. The handicapped child will need greater encouragement to use her available physical and mental abilities to the fullest. Handicapped children need to know that their ideas are appreciated and that they can reach meaningful yet realistic goals. They must be made aware that doors are not closed to them merely because of their physical problem. The professions are open to the physically handicapped, as are occupations at every level. (Indeed, we have had a President of the United States who was paralyzed by polio.) Public foundations dealing with the handicapped have designed programs to show people how to run their homes effectively. Many enjoyable recreational activities can be learned, from those that involve personal participation to those needing only passive spectator appreciation. In effect, long-range goals are limited only in occupations where the affected part of the body is involved. In large part, the adjustments needed for the handicapped in terms of occupational planning must be provided by society in its change of attitude and modification of physical facilities.

For the individual who cannot plan on going out to work, there are many sources of income that can be developed at home. These include securities and investments services, typing or bookkeeping services, advertising, direct sales, mailing or labeling services, appointments or other telephone answering services, and travel agent services. Adaptation of equipment to the needs of people with arm as well as other body involvement makes it possible for the intellectually able but physically disabled to perform a wide range of activities.

Modification of Education and Facilities

At the preschool level, handicapped children can and should obtain the same developmental stimulation in the areas of self-expression, rhythm, art, conversation, prereading activities, arts and crafts, self-help procedures, and peer-group activities as other children their age. Physical education and motor activities can be modified according to a child's needs. An effective preschool program will help prepare the child for entrance to regular public schools.

When it comes time to enter public school, however, many questions come up. How will the child get to school? Transportation for the handicapped child requires both a bus with hydraulic lifts for children in wheelchairs and a driver who is cheerful, helpful, and sensitive to the needs of his special passengers. Are there steps at the school entrance? Are doorways wide enough to permit wheelchairs to go through? Are there ramps as well as stairs to permit easy mobility from one classroom to another? Ideally, a school physical plant that will be used by orthopedically handicapped children should be one story (or, if several stories, it should have elevators as well as ramps), with rest areas for those children who need rest periods, larger doorways and classrooms to accommodate wheelchairs and other special equipment, modified restroom facilities, drinking fountains that are either adjustable in height or otherwise modified to permit children of various sizes and conditions to use them, and special therapy rooms so that education will be minimally interrupted by treatment. Sand and water tables for young children in wheelchairs have to be shallow as well as at a comfortable height, with room for the chair to slide under or into a niche.

Case in Point

In the world outside of school, public facilities should reflect an awareness of the need to reduce architectural barriers for the handicapped. Revolving doors pose problems, as do self-service elevators. Restaurants lack appropriate seating-eating facilities. High street curbs pose problems, although in some cities this challenge has been met through the provision of ramped curbs. (See Figure 6-1.)

Public transportation, with its high steps at bus doorways and long flights of stairs associated with subway and elevated trains (plus steps on the trains themselves), poses annoying if not impossible challenges to the individual in a wheelchair or on crutches. Public telephone facilities, either the telephone booth or the open-air phone, are completely inaccessible to those in wheelchairs also. One possible remedy for this problem has been developed at the Franklin Institute Research Laboratories. By means of levels and with the aid of foot clamps, the person is raised to a standing position, enabling him to reach the coin slots and telephone receiver. (See Figure 6-2.)

Within the past few years, growing sensitivity to these problems has become apparent. Department store and other parking lot operators have marked off spaces close to building entrances for the physically handicapped. More restrooms have one or more extra-wide cubicles with handbars for the wheelchair-bound. Public telephone facilities in hotels and airports include telephones set low enough for use by the physically handicapped.

Blackboards should be projected out from the wall to permit children in wheelchairs to take their turn at the board with a minimum of awkwardness as their chairs slide under the blackboard ledge. At the McDonald Comprehensive Elementary School in Bucks County, Pennsylvania, for example, even the cafeteria tables have been modified so that children in wheelchairs can sit at them comfortably and eat with other children in the school. Such integration with non-handicapped children is a tremendous aid to psychological and social adjustment.

Figure 6-1.   Boston Streetcorner with Sign for Wheelchairs and Ramped Curb
(Photo courtesy of Stock, Boston)

Figure 6-2.   Elevating Wheelchair (Photo courtesy of the Center for the Enrichment of the Capabilities of the Handicapped, Franklin Institute Research Laboratories. The Stand-Up Wheelchair is patented by Peter W. Bressler and manufactured by the Overly Manufacturing Company, Greensberg, PA)

Whether the child is in a segregated or integrated school, it is obviously important to have quick and easy access to safe exits in case of an emergency. A team of classmates ought to be prepared to help the orthopedically handicapped child move quickly in such a situation. The child should not be excused from fire drills on the grounds that "it's just a drill," for he needs the practice to become familiar with the emergency procedures, and participation will reduce his "difference" from classmates.

At school, the handicapped child finds writing an important classroom task, and possibly an impossible one due to paralysis or tremors in the hands or fingers. Typewriters should be provided and instruction in their use given, so that written assignments can be prepared. Tape recorders can be used for taking notes that are then transcribed at home on the typewriter. An automatic page-turning device, operated by pushing a switch or a button, will reduce the frustration or embarrassment caused by lack of manual dexterity. Other helpful devices include the use of push buttons or foot pedals rather than switches or levers, one-handed rolling pins, left-handed scissors, touch latches on cabinet doors, nonslip bases on equipment, and lapboards.

Participation in group activities, according to the individual's talents and interests, is important to the psychological well-being of the handicapped youngster. If her physical condition inhibits playing a guitar or wind instrument, playing the cymbals on cue may be within the child's capabilities and will have therapeutic value as well in the area of muscular control. If there is no appropriate role in the class play, she can exercise certain muscles and have a part in the production by pulling the curtain ropes, or can be the prompter, director, or property woman. During physical education periods, handicapped children can participate in an adaptive physical education program. If enough children in this category are present in a given school or district, they can have their own teams and "Olympics," as handicapped adults do. Swimming offers therapeutic and recreational values and is another area in which the handicapped youngster can relate to nonhandicapped peers. At the same time, school personnel must remember that many of these children are physically weak and provide ample opportunities for rest. Further, if the child can't actively participate, an understanding of various sports can lead to many pleasant hours as a spectator.

In art courses, the child with inadequate arms or hands can learn to paint or draw with the brush or other tool in his mouth or toes. If the disability does not involve the upper limbs, there should be no problem other than having a work area appropriate in height and other dimensions on which he can work. Similarly, industrial arts activities need to be adjusted for work surface adaptability but should need no other modifications for those children who can use their upper limbs freely. Where there is arm or hand disability involved, however, the physical therapist and art or industrial arts teacher should plan appropriate beneficial and enjoyable activities together. This team approach, in fact, should be implemented in as many areas as possible.

Arrangement of the academic program should include special library privileges as needed, use of the diagnostic and vocational services of vocational rehabilitation specialists, and ample time for movement from one location to another. Both the affected students and their teachers should be aware of and plan for rapid movement in emergency situations. Assignment of handicapped students to particular course sections and curricula should be based on their mental abilities primarily, although some realistic consideration of available physical facilities, teacher attitudes, and physical handicaps should enter into the class assignments.

Educational and other professional personnel, therapists, recreation and physical education specialists, bus drivers, and cafeteria workers should all work together in making the school environment compatible to the handicapped child's physical and emotional needs. Each can contribute to the acceptance of the child and the handling of problems she brings to school.

Instruction is available for the homebound or hospitalized child in most large school districts, and hospitals with long-term patients of school age often have a small school on the premises, with teachers meeting their pupils either in a classroom or at their bedside. Physical incapacity should not and need not create a mental "vegetable." If children are unable to go out to meet the world, it can be brought to them through books, films, tape recordings, and educational and commercial television.

Case in Point

"Ham" and Citizen's band (CB) radios can also increase the handicapped individual's contact with the outside world and often are critical aids in an emergency. One newspaper story reported an instance where a female student in a wheelchair found herself alone in a college building with no way to operate the elevator buttons. After she was "rescued" several hours later, it was decided that a CB radio would be attached to her wheelchair so that she would not be stranded again.

From the *Tucson Citizen*, December 29, 1977

Teacher Preparation

There are a number of teacher certification programs available across the country in the area of teaching the orthopedically handicapped. Courses included are the usual ones in development, educational psychology, and teaching subject-matter content, plus those emphasizing modifications relevant to physical disabilities and the psychology of exceptional children. Experience in recreation or camp programs for the orthopedically handicapped is extremely useful in broadening the teacher's understanding of the physical and psychosocial needs of the children.

The teacher must be able to accept but not be blinded by physical limitations. She should be warm, flexible, adaptable, and not easily panicked by emergencies. The therapists and special physical education personnel will, of course, need to have physical strength for lifting and moving these students in addition to other personal traits.

In recent years, educators generally have focused on the "whole child." For the handicapped, this means looking beyond the medical problem to view the child as a learner among other learners, a child among his peers. Adjustments to the medical problem are just that—adjustments. Depending on the severity of the child's handicap, it may be necessary only to have resource teachers in the public school. A greater challenge may be educating regular classroom teachers to be sensitive and sympathetic to the child's needs but not pitying or overindulgent.

7

Hearing-Impaired Children

Group Characteristics

The hearing-impaired category includes all of those who have difficulties in hearing, whether the loss is mild or profound. Those with severe hearing loss either do not acquire speech spontaneously (if deafness was present at birth or occurs at a very early age) or lose speech and language skills if the impairment occurs later in childhood. Other terms used include acoustically handicapped, auditorially handicapped, and hard of hearing. The Conference of Executives of American Schools for the Deaf defines the deaf person as one with a hearing loss, usually 70 decibels or greater, that precludes the understanding of speech through the ear, with or without a hearing aid. The hard-of-hearing person, with a hearing loss of 35 to 69 decibels, has difficulty understanding speech through the ear alone, with or without a hearing aid.

For educational purposes, the hearing impaired are divided into four categories. All of these children routinely require special speech and hearing assistance. Those with mild hearing loss (35−54 dB) do not usually need special class or school placement. Children with moderate hearing loss (55−69 dB) occasionally require special placement and usually need assistance with language. Both the severely hearing impaired (70−89 dB loss) and the profoundly impaired (90 dB loss and beyond) routinely require special class or school placement, language assistance, and educational assistance (Moores, 1978, pp. 5−7). It is also possible to view the hearing-impaired child in terms of how much usable hearing he has, and his speech and language skills. According to Table 1-1, there were 49,000 deaf children and 328,000 hard-of-hearing children in this country in 1975−76. Although 92 percent of the deaf children were being served, only 20 percent of the hard-of-hearing were in appropriate programs.

In many cases, the cause of hearing loss in unknown. The most commonly reported causes are heredity (genetic), rubella during pregnancy, prematurity, Rh incompatibility, and postnatal meningitis. The genetic factor may be obvious if one or both parents is deaf, but assumed (possibly in error) if the parents and siblings of the child have normal hearing but there are other relatives who are deaf.

Whether congenital or occurring in early childhood, hearing loss affects both the learning and retention of speech, and this, in turn, affects most other areas of the child's functioning. Much current research is focused on the effects of restricted hearing ability on intellectual functioning specifically. Other research is centered on the value of mainstreaming for the hearing handicapped. There is genuine concern that neither the classroom teacher nor the curriculum will be appropriate for the child, and that needed support services will not be sufficiently available.

The average I.Q. score (on standard intelligence tests) of children with severe hearing impairments is about 90. This possibly is due to the nature of the tests: Some tests do not adapt well to use with the hearing impaired. However, these children's developmental lag in communications skills tends to retard their entrance to school and to keep them behind by three to five years academically. Even those children with more adequate test scores may appear "backward" because of their difficulties in communicating. Their motor and computational skills do not lag that far behind.

There are a number of understandable personal and social adjustment problems among the severely hearing impaired. They tend to be less emotionally stable than those with normal hearing, and, of course, they have difficulty in comprehending and being understood. Frustration resulting from these communication problems can lead to temper tantrums, withdrawal, and inadequate or inappropriate performance. Behavioral symptoms include apparent chronic inattention, failure to respond when spoken to, and very delayed or poorly articulated speech. Because these symptoms may be misinterpreted as signs of

---

Case in Point

The range of sound is 1−130 decibels (above 130 decibels, sound is replaced by the sensation of pain). Continuous exposure to sound above 90 decibels has been shown to cause permanent damage to hearing. By way of illustration, some commonly heard sounds and their decibel impact, taken singly rather than combined as they frequently are in the environment, are:

Rustle of leaves in a slight breeze	10 decibels
Average house sounds	45 decibels
Average conversation	65 decibels
Loud rock music	115 decibels
Thunder	107 decibels
Telephone (medium ring)	85 decibels
Turbojet engine	175 decibels
Motorcycle	110 decibels

autism or retardation, audiometric and other tests are necessary for clear diagnosis. Diagnostic errors and subsequent inappropriate "treatment" in early childhood can create unnecessary additional emotional problems.

Hearing impairments are the least visible physical handicap, and others may view the hearing-impaired child's "different" behavior, and therefore the child herself, negatively. Lack of mutual understanding leads to suspicions on the part of the hearing-impaired individual that others are talking about her and dislike her; aggravated instances lead to almost paranoid behavior. As suggested in Chapter 2, the inability to hear may prevent or delay the development of a good parent-child relationship and a positive self-concept, compounding the possibilities of emotional maladjustment in adolescence and adulthood.

Group Goals

The primary goal for the hearing-impaired child is effective communication with other people. Early diagnosis is important, because the child can participate in special programs that will minimize the loss in intellectual and communications functions. Doctors and parents should not shrug off lack of response to verbal cues as inattention or contrariness, nor delayed speech as a general or specific developmental lag.

Ideally, of course, hearing tests might be administered shortly after birth as they are in Luxembourg, where infants are routinely tested at 5 days and again at 6 months, permitting early diagnosis and planning for those whose hearing is impaired. If a child is found to be deaf, the mother is brought to the school for the deaf (the Logopedics School) for a three-day training period in which she is taught how to speak to and work with her child. Her work continues until the child enters the Logopedics School at age 3 (Polis, 1973). At the Johns Hopkins clinic in Baltimore, the John Tracy Clinic in Los Angeles, and the Pennsylvania State University clinic, for example, mothers are also required to participate in the special training sessions so that they can work with the child at home.

During the school years, the hearing-impaired child may live at home and attend special classes or schools, or live at a special residential school for the deaf and go home on weekends and holidays. Some may be able to work gradually into regular classes. For some, college is a possibility, either at the federally funded Gallaudet College in Washington, D.C. or at any other college. Technical programs for the deaf are available at the National Technical Institute for the Deaf at the Rochester Institute of Technology and in three regional programs at postsecondary institutions in New Orleans, Seattle, and St. Paul (Minnesota). All of these programs are federally funded. Obviously, educational attainments will vary according to abilities other than hearing and will depend on the nature of available educational facilities.

The vocational goals for some of the hearing impaired will be the same as for hearing youths. For others, however, realistic goals will be the semiskilled occupations that require minimum verbal communication. The state vocational rehabilitation office can be a valuable resource for guidance and training.

To encourage a relatively normal adult social life, the hearing-impaired child should be raised in a speaking environment and encouraged to speak for herself as much as possible. Like any child, she needs affection and attention to promote emotional well-being. Frequently, the deaf and hard of hearing form their own groups, being more comfortable with peers who have similar difficulties, and ultimately marry and have children (who may well have normal hearing). Summer camp programs also encourage interaction with peers and ease personal and social adjustment problems. New communication techniques also make it easier even for those with profound hearing loss to deal with normally hearing people, a much desired goal. Undergraduates at Gallaudet are also learning "street law" in a special project of the National Center for Law and the Deaf. This training will help them as consumers and tenants as well as in dealing with the police and the courts.

Modification of Education and Facilities

In 1954, Gallaudet College, mentioned earlier, was designated as the successor to the Columbia Institution for the Deaf, originally created by Congress in 1857. In 1966, a model secondary day and residential school for the deaf, to be established and operated in cooperation with Gallaudet College, was authorized and funded by Congress. A few years later, Congress authorized Gallaudet to establish similar facilities at the elementary level (the Kendall Demonstration School). A preschool program is also being developed. Together with the technical-vocational programs, these facilities serve as models for other programs for the hearing impaired and as teacher-training facilities.

Techniques of educating the hearing impaired depend upon the degree of functional hearing loss and the presence or absence of other abilities. In general, a primary concern is to teach the child to communicate effectively, whether through speech, writing, sign language (see Figure 7-1), gestures, or finger-spelling. The hearing-impaired child must be taught to attend to the communications of others as well, through *their* use of speech, body language, gestures, sign language, finger-spelling, or written cues. Auditory training, lip-reading, and cutaneous (touch), kinesthetic (movement), and visual cues are all part of total communications instruction. Greater visual acuity is not an automatic compensation for hearing loss, but must be taught. Opportunities for problem-solving and eye-hand coordination must be provided. The teacher must acquire some familiarity with the meaning of common gestures and facial expressions (body language) in the child's native culture. Circular or semicircular classroom and mealtime seating usually best enables each person to see everyone else's face and facilitate lip-reading.

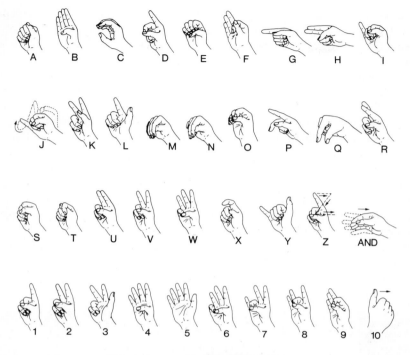

Figure 7-1.   The Manual Alphabet

Speech instruction varies, too, with the severity and time of onset of hearing loss. Those children who cannot master oral speech are usually taught the manual alphabet, although this limits their communication with the hearing world. Lip-reading is also taught, although this, too, presents restrictions. The deaf person can usually grasp only about 25 percent of the words said to him by a normally speaking person. Phrases and short sentences, spoken clearly and slowly, encourage and aid lip-reading. Specialists recommend that language be used spontaneously rather than practices with dull, repetitive drills. As in other learning situations, meaningfulness enhances learning.

Obviously, it is important for one to face the hearing-impaired listener while speaking to him. In the classroom, face-to-face communication is made easier if the children's chairs are elevated enough to put them at eye level with the teacher's lips. In some specially constructed facilities, chairs are mounted on a pole so they can be raised or lowered as needed. When the child responds to sound, at home or at school, he should be reinforced for his efforts so that this desirable behavior will occur more frequently.

Newer techniques include "cued speech," a combination of hand signals in the vicinity of the mouth to supplement and clarify lip-reading, and the "verbotonal" method, which uses infrasound to improve speech production. The Phonic Ear apparatus shown in Figure 7-2 magnifies sound so that verbal instructions can be heard even over distances of several yards. The teacher speaks into a microphone and the student receives the sounds through headphones and a small amplifier worn on her chest.

The use of films and videotape for the deaf, to promote their educational and cultural development, is encouraged under congressional legislation (1970). Many of these filmed materials are made with captions or titles so the nonlipreader can follow the narrative. But it is also desirable to use uncaptioned films to prevent lip-readers from becoming "lazy" in this skill. A few television stations now have a special newscast which combines a sign language "translation" while the regular news reporter speaks. The National Theater of the Deaf provides a fine opportunity for deaf people to enjoy theatrical presentations.

In the classroom, group hearing aids, combining a central source of amplification with binaural earphones at the listening stations, convey either the teacher's or classmates' voices or sounds from other audio equipment. Tape recorders and Language Masters permit some children to hear prerecorded speech and increase their own fluency. Hearing aid vests for children up to 10

Figure 7-2. **The Phonic Ear** (Photo courtesy of HC Electronics, Inc.)

years old or so are available that enable the child to wear bulky body hearing aids comfortably. Acoustic puzzles, using tape-recorded sounds, are combined with reinforcement techniques to teach hearing-impaired preschoolers such sounds as male and female laughter, a dog's barking, the difference between scolding and crying sounds, and so on. This training helps children to interpret speech rhythms when they cannot hear the actual words. The overhead projector, which permits the teacher to face the class while speaking, is another significant tool. Filmstrips, books, pictures, and printed words or symbols provide supporting visual stimulation which, even without auditory accompaniment, is a valuable aid for learning and communication. Family or school-sponsored field trips to stores, the zoo, even an amusement park, help the child to expand her vocabulary.

The hearing impaired, like other exceptional children, derive great benefits from art, music, and physical education classes. Art permits the expression of feelings and the development of talents for which sound is unnecessary. In music, the hearing-impaired child can respond to and learn rhythm, although she may not hear the melody itself. The ability to detect rhythm can be combined effectively with speech and language therapy.

Although the hearing-impaired child may not be able to hear a starter's gun, she can respond to a visual signal to begin a race. Through visual cues, in fact, she can learn a variety of sports, and, again, rhythm can be an effective aid in physical fitness exercises. Many deaf people are successful dancers, adapting their movements to vibrations in the dance floor that they literally perceive through their feet. Given instruction in the fine points of a game, the hearing-impaired child also can become an active and enthusiastic spectator, an "activity" that will give her another means of interacting with her hearing peers.

When hearing-handicapped youngsters are integrated into regular classes, the noise level of the classroom must be kept at a minimum if they are to use whatever hearing is available to them. A naturally lively and relatively noisy class, however, will find it difficult to adopt a radically different style. It is best for all concerned if the hearing impaired are placed in usually quieter classes.

Another area in which both home and school have serious responsibilities is in safety instruction. Although every young child needs to be taught to cross the street with the green light, this is even more essential for the hearing-impaired child who cannot hear a car approaching. Visual signals to supplement the fire gong are necessary at school. They are also useful adjuncts to the doorbell and telephone at home. In addition, the telephone company has special amplifying equipment that can aid the hearing impaired in telephone communication. Another telephone aid developed uses a combination of teletypewriters and telephones plus a device that permits conversion of spoken messages into typed messages and vice versa.

At home and at school, the hearing-impaired child should be given responsibilities and sent on errands. As she grows older, she will need to be taught the skills that are assumed to be common knowledge in the larger society—how to pay bus fare, what a ''coffee break'' is, where to seek information. Interaction and friendship with peers who can hear further dispels the isolation felt by many of the hearing impaired.

Teacher Preparation

Preparatory programs for educators of the deaf can be found in many colleges and universities. If combined in part with the training given to future speech therapists, the student gains additional insight into the deaf child's speech problems. Special teaching techniques are necessary even for the basic subjects, and training in remedial speech methods further prepares the prospective teacher of the deaf for the realities of the classroom.

At Western Maryland College, where deaf and nondeaf students study to become teachers of or social workers with the deaf, total communication is stressed to facilitate integration of the deaf into the hearing community (Wood, 1974). Extensive student-teaching opportunities generally are included in these programs, because so many of the professional skills must be modified. Familiarity with and understanding of the emotional problems of both the hearing-impaired and the normal child are also essential if teacher-student rapport is to be established and effective. Again, the personal qualities of warmth, patience, and acceptance without pity are highly desirable for these teachers. The special teacher today also needs to be able to work cooperatively with the regular classroom teacher—coordinating lessons and goals, sharing special skills and information about teaching the hearing impaired, and reducing possible sources of irritation or rejection by the teacher.

8 Visually Impaired Children

Group Characteristics

Legally, people are classified as blind when *corrected* vision in their better eye is no more than 20/200 or when their visual field is no greater than 20° (tunnel vision). Educationally, the blind are those who must be educated primarily through auditory, cutaneous, and kinesthetic senses—about 1 in 3,000 school children. There are, in addition, partially sighted children (corrected visual acuity 20/70−20/200)—about 1 in 500 school children—who need special education. Altogether, there are roughly 66,000 visually impaired children (see Table 1-1, Chapter 1) who need special education.

A leading cause of blindness is heredity, although specific genetic factors cannot always be determined. German measles (rubella) and other diseases during pregnancy may also cause a baby to be born blind. Premature babies are often given oxygen to help them breathe and prevent disease or brain damage. This treatment, however, frequently results in a condition known as retrolental fibroplasia (RLF) which leaves the infant blind. (As a result, oxygen levels were reduced to avoid blindness due to RLF. It was subsequently found, however, that brain damage or death could not be prevented at these lower levels, so the oxygen level has again been raised, resulting in an increase in blindness due to RLF [Chase, 1974].) Tumors, infections, and injuries are other causes of visual handicaps.

Whether a child has been blind from birth or is blinded later from illness or injury will affect the educational methods used. Depending on the age of the child when blindness strikes, however, enough experiences may be remembered to ease the transfer in learning techniques.

Developing defects and severe reduction in vision present a variety of symptoms: chronic eye irritations, double vision, excessive caution in walking or running, abnormal inattention during vision-oriented school work (maps, blackboard activities, and so on), excessive blinking or unusual head positions while reading, and several others. "Lazy eye," or amblyopia, can be treated effectively if detected by physical examination before or at the time of entrance to school but usually does not require special education placement.

The blind child has normal growth patterns generally, except in the area of motor performance where, understandably, there is some delay in the development of independent mobility. There are few intellectual impairments linked to blindness, except in cases of genetic or common environmental causes. In fact, the average I.Q. of the blind is 99 on the Hayes version of the Stanford-Binet intelligence test. Cognitive limitations may arise, however, from negative educational experiences as well as from the obvious problems in reading or otherwise acquiring visual information. Speech development may be slower than for the sighted, due to poorer lip movements and fewer gestures. This merely reflects the lack of visual models by which most of us master these aspects of speech; there is no other language deficit peculiar to the blind.

For blind children, the greatest threats to emotional well-being are overprotection and rejection. If they are permitted and encouraged to develop physical independence, they can have feelings of competence. If, on the contrary, they are led everywhere, seated frequently to wait quietly while others are active, or perceived and treated as retarded when they are not, they will have no feelings of competence, power, or significance to others. Frustrations may lead to aggressive behavior (tantrums, fighting, breaking objects), but this can occur with any child who is pushed beyond her ability to handle a situation. Blind children do not seem to have the tendency toward specific emotional problems, however, that is seen in the hearing impaired.

Group Goals

The blind who are normal in all other respects can have the same life goals as sighted individuals. With ability, encouragement, and guidance, they can attend college and even professional school. Careers in law, teaching (where

Case in Point

Gilbert Ramirez, the first Puerto Rican to sit as a justice of the New York State Supreme Court, is blind. Sighted as a youth, he went blind in his twenties, and was told that he could learn to weave brooms. He taught himself typing, however, obtained a job, and subsequently completed the four-year course at Brooklyn Law School in three years. Ramirez served in the state legislature for three years and then as a family court judge before being elected to a fourteen-year term on the State Supreme Court.

Philadelphia Inquirer, November 19, 1977

state certification laws or institutions of higher education permit), social work, psychology, and many of the creative arts are all within reach. Broom-making and piano-tuning, two traditional occupations for the blind, are not and should not be the upper limits of the blind youth's aspirations. Vocational/career training, preferably with sighted children, should be part of all blind students' vocational programs.

If not overprotected or encouraged to indulge in self-pity, the blind and partially sighted can lead normal personal and social lives. They can and do marry and have children. To achieve these levels of normality, the blind child needs the love, acceptance, and encouragement by her parents and others that will develop her self-security and self-motivation.

Modification of Education and Facilities

The parent of a blind infant needs counseling to work out feelings of guilt and to face the reality of the family situation. Early intervention also reduces the possibility of environmental privation leading to retardation, an unnecessary compounding of the child's difficulties. Very important is the development of the normal parent-child relationship, with encouragement of infant response to the parent's voice rather than his or her face. The blind baby, like any other, should be talked to, handled, and encouraged to develop in all areas. Extra attention to sensorimotor development is particularly helpful.

At the nursery school level, in addition to the usual activities and routines, the blind child needs extra opportunities for tactual stimulation (books with variously textured fabric samples; a variety of work materials such as simple puzzles of basic shapes, blocks, paste, and fingerpaints), coordination exercises, outdoor recreation, and much individual attention. Whenever possible, she should be part of a group of both sighted and blind children to enhance her self-confidence and social relationships.

Training in the use of Braille should begin early. Early auditory training to increase attention to small cues and facilitate use of tape recording and phonograph equipment is also important.

In addition to Braille, a portable electronic reading aid, the Optacon, also enables the blind to read a wide range of printed material. A miniaturized camera in this relatively new device reproduces letter images on a tiny screen that provides tactile stimulation. The blind reader can feel the image with one fingertip. For the 80 to 90 percent of the blind who do not read Braille, this is a useful instrument, despite the limitations of the early models. Other devices are being developed for blind diabetics whose fingertips lack the sensitivity needed to read Braille or the Optacon.

Although classwork should emphasize academic learning, other aspects of

---

Case in Point

Training programs for volunteers permit more books of all kinds to be reproduced in Braille. Special tasks include the printing of religious texts in Braille, enabling, for example, a blind young woman and a teen-aged boy to follow and participate in congregational worship. The size of Braille texts, a result of the heavy paper needed for the raised dots, makes their use more difficult for children. Texts are available in any subject and at any level, or can be custom-made, enabling the blind child to keep up with her peers. Other diligent volunteers read texts onto audio tapes, also helping the blind to expand their horizons. These "Talking Books," whether provided by local volunteers or by the American Printing House for the Blind, are used also by older adults becoming blind or recovering from eye surgery.

---

education should not be neglected. Continued opportunity to learn by touch (models, textures) is essential and should be encouraged also in art programs, using three-dimensional materials, and in learning to type, cook, and use hand and small machine tools. Electronic technology has made possible other helpful devices such as sound-emitting, light-sensitive rods that can differentiate different denominations of paper money, sonarlike mechanisms that make the blind individual aware of the location of persons and objects, and even talking calculators. Each of these devices helps the blind child or adult to function more independently in the seeing world.

Field trips offer further opportunities for stimulation and learning. Facilities designed especially for the blind, such as the Brooklyn Botanical Garden and the University Museum, University of Pennsylvania, are particularly stimulating and gratifying. Some art museums, such as the Krannert Art Museum at the University of Illinois, arrange special tours and exhibits at which the blind person is able to touch a variety of art objects and experience their texture, weight, shape, and proportional relationships. The arboretum in San Francisco's Golden Gate Park includes a garden for the blind. The plants, set so they can be reached without stooping, are meant to be sampled. Leaves can be picked, felt, crushed, smelled, and even tasted.

Adaptive physical education can lead to physical fitness, enable the blind child to participate in family and community recreation activities, help develop spatial orientation and thereby improve mobility, and provide the youngster with sports information that she can use as a social skill. Whenever possible, the blind child should participate in activities with sighted companions. Buell (1966) offers detailed suggestions for such a program. Several Scout troops for both boys and girls also contribute to the goal of normal social development. Many activities at camps for blind children are normally associated only with sight,

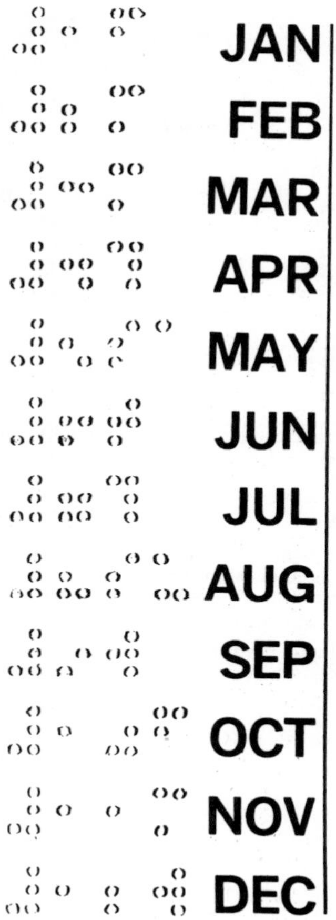

JAN Printing a complete calendar in Braille would take many times more space than a regular calendar. Therefore, the Braille calendar indicates only the day on which the first of each month falls.

FEB

MAR

APR

MAY The Braille calendar at left reads 1F, 2M, 3M, 4TH and so on, indicating the first day of the first month is a Friday, the first day of the second month is a Monday, etc.

JUN

JUL

AUG By knowing what day of the week the first day of a month is, all other days can then be determined.

SEP

OCT

NOV

DEC

Figure 8-1.   The Braille Calendar

such as archery (balloons on the target and assistance in aiming the arrow make this possible), horseback riding, tumbling, swimming, and water-skiing. Experimental electronic devices embedded in baseballs have also been designed to permit participation in this sport. Where facilities and funds permit, these, too, can be adapted to the school's physical education program or extracurricular schedule.

From early childhood on, the blind child needs to learn how to cope with social demands, his dependency feelings, and other people's attitudes toward his handicap. Many attitudes toward the blind seem to stem from ignorance and anxieties. Pity, cruelty, rejection, and teasing are too often exhibited toward the blind child. When these reactions are demonstrated by other children, they usually reflect family attitudes. The blind adolescent has a particularly difficult time in resolving the conflicts between his dependency and the rebellion against

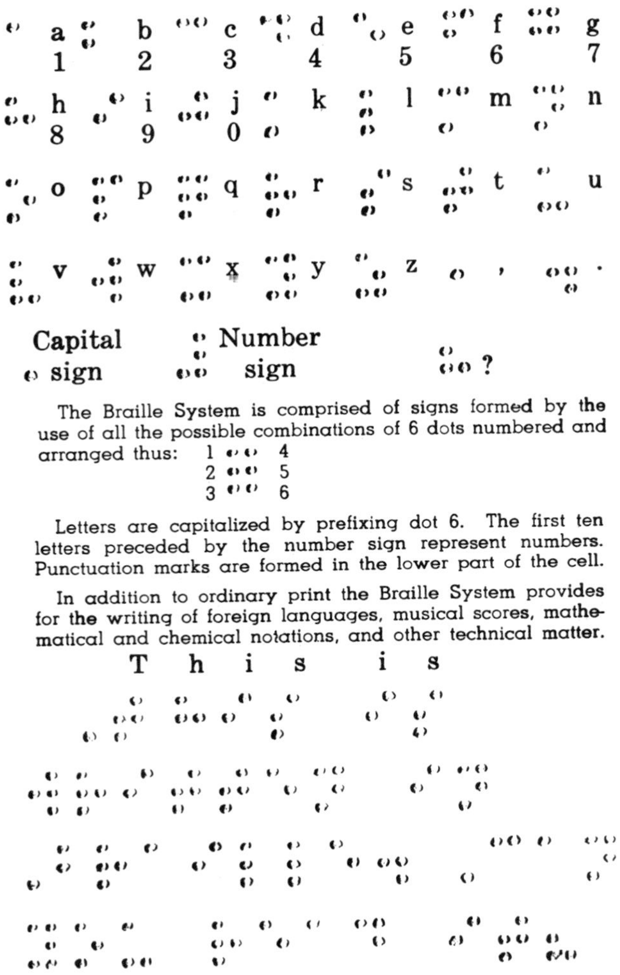

a b c d e f g
1 2 3 4 5 6 7

h i j k l m n
8 9 0

o p q r s t u

v w x y z , .

Capital   Number
sign   sign   ?

The Braille System is comprised of signs formed by the
use of all the possible combinations of 6 dots numbered and
arranged thus: 1   4
                 2   5
                 3   6

Letters are capitalized by prefixing dot 6. The first ten
letters preceded by the number sign represent numbers.
Punctuation marks are formed in the lower part of the cell.

In addition to ordinary print the Braille System provides
for the writing of foreign languages, musical scores, mathematical and chemical notations, and other technical matter.

T   h   i   s   i   s

Figure 8-2.   The Braille Alphabet and Numbers

parents that is normal at this age. Rebellion against those on whom the adolescent is so dependent creates feelings of guilt and resentment. He needs to have an
opportunity to explore and express his feelings in this regard and about his
handicap generally. The teacher or counselor can be most helpful in this area.

Personal grooming is important, too. The blind youngster needs to be aware
that she is seen by sighted people, who do judge by what they see. A neat appearance will be expected in both social and occupational situations. Knowing that
they are well-groomed gives the blind additional self-confidence.

The partially sighted child needs many of the modifications designed for the blind, but does have the advantage of some sight. She needs large-type reading materials, glare-free working areas and materials, and opportunities to participate in physical education, art, home economics, and other nonacademic activities adapted to her abilities. Typewriters with large-size type will be helpful both to the classroom teacher in preparing materials and to the student herself in completing assignments. Pencils should have heavier and thicker lead for easier reading. Illustrations should be clear and well-spaced for easier perception. Desks with adjustable easel tops, heavily bas-reliefed maps and charts, and manipulable materials are other learning aids for the partially sighted pupil.

The partially sighted child can be assigned to regular classes and participate in many activities with her peers. She can go to a special teacher or resource room or work with the guidance of an itinerant teacher on tasks requiring close visual effort. The special teacher and regular classroom teacher should have frequent conferences to coordinate their teaching approaches. For example, the special teacher has the resources to arrange for having class lessons put into Braille, the knowledge of the blind child's abilities with which to persuade the regular class teacher or others that the child can participate in a debate, and the sensitivity to explain blindness to a child's seeing classmates.

If the visually impaired student is in a regular classroom, two extremely important matters are orientation and safety. The youngster should come to school for a few days before classes open, if at all possible, in order to become familiar with the classroom arrangement and facilities, corridors, stairways, and other areas she will use. Safety involves thoughtfulness on the part of all—pushing chairs under tables or desks, telling the student of furniture rearrangements, closing or opening doors completely, and so on. Provision must be made for such emergencies as fire drills. Auditory alarm signals must supplement visual signals. A navigable safety route should be practiced, and a "buddy" system with sighted classmates is advisable.

In a special educational setting, handrails along the walls as well as stairways, easily reached and grasped door handles, and systematic storage facilities make it easier for the vision-impaired child to move about on her own and find

This is regular size print used in most news publications. To read it is a strain for people who have poor vision.

This is the size print used in the Large Type Weekly. See how much easier it is to read.

Figure 8-3.   Large Print Type

supplies without assistance. A textured tile path will help the blind child to find her way down the hallways with minimal assistance and fewer bruises from bumping into walls. Corners may be curved rather than angled, again to reduce the possibility of injury. Any reduction in the need for help from others also reduces the vision-impaired child's feelings of dependency, and she does need this emotional lift.

The blind child needs the same warmth and acceptance from the teacher as do other children. The considerate teacher will give specific verbal directions and instruction and avoid embarrassing situations by informing the student quietly and informally of her presence or impending absence.

Although the blind youngster may have many abilities, she is too often perceived as almost completely helpless. By doing too much for her, others only contribute to a negative self-esteem. Striking an effective balance is the touchy task of both teachers and parents.

Teacher Preparation

Relatively few college programs in this country prepare people to teach the blind and partially sighted. Beyond the usual foundation courses in psychology and education in the professional program, the prospective teacher of the visually impaired needs to understand the development and psychology of the exceptional child in general and the blind in particular.

Special methods courses will emphasize materials involving the auditory, tactile, and kinesthetic senses, as well as the variety of educational media available for the partially sighted child. Coursework in the anatomy, physiology, and hygiene of the eye; principles of physiological optics; and study of eye diseases will contribute to the teacher's understanding and ability to deal with the physical problems of the visually handicapped. Training in music, art, and adaptive physical education give the teacher added means for enriching her students' education. (There are very few professionally trained instructors available for the mobility training—crossing streets, using subways and buses, and so on—that gives the blind child additional freedom, independence, and self-assurance.)

Frequent and prolonged contact with visually impaired people will greatly increase the prospective teacher's confidence and expertise.

Coursework and experience, where possible, in dealing with the emotional problems of the visually impaired and interacting with their parents is especially helpful. The blind child is much more apt to achieve her goals if the teacher succeeds in gaining the cooperation and support of the child's parents. Great frustration is in store for student and teacher alike if classroom learning is undone or ignored in the home. Finally, added to the usual personal and professional qualifications, the teacher should have the initiative and resourcefulness to develop materials and activities that will benefit the student.

9 Multiply Handicapped Children

Group Characteristics

A multiply handicapped child has two or more disabilities to overcome. These may include auditory and visual impairment (deaf-blind), retardation and cerebral palsy, aphasia and deafness, and many other possible combinations. Such difficulties may be present at birth as the result of the rubella epidemics of the mid-1960s, prenatal drug effects (especially thalidomide), the Rh factor, and other congenital conditions, or may arise after birth due to injury or illness. Psychological disturbance is a common additional handicap, an outgrowth of the many frustrations suffered by the multiply handicapped.

Among the most severe cases are those suffering two or more sensory impairments, because the sources of stimulation to which the child can respond are so limited. Helen Keller, however, is the classic example of an individual who overcame auditory, visual, speech, and psychological handicaps to lead a relatively independent and productive adult life. The child whose develoment is severely hampered by cerebral palsy and who is also retarded and blind or deaf has decreasing chances of learning even the rudiments of self-help. Despite the right-to-education rulings in several states, such a severely handicapped child can profit so minimally from even special education classes that, in the absence of a combination of good day programs and unusual parents, residential placement is generally best for the child, his parents, and his siblings.

The Office of Education estimate for 1975—76 was that, of 40,000 multi-handicapped children, only 16,000 were being served by day-care programs or schools. The location and learning activities of the remaining children are unknown.

Group Goals

The educational goal for the multiply handicapped child is clear and basic: Help him use the abilities he has.

The establishment of model centers for deaf-blind children was authorized by an act of Congress in 1960. These centers were to provide diagnostic and evaluative services; develop programs for the children's adjustment, orientation, and education; and develop effective consultation services for parents, teachers, and others involved with deaf-blind children. The centers are scattered throughout the country and can be located through a local branch of one of the agencies listed in the directory at the end of this book.

In one preschool program for deaf-blind children, positive changes in behavior were sought in eight areas of child development: "a) eating and drinking, b) dressing, c) toilet training, d) muscle tone and posture, e) locomotion, f) play, g) self-stimulation and attention to external stimuli, and h) adaptive reactions" (Calvert et al., 1972, p. 419).

In a cerebral palsy center for severely multihandicapped young school-age children, similar goals, with the exception of toilet training, were established.

In a school for the multiply handicapped blind, self-help, adaptability, mobility, and physical conditioning are stressed, and the child is exposed to as much academic learning as she can handle. Those whose learning potential is evaluated as normal are transferred to public school classes for the blind as soon as they are ready for this move and as long as the physical facilities of the receiving school are adequate to their needs.

In a center for preschool retarded and orthopedically handicapped children, the same goals are set. The retarded trainable or educable may be transferred to special public school classes.

Although we are not principally concerned here with the family of the multiply handicapped child, one also must work with the parents and perhaps siblings and/or grandparents for maximum benefit to the child. The family often needs help in dealing with feelings of guilt, inadequacy, and hopelessness, and in facing the realities of the situation. The major goal is to help the family in its efforts to help the child. Too often, progress made in the special program is undermined by rejection, lack of reinforcement, or other negative attitudes at home.

Modification of Education
and Facilities

It is unlikely that many of the multiply handicapped will be mainstreamed. However, it is possible that some such children can spend some school time in regular classes. These might include the orthopedically handicapped with mild retardation or speech problems, the partially sighted with a specific learning disability, and children with similar combinations of limited handicaps.

Many of the educational and facility modifications discussed in the individual sections on the physically different apply to the multiply handicapped. A complication, however, is that modifications appropriate for one handicap may not be practical when a second and a third disability are present. For example, there is some research evidence that colorblindness occurs in the deaf more frequently than would be expected (Frey and Krause, 1971). Although color is generally a good educational tool, its use might have little value for the deaf retarded.

A psychologically therapeutic atmosphere—personal warmth, responsiveness, and acceptance—is a requisite for even the most severely multiply handicapped. The aphasic cerebral palsied child can learn to smile, to move limbs voluntarily, and to respond in little ways to stimulating people and objects. Each bit of progress in one of these areas can't help but be reinforced by the excitement of the child's teachers. The deaf-blind child whose mental abilities are unimpaired needs much psychological support if he is to function intellectually and socially in spite of his physical constraints.

Multiply handicapped children, particularly those with aphasia and hearing problems, generally also have communication problems. In a demonstration program, however, multiple daily therapy sessions and therapeutic materials related to classroom language concepts brought improvement in many cases (Doob, 1968).

Case in Point

Modern technology can enhance the receptive and expressive activities of the multiply handicapped to a considerable degree. The Seattle public schools, for example, employ a team headed by a neurophysiologist, an electrical engineer, and an electronics technician to design and build equipment that will enable a child to maintain head balance, develop muscle control, and convert auditory stimuli into visual patterns for speech improvement.

From V. Hedrick (1972)

Clearly, noneducators and special education personnel must work together imaginatively to modify the educational situation for the unique needs and problems of each multiply handicapped child. A multifaceted approach is essential to the multiply handicapped. Music can be used in many ways—to stimulate movement, teach rhythm and concepts, relax, and so on. Art is another activity for many of these children. However, because each child's combination of handicaps is unique, one program can hardly serve the needs of any group of children, nor can the same goals be set for all children. Taking one step alone may be a major achievement for one child, and moving a finger voluntarily may be the ultimate goal for another. Some of the multiply handicapped may profit from instruction in reading and other academic subjects, but this is often, for them and their teachers, a long, long road.

Teacher Preparation

An examination of a list of certification programs in colleges across the country reveals none specifically oriented to preparation for teaching the multiply handicapped (Vernon, 1969).[1] There have been, however, teacher training programs for working with the deaf-blind at Perkins School for the Blind (Massachusetts), San Francisco State University, George Peabody College for Teachers (Nashville, Tennessee), and Michigan State University. The Center for Multiple Handicapped Children, operated by the New York City Board of Education, is also a training center for teachers of the handicapped, paraprofessionals (many of whom are themselves handicapped), and interns from the New York Hospital Medical Center.

Most of the preparation must come from on-the-job training, and prior experience with singly handicapped children is considered very valuable. A teacher of the multiply handicapped probably needs more patience, versatility, resourcefulness, and compassion (but not pity) than is required of teachers of any other group. A strong academic and experiential background in early childhood development is a definite asset, too, since this is the level at which most of the children function.

---

[1]Note: In 1978, there were still no such programs to the author's knowledge.

Four

Oral Communication Difficulties

Two large groups of children have difficulty with oral communication. One group suffers from such speech impairments as stuttering, vocal disorders, or inadequately developed speech. The other group consists of the language handicapped, those who speak little or no English and may also have a poor command of their native language.

Although the sources of their problems are quite different, the children in these groups share a common difficulty—they cannot make themselves understood. This not only frustrates them and those to whom they are trying to speak but also can lead to mistaken impressions that the child is slow, retarded, emotionally disturbed, or otherwise handicapped. The inability to communicate effectively can have long-term negative effects on the child's personality and ultimately on his career plans.

There is legislative support for programs for the language handicapped, and there have been speech therapy programs in the schools for decades. As a result of right-to-education laws, more children in these two groups will enter and remain in the school population; support for special education in the oral communications area will have to be increased correspondingly.

One key to interpersonal, and even international, conflicts is ineffective communication. Because speech is the basis of much of our interaction with other people, and ineffective communication hinders learning as well as social activities, effective remediation is crucial.

10 Speech-Impaired Children

Group Characteristics

A lisp is cute in a toddler or temporarily toothless 6-year-old, and the stammer of a young child groping for a word is understandable, but the persistence of these speech characteristics in older children and adults is neither cute nor generally acceptable. The wide range of speech impairments varies from the relatively simple articulation disorders to those caused by organic dysfunction. Almost 2,300,000 children, the largest group of exceptional children counted by the Bureau of the Handicapped, are speech impaired.

Speech impairments, because they are disturbing, distorted, and restrictive, handicap interpersonal relationships. The inability to communicate freely inhibits emotional expression, a frustration that ultimately affects the individual's personality and social behavior. It can also interfere with learning. The often-admired "strong, silent type" may behave that way because his speech is impaired, and the quiet child in the back row may sit there to avoid being called on and thus forced to expose a speech impairment before the class.

Speech problems may arise from emotional, physical, environmental, or intellectual factors. For example, delayed onset or inadequate development of speech can have intellectual causes (retardation), physical causes (retarded maturation of the speech apparatus or hearing loss), environmental causes (no response to the child's early speaking efforts), emotional causes (anxiety about parental reaction to speech behavior), or some combination of these. Articulation problems, creating inaccurate, incorrect, or unclear sounds, may be due to physical impairment or the lack of good speech models in the environment. Vocal disorders—volume, pitch, quality, and rate of speech—are often caused by other physical handicaps or emotional factors. Fluency problems (stuttering) frequently are a response to anxiety (which increases as stuttering increases).

Some speech disorders, particularly those related to articulation, or the production of speech sounds, are self-correcting by the time the child is about 10 years old, if she *hears* correct pronunciation. The normal stammer and stutter of the 3- to 5-year-old may also be self-correcting if the child does not develop additional behavioral problems. Overconcerned parents should be reassured that normal maturation can solve these problems. Organically based speech disorders, however, which stem from cleft palate, cerebral palsy, hearing loss, or aphasia, are generally not self-corrective and require a variety of therapeutic techniques for remediation. Obviously, the earlier these more severe conditions are discovered, the more the child can be helped to achieve effective speech. Surgery to repair the cleft palate, communications instruction for the hearing impaired as suggested in Chapter 7, and other more extensive therapies are, however, beyond the scope of this book.

Group Goals

The goal here is, simply, to help the speech-impaired child achieve more effective oral communication. For those whose speech cannot be improved substantially, some adjustment in vocational goals may be necessary. Consideration must be given, too, to reducing the social and emotional problems either caused by or resulting from the child's speech disorder. Reduction of these problems should involve the parents as well as the child.

Modification of Education and Facilities

For children whose speech impairments are due primarily to emotional factors, learned behavior, or mild physical dysfunctions, remedial assistance usually consists of clinical therapy, once a week for an hour or so, with the speech therapist and exercises to practice at home. Essentially, new learning must take place to break down poor speech habits. It may also be necessary, however, to schedule psychotherapy sessions to eliminate the emotional problems suggested earlier. For a few children, minor surgery may be the appropriate remedy.

Looking first at the articulation disorders, the most common type of speech impairment, we find children who omit initial or final consonants ("ste" for "step"), substitute one sound for another ("wittle" for "little"), distort sounds through slurring or lisping, or add sounds to words. Some children have not been stimulated to modify, or are encouraged to maintain, their babified speech by a parent who thinks it's "cute"—for example, "telebision" for "television." In other instances, these speech errors reflect exposure to others' faulty articulation, as when the "g" is omitted in words that end in "ing." If other children in the class speak correctly, they may tease or ridicule the child who makes these errors. Some children will then emphasize the errors, rejoicing in the attention that this brings them, while others will hesitate to speak at all for fear of being laughed at.

The speech therapist uses a number of methods to correct the errors and provides psychologically sound guidance for improving both speaking performance and peer relations in the classroom. Correct tongue placement and mouth movement, drill on sounds, the Language Master, audiotapes, pictures, and her own example are among the therapist's techniques.

Stuttering in older children appears to be closely related to parental sensitivity to the child's speech (Johnson, 1958). If the parent perceives the child as a stutterer, she often becomes one. (If true, the principle ties in with Rosenthal's theory (1968) that we perform academically as others expect us to and Sullivan's theory (1953) that we develop a self-concept based on the reflections of significant others.) As the child begins to perceive herself as a stutterer, she becomes more anxious, often adding blinking, tics, or extra vocalizations to her speaking behavior in an effort to avoid, prevent, or release the stuttering. That is, responding to parental or teacher concern and attempting to avoid speech disfluencies, the child becomes anxious and exhibits additional disfluencies.

What is to be done? The therapist first needs to observe carefully what behaviors precede or accompany stuttering and then replace these with behaviors that will enhance fluent speech. The cooperation of the child's parents, teacher, and even his classmates should be enlisted to help him change his self-perception as a stutterer. They will also be taught how best to respond when stuttering occurs. Frequent injunctions to "speak more slowly," "hold your breath," "start again," and so on only tend to increase the child's self-consciousness and, therefore, his disfluency. Positive reinforcement for improved speech is far more effective in the long run. Psychotherapy that helps to reduce conflicts, decrease anxieties, and improve the child's general emotional adjustment is also likely to relieve the stuttering problem.

Problems in the use of the voice can be similarly reduced by the speech therapist. Here, however, physical factors frequently are involved. The child with cerebral palsy or a hearing impairment, for example, may speak too softly (because this is how she hears others), too loudly (because others shout to her), or

---

Case in Point

Unlikely as it may seem, participation in debating team activities may be helpful to the stutterer. Attention is focused on the ideas to be communicated, and debaters are urged to speak slowly and deliberately. This style gives the stutterer time to "face" troublesome words without emphasizing his special need to pause or make a "dry run" to avoid disfluency.

After Wingate (1976)

with insufficient variation in pitch and volume. One-to-one instruction by the speech therapist can correct these problems over a period of time. Practice with audiotapes is also helpful.

Music is a valuable technique for including children with remedial speech impairments in class activities. As part of a singing group, their lisps and stammers tend to fade, partly because the attention is focused on the words of the song rather than on individual production of sounds. Children with foreign or regional accents also seem to lose these during singing.

Teaching a foreign language to a child with speech problems also has interesting effects. If the problems are emotionally rather than physically based, they may disappear in the second language. On the other hand, problems with a physical basis continue in the second language, and the foreign language teacher must be aware of the child's difficulties and respond to them diplomatically and sympathetically. Whether or not to encourage or insist that the child participate in individual oral drills must be decided on an individual basis, for some children will be able to do this and others will lose even more self-confidence.

Although no drastic architectural changes are needed for the speech impaired, a number of aids should be present at school and, where possible, at home as well. A large mirror enables the child to see that she is placing her tongue correctly or to observe and eventually eliminate undesirable mannerisms that accompany her speech. Puppets enable the child to speak without being seen, yet force her to speak clearly so that the puppet's actions and story can be understood by listeners. The Language Master permits the child to hear both correct speech sounds and her delivery of the same sounds while she sees what she is to say (object, word, or situation). Tape recorders, phonograph records, videotape and other film materials, and the Peabody Language Development Kits are also effective with the speech impaired.

In the case of organically based speech disorders, additional techniques may be needed. The child with a cleft palate, for example, needs both surgery and speech therapy to reduce nasalization of vowels and unclear consonants. The child with cerebral palsy frequently needs exercises in motor coordination and muscle control along with corrective speech exercises. Children with hearing loss, to hear and produce speech correctly, must have access to amplification equipment.

For all of the speech impaired, it is very important that children be accepted as worthwhile to themselves and others. Everyone who relates to them should encourage their verbal participation without embarrassing them and give them nonverbal responsibilities which contribute to group projects and their own learning. In other words, a speech problem should not be a reason for avoiding contact with others; emphasizing the speech-impaired child's assets and encouraging her to share them provides her with access to social interaction. There is little question of having speech-impaired children in regular classes. They have always been there. For decades, they have spent an hour or so a week with the speech therapist, slipping in and out of the classroom with little attention from their peers because "going to speech clinic" has been so routine.

Teacher Preparation

In public school systems, children with speech impairments usually work with an itinerant trained speech pathologist or therapist. The speech therapist should have followed a special college program that includes course work in anatomy and physiology (particularly of the speech and hearing apparatus), corrective techniques, diagnostic methods, psychology courses emphasizing problems of adjustment and mental health, and supportive courses in education that help her work more effectively with the classroom teacher. In small school districts without a speech therapist, the classroom teacher should be provided with inservice courses to learn something of the symptoms, causes, and emotional by-products of speech disorders and what to do about them. Training in art, music, and the uses of instructional media give the teacher additional techniques for work with the speech-impaired child. It is important, too, that the teacher speak correctly, and in some states this is a qualification for teacher certification.

11 Language-Handicapped Children

Group Characteristics

The language handicapped are more commonly referred to as bilingual. This is not entirely accurate, however, because bilingualism, first of all, is the ability to speak two languages with equal skill and, second, implies fluency in both languages. Language-handicapped children, however, frequently are unable to speak and/or comprehend standard English fluently and have variable proficiency in another language. Language-handicapped children in the United States may be American Indian, Cuban refugees, French-Canadian, Mexican-American, Puerto Rican, and Chinese, among other, less frequently identified groups. Children from isolated Appalachian areas, where spoken English is a dialect used a few hundred years ago; from French-descended Creole settlements in Louisiana; from the very rural South; and from urban ghettos, who also speak a nonstandard English dialect, may also be language handicapped.

All of these children present a challenge to the teacher, an "outsider" from their point of view, who speaks standard English and expects them to do so, too. The lack of communication is a mutual problem. Even if the teacher can speak the second language or dialect, she is usually unfamiliar with the idioms or patois unique to the children's reference group. Add to this the complication that the child may not even speak his native language at a "standard" level, and you have what Anastasi and Cordova (1953) call "language bifurcation"—that is, inadequate mastery of either language. This is the common problem of these children when they attend school. They cannot profit from traditional instruction because they and their teachers simply do not understand each other.

There are several additional problems related to this communications barrier. For example, many school districts with a fairly large number of so-called bilingual children do not permit these children to use their native language at all during school hours, including recess periods. This practice not only makes them resent the school and its authorities but also strikes a blow at their self-esteem, for they are made to feel ashamed of their families, their culture, and themselves and inferior to the dominant culture of the school.

Case in Point

Pablo, age 5, was referred to the diagnostic facility because he spoke very little at the Get Set Center and appeared to be either retarded or emotionally disturbed. Small but sturdy, he was reluctant to take the examiner's hand at his first visit and shuffled his way along the corridor with his head down.

Pablo was given the *Wechsler Preschool and Primary Scale of Intelligence* (WPPSI) in English, as well as several other tests. The WPPSI was of particular interest because of his irregular performance on the subtests. For example, Pablo could not "name two animals," but knew that milk came from an animal called "a cow" and defined a donkey as "an animal." He did not know the days of the week in either English or Spanish. He could subtract, having failed easier addition problems. On almost every subtest, he passed several difficult tasks, having failed easier ones. Was this variable performance the result of a language or an experience deficiency? Repetition of several of the questions in Spanish at a second testing session suggested the latter, for Pablo still missed the questions.

Despite errors, Pablo earned verbal subtest scores in the range of 7 to 10 (Verbal Scale I.Q. of 91) and performance subtest scores in the range of 8 (Mazes) to 14 (Geometric Designs) (Performance Scale I.Q. of 111), and a Full-Scale I.Q. of 101. As Pablo carefully printed his name, and about two-thirds of the alphabet, he said that his 12-year-old brother had taught him letters and some of the arithmetic concepts.

Pablo's brother, mother, and father all speak some English, but only his mother apparently speaks to him regularly in English. Since she is employed, his primary caretaker is a Spanish-speaking grandmother. No one in the family appears to have a good command of either language, resulting in true language bifurcation for Pablo. Despite his ability to function within the average range, he will become handicapped without language instruction and an expansion of his experiences.

A Massachusetts law, however, mandates instruction in the second language wherever it is needed. And a Supreme Court ruling in January 1974, in the case of non-English-speaking Chinese children in San Francisco, ordered special instruction in the English language to prevent these and other so-called bilingual children from becoming handicapped second-class citizens. Funds for bilingual education projects are available under Title VII, Emergency School Aid Act. Consideration should be given when planning such projects to the children's preferred (most frequently spoken) as well as dominant (native) langue while they are receiving English language instruction.

A second problem engenders emotional conflict. To many of the children and their parents, being forced to learn standard English is a rejection of the environment in which they have developed and been cared for during their preschool years. The children feel caught in a painful dilemma: be rejected by the schools or reject their families. Furthermore, when the parents and peers of one of these children do not seek upward mobility for her or for themselves, the child who tries to accommodate her language to that desired by the school becomes a social outcast. She is seen as "uppity."

In addition to these psychological conflicts, the child may experience considerable anxiety in her attempts to speak English correctly. This frequently leads to speech impairments, particularly stuttering and stammering. In her efforts to listen to and hear English words correctly, furthermore, she may become so involved with the individual words that she fails to grasp the concept or thought being discussed. Her lack of ability to communicate effectively also handicaps her relationships with other children in the school, again devaluating her self-concept.

In most cases, language-handicapped children come from lower-class families and belong to one of the cultural minorities previously mentioned. Their lack of academic achievement and inability to communicate effectively often lead them to terminate their schooling prematurely. This, in turn, limits their job opportunities and socioeconomic mobility, tending to doom them to the same borderline economic existence as their parents have had. The interruption of this cycle would benefit the individual and society as a whole.

Case in Point

An unusual variety of language handicap, unrelated to "bilingualism," is *idioglossia* or twin speech. In the case of identical twin girls, aged 7, the children speak a self-designed language that is unintelligible even to their parents. Thought to be mentally retarded, it has been discovered that the girls understand English, German, sign language, and a little Spanish, but prefer to communicate in their private language. In therapy, they have been found to be mentally alert and quite capable of learning.

Howes (1977)

Group Goals

The obvious goal for the language handicapped is to teach them English as it is spoken in the larger society so that they can profit from learning experiences in both school and less formal settings. Beyond this primary goal are others common to all children: enabling them to optimize their abilities and enhance their self-concept. The latter effort should include maintenance of skill in the native language so that the individual can communicate effectively in both languages.

True bilingualism is an occupational asset in many fields: foreign service, law enforcement and corrections, social work, teaching, politics, and international commerce are just a few examples. It is also a social asset (and sometimes a necessity) in many communities, particularly in Canada, where bilingualism is the law of the land.

Modification of Education
and Facilities

The most direct way to deal with the language handicapped would be to teach them standard English before attempting other instruction. In this instance, however, the most direct approach is not necessarily the easiest, the most correct, or the most effective. The psychological conflicts cited earlier inhibit learning standard English. Many children are bored by a chronic daily diet of English instruction. The newly arrived teenager, particularly, rejects being given only simple language instruction, because she knows that she will fall several grades behind her age peers. Educational modifications, then, must be tailored to the needs—in terms of age, prior formal learning experiences, and family environment—of the individual child.

It should be recognized at the outset that all children tend to exhibit one set of behaviors in school and a somewhat different set outside of school. This applies to language as well. The language handicap tends to be intensified in the child's dealings with school personnel and other authority figures. He generally communicates quite effectively away from school. One possible technique to reduce the communications and learning barriers is to modify the attitudes of school authorities so that the child is encouraged to speak more to adults in her natural idiom and thereby increase her overall frequency of communication.

It is essential that the standard English speaker articulate clearly and pronounce words correctly, or the listener will simply exchange one kind of nonstandard language for another. When it is difficult for the learner to pronounce a particular speech sound—for example, because it doesn't exist in his native language—the speech teacher should be called on for assistance. The child who must continue to flounder is apt to feel both frustrated and humiliated.

It is highly probable that the child comprehends standard English better than she speaks it (true for all of us), and, for this reason, standard English, rather than the nonstandard idiom, could and perhaps should be used by the teacher. There often are, however, multiple terms for the same object or concept, and the teacher will need to know any regional preferences (which are preferences, not language errors). It is quite possible for the child to be familiar with an object but become confused when an unfamiliar label is attached to it. This confusion can lead to depressed scores on intelligence tests, resulting eventually in labeling the child as retarded, as well as misinterpretations of teacher's directions.

With regard to testing, a little latitude in individual testing might be appropriate: going back to missed items and using an alternate term (for example, instead of "show me the stove," ask "show me the oven"). Figure 11-1 shows sample alternate terms. Appropriate comments can then be added to the test results summary. This practice, often followed by clinical psychologists when they suspect the validity of test results, is not done often enough in school testing.

Alternate terms are also appropriate when testing in Spanish, because different Spanish-speaking countries often use different words for the same object.

Nonetheless, the language handicap must be reduced. The strongly motivated child, immersed in an English-speaking class and given individual tutoring, should learn the language fairly quickly. In other cases, however, as mentioned earlier, a variety of techniques are needed to make language learning desirable to and effective with the child. The primary task, therefore, is to stimulate the child's motivation.

The principles of behavior modification find ready application here. Positive reinforcement for attempts to use the desired vocabulary or syntactical (grammatical) structure helps to increase the frequency of this behavior. Since it is unlikely that the language-handicapped child will be completely successful in her

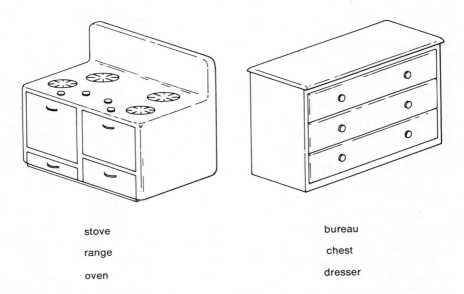

stove	bureau
range	chest
oven	dresser

Figure 11-1.   Regional Synonyms

first efforts to speak standard English, reinforcement must be given as she approximates and approaches the goal—a process called "shaping."

The desire to learn standard English will also be increased if language instruction is embedded in a functional context rather than an abstract and isolated situation. That is, there is a need to demonstrate to the child that what she learns will be immediately useful and beneficial to her. A girl interested in athletics, for example, might respond best initially in a sports setting where her ability to comprehend and use the appropriate terminology will enable her to participate in the game. While playing, she will acquire additional incidental vocabulary.

Although a full day of sports is obviously impractical, this is an opening wedge to further language instruction. A classmate playing the same game can be asked to serve as a "buddy" and help to acquaint the language-handicapped child with both the general vocabulary and sports teminology. The buddy system is effective for both sexes and can be used wherever the student body consists of standard and nonstandard English speakers. The buddy's background may be very similar to the new student's, but he will have achieved greater fluency in English.

As a practical matter, the buddy, tutor, or teacher should first acquaint the language-handicapped child with the names of the teacher and his classmates, the parts of the classroom and school building (including the important distinction between the words identifying the restrooms), titles of subjects, procedures in the school, and even names of members of his family and their relationship to him. In how many schools does someone actually take the time to do this for any newcomer, let alone one who doesn't speak the same language?

Arithmetic, except for word problems, can be taught in almost any language since the numerical symbols remain the same. It is also a practical subject since the fundamental processes can be helpful in a variety of school and home activities. If the only available teacher speaks only standard English, she will have to use a great many visual examples to supplement oral instruction. If there is an available bilingual resource person, however, instruction can be given in both English and the other language or dialect. The primary point is that the child can be actively learning rather than passively sitting in a classroom absorbing little and falling further behind her classmates. Furthermore, the growing lag in academic progress strikes at the child's sense of competence and reduces her self-esteem as well as the respect other children have for her. This problem has been too common where language-handicapped children are concerned.

Resource persons can be bilingual teachers, volunteer student tutors who will work with the child on an individual basis, or adult members of the community. If at all possible, such special instruction should be on a daily basis to enable the child to keep up with her classmates. Bilingualism is desirable, but not necessary. In fact, in one project, college students who spoke only English worked with Puerto Rican children, teaching them vocabulary, numbers, and eventually reading. Several of the college students later reported that they had learned some Spanish during the tutoring process and that their willingness to learn increased their rapport with the children.

If the child's interests can be ascertained, initial vocabulary and reading instruction can be geared to those interests. Additional materials can be introduced as the youngster, reinforced by a few successful attempts, seeks to learn more words and expand her interests. Many books are now available that combine high interest level with a simple vocabulary. These books can be read to younger children so that they hear and learn the sounds and structure of English before attempting to read the words themselves. Profuse illustrations, either in the books or as adjuncts to instruction, are also beneficial. Publishers have already marketed bilingual editions of common fairy tales that are attractive to primary-age children and aid their transition from one language to another.

Another technique that helps the language-handicapped child work at the same level as her classmates is to translate assignments into her own language and permit her to complete them in that language. A bilingual resource person can assist the teacher in such tasks. A variation of the ''experience chart'' used with beginning readers is also helpful. Ordinarily, the experience chart is a reading vocabulary derived from a story told by the child and written down by the teacher. For the language handicapped, the English translation can be placed beside the student's own work, and she can match the principal words in each as vocabulary instruction. The inability to express one's ideas in standard English does not mean that the ideas don't exist.

If the class, of whatever grade level, is working on social studies, the language-handicapped child can be drawn into this activity, too. Flash cards can be made from the experience charts and placed in a ''word file'' for the child to study on her own. Illustrated flash cards, with a drawing or picture on one side and the English word on the other, can also be placed in the file for study and reference. If the child cannot express her thoughts in English, she can draw from the file her responses to questions. She will understand the question if a few other students are asked before she's called on and if there is a visual supplement to the verbal question. If the class discussion is related to her national or subcultural heritage, she can be a resource person for the class, contributing to both her classmates' knowledge and her own self-esteem.

Art and music are often said to be universal languages. Certainly they are important media for integrating the language-handicapped child into the class and bringing her closer to the curriculum. Her competence in these areas can also help her socially. Physical education, a particularly visual activity, is another school requirement that the language-handicapped child can meet. Gestures and demonstrations usually supplement verbal instruction here, so that, apart from a slight increase in the use of these methods, no modification in instruction is necessary. Similarly, in home economics classes, diagrams and pictures labeled in English can supplement verbal instruction in cooking and sewing. Industrial arts also meets current and future needs and can be handled in much the same way. With the ''machismo'' concept of the Spanish culture, such sex-linked courses should probably follow tradition, but otherwise there should be no barriers to integrating the sexes in these fields. All of these subject areas provide means of integrating the language-handicapped child with her classmates and offer opportunities for her to demonstrate her capabilities.

Classes composed entirely of language-handicapped children require additional methods of instruction. Respect for the environment from which the children come is particularly important. Rather than expecting the children to "forget" their native language and use standard English when they enter the classroom, instruction initially can be in the native language with English taught as a second language. A wide variety of methods, including Peabody Picture Vocabulary Kit cards, music, rhymes, and some of the techniques common to foreign language instruction, are used in such programs.

Such programs reflect a new concern for including the subculture in the curriculum rather than automatically rejecting it as "nonstandard." This has been particularly crucial in the schools for Indian children of the Southwest. Their values, practices, and concepts of interpersonal relations frequently differ considerably from those of the national culture. In years past, everything Indian was viewed negatively by the schools established to teach these children. The conflicts between the two orientations were too great for the children to manage, and the consequence was high rates of emotional disturbance and dropout. Today, the legends and practices of the Indians are interwoven with those of the larger society to present a more rounded curriculum with which the children can live comfortably.

Enrichment, used in urban ghetto schools for nearly two decades as a means of overcoming language and cultural differences, will be discussed further in Chapters 12 and 13.

Teacher Preparation

The prospective teacher who wishes to specialize in teaching the language handicapped will find it difficult to locate regular college courses specifically designed for her interests. A number of institutions offer Teaching English as a Second Language (TESL) but, aside from this, expect the student to work toward the usual elementary or secondary teaching certificate. Northern Arizona University prepares students to work with and teach Indians in the Southwest and includes laboratory experience on the reservations. The VISTA and Teacher Corps programs offer some on-the-job training, with language instruction, in Appalachia, urban areas, and the Southwest.

Solid preparation in language arts, music, arts and crafts, sociology, anthropology, and Teaching English as a Second Language is strongly recommended for students wishing to work with the language handicapped. The child development courses usually found in teacher preparation curricula should be supplemented with cross-cultural studies for knowledge of varying child care practices and parental attitudes. There is great need, when working with both the language handicapped and the culturally different, for positive and constructive interaction among teacher, parents, and the community. Experience in working with staff members from other disciplines, such as social work, human relations, psychology, and anthropology is also useful, for a team approach is frequently applied in working with these children and their parents. Other members of the team include the speech therapist and teachers of nonacademic subjects.

In terms of personal characteristics, the teacher of the language handicapped needs a great deal of patience and the willingness to invest more time and effort than any teachers' manual calls for.

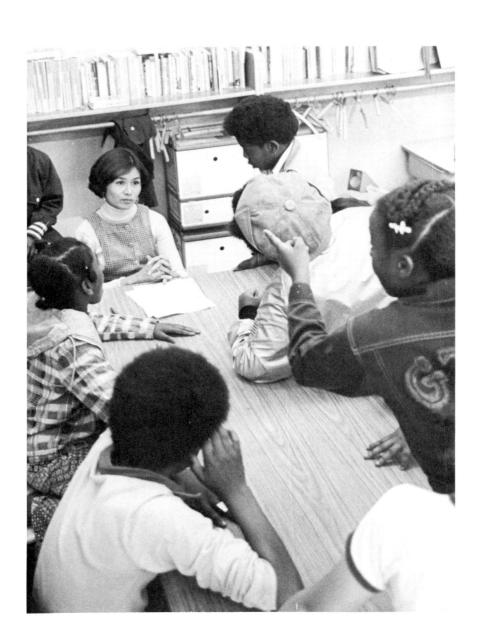

Five

The Culturally Different

Some cultural groups in the United States are at an economic disadvantage because they cannot compete effectively in the labor market. Others face a language disadvantage that primarily inhibits their interaction with the majority. Still others must confront racial or national prejudice that places them at a social and economic disadvantage. Almost all of these groups, because of their differences from the majority culture, are at an educational disadvantage.

Several terms are used, almost interchangeably, for groups that do not fit the white, Anglo-Saxon, middle-class national image. The accuracy with which they describe these groups is open to question. Calling them "culturally deprived" implies that these are groups without a culture or way of life. Of course, this is not the case, as each minority group has its own set of attitudes, values, special holidays, and so on. "Culturally disadvantaged" poses similar difficulties. Great differences between majority and minority cultures may place the minority at a disadvantage in a number of areas, but the term implies that it is the *culture*, not the minority status, that is disadvantaged. The most appropriate term, then, appears to be "culturally different."

New pride in one's culture, without apology for its difference from the majority culture, has meant revision of textbooks and curricula. But it has not yet had such an extensive effect on classroom atmosphere and teaching techniques. For the culturally different, whether the difference is racial, ethnic, or socio-economic, special education can play an important role in reducing the gaps between the home and the larger society. Respect for the child as an individual and for her family and home are important if she is to develop the self-image and self-confidence so vital to success in the learning situation. We are belatedly realizing that diverse groups in the school population should be regarded by school personnel as a challenge rather than a burden. Instead of condemnation to a marginal existence because of conditions into which they were born, these children surely have their right to education, in the fullest sense of the word.

12 Learning-Disadvantaged Children

A departure from the general format is necessary in this chapter because there is so much controversy about how and when to work with the learning disadvantaged. Common to these children is their lack of opportunity to learn the skills acquired by most children in our society. A large number receive too little stimulation because of parental inadequacies. These are not only the poor, the "hippies" or dropouts from society, the culturally different, the alcoholic, or the emotionally disturbed parents. Inadequate stimulation can be found in middle-class homes where socially or professionally preoccupied parents delegate their child-raising responsibilities to persons whose primary job is housekeeping or baby-sitting, but not child-rearing. Daily "interaction" with an inadequate parent-surrogate, combined with benign neglect by the parents, can be as great a disadvantage to the child's development as more obviously negative environmental situations.

A second group of learning-disadvantaged children are in residential institutions that provide only the essentials of housing, food, and general physical care. These children have been abandoned, removed from their homes by welfare agencies, or incorrectly diagnosed. A third group of learning-disadvantaged children live in communities so geographically isolated and often so economically deprived as to severely limit any opportunities for learning.

Prevention or Compensation

The principal remedial approach to such disadvantages is compensatory education, which, however, has evoked considerable controversy. Jensen (1969) criticized expenditures for Head Start and similar compensatory programs on the grounds that genetic intellectual differences among the races were substantial enough to invalidate any efforts at improving intellectual performance. Most psychologists and many behavior geneticists disagree with this point of view. It is true that a number of research studies show that the effects of compensatory programs fade by the end of first grade; the programs are therefore perceived as futile. The question, however, is whether the nature and quality of first-grade instruction are appropriate for these children. Compensatory education, still widely touted and supported, is nevertheless in question as the best way to work with the learning disadvantaged. It is, after all, "after the fact" action.

Many psychologists and educators believe that preventive educational methods are more desirable, just as they are in medicine. Intensive and extensive programs during infancy and early childhood would seem a wiser financial investment than prolonged rehabilitation or welfare for the learning-disadvantaged adult. This is a philosophy practiced widely in Scandinavia, where children—the nation's future—are considered a worthwhile investment in money, time, and effort from infancy on.

Child development specialists consider the first years of life crucial to overall development. They point to critical periods in infancy and early childhood when, if what is to be learned is not learned, the pace of development and learning may be permanently altered. The preventive approach is based in part on these theories. It is also an attempt at positive intervention in the infant's and young child's exposure to family attitudes and cognitive styles, linguistic experiences, home conditions, and nutrition. Many children evaluated as intellectually retarded in the school years may have had the potential to perform at a gifted level but were handicapped by one or more family situations listed above.

A few programs begin with infants, or the mothers of infants, rather than preschoolers. One such program, under the direction of Boyd McCandless (Emory University, Atlanta, Georgia), is a parent-child development program. Its emphasis is on training the mother in all areas of child development. Children of participating mothers range in age from 3 months to 3 years. In addition to principles of child development, mothers are taught reinforcement techniques, the value of play experiences, nutrition, and homemaking skills.

Several large school districts have similar programs for adolescent unwed mothers and their infants. While the mother learns child-care practices and progresses toward high school graduation, her infant is cared for and provided with a variety of stimulating experiences in the school's day-care or nursery center.

In another program involving infants, under the direction of Rick Heber (University of Wisconsin at Milwaukee), trained specialists go to the home daily when the child is a few weeks old and provide stimulating experiences. The mothers of these children are retarded both measurably (I.Q. 70–80 and below) and functionally. When the infant is 3 to 4 months old, he is brought to the Infant Education Center on the Milwaukee campus for several hours daily. Stimulation is provided in language, visual and motor skills, music, art, science, and creative thinking. For the first two years, the child is instructed on a one-to-one basis. At age 2, small group instruction begins with a 2:1 child-teacher ratio that increases to almost 4:1 by age 4. At the same time, the mothers of the children are encouraged, but not required, to participate in a center-run homemaking program.

With their program beyond its fifth year, Heber and his associates have found that the first groups of children with whom they worked measure and function at average or better levels of performance. They appear to have flourished in spite of the inadequacies of their parents. An evaluation of the program showed that "at 42 months of age, the children in the active stimulation program measured an average of 33 I.Q. points higher than the children in the control group, with some of them registering I.Q.'s as high as 135. Equally remarkable, the children in the experimental program are learning at a rate that is in excess of the norm for their age peers generally" (Strickland, 1971, p. 7). Published criticisms of this program question the adequacy of the data provided. In 1976, Heber reported that the experimental group, after three years in regular schools, was still maintaining an I.Q. advantage over control group children in excess of twenty points. Some adjustment problems were experienced by children in the experimental group, although not as many as might have been expected (Trotter, 1976, pp. 4–5, 19, 46).

There is slow but growing acceptance in the United States of the idea that public responsibility for children's education begins at birth. This policy has been practiced abroad (in Sweden, Russia, and Israel, for example) for many years, but has only recently caught the attention of legislators here. Even when bills have been enacted for comprehensive child development programs, which would combine parent-effectiveness training and stimulating experiences for the infant and young child, funding is inadequate.

B. L. White, who, with Jean Carew Watts, is codirector of the Harvard Pre-School Project, makes the point that more money spent in preventive intervention may ultimately mean less expense for remediation and special classes at the elementary and secondary levels (1972). In the Harvard project, different patterns of growth from the ages of 1 to 3 years were observed in visits to the subjects' homes. Two principal behavioral differences became apparent in the research: (1) mothers of toddlers who exhibit superior growth talk a great deal directly to their children, and (2) they enjoy their children. These two behaviors did not characterize the mothers of children who were developing poorly.

A third program, described in the Case in Point, is primarily preventive and secondarily compensatory. Although its emphasis is on reducing potential emotional disturbance, it simultaneously succeeds in reducing early experiential disadvantage.

Under the auspices of the National Program on Early Childhood Education, T. R. Risley, at the University of Kansas, has designed an infant day-care center that emphasizes more efficient assignment of staff responsibilities and increasing interaction with their infant charges. This project is small (twenty infants, aged 2 to 12 months) but develops techniques for similar centers as they are established across the country.

Case in Point

"When Carol came to the Center for Preschool Services in Special Education from an inner-city Get-Set program she was 3 years old, but she could neither talk nor recognize herself in the mirror. Her mental development was that of an 18-month-old.

"After seven months at the Center she talked and did appropriate preschool work. Now, at age 5, Carol has outgrown the Center and is ready for a special kindergarten program in a private school that offers a strong program in language development. This all sounds encouraging, but the best school for Carol is 30 minutes away by train, and she is too young to travel there alone. Her mother works, so Carol needs not only a scholarship but free transportation. . . .

"Preschool day care programs serve many thousands of city children from disadvantaged families. Hundreds of these children are presently failing to develop adequately and hundreds more will fail in future educational situations. . . ."[1]

The Center for Preschool Services is a demonstration program with a multidiscipline approach that stresses interventive psychoeducational procedures for preschool children who, untreated, may become failures in school and society in only a few years. Using appropriate therapeutic techniques as well as the better nursery school stimulation experiences, it aims to prevent serious emotional disorders and enhance learning ability. The program also trains teachers from the Get Set day-care centers to help them recognize children who might benefit from this program and participate in their long-term therapy.

The Get Set, Head Start, and other compensatory programs try to provide experiences common in middle-class homes but not in the homes of the poor, the culturally different, and the retarded. Teacher-to-pupil ratios are very low, and federal funding provides the main support for facilities, staff, and equipment. Included in the programs are a variety of sensory-stimulating experiences, language training, field trips, socialization, and usually one or more nutritious meals. As noted in Table 12-1, analysis by University of Illinois personnel reveals five basic approaches to these programs. The duration of these programs varies from one summer to two years, and they usually take children when they are 3 to 4 years old.

"After one year of preschool intervention the findings indicated that the Ameliorative, the Direct Verbal, and the Traditional groups had made signifi-

[1]*The Franklin Institute News*, Spring/Summer 1972, 12–16.

Table 12-1.   Illinois Project Program Descriptions[1]

Group	Number of Children in Program	Program Description[2]
Traditional	25	Project-operated, self-contained class of disadvantaged children. Emphasis on personal, social, motor, and general language development through incidental and informal learning opportunities.
Community integrated	16	Same as above except disadvantaged children were integrated into community operated traditional preschool classes of predominantly middle-class children.
Montessori	13	Under Montessori society control; emphasis on sensory training and psychomotor learning through independent manipulation of didactic materials.
Ameliorative	24	Cognitive approach emphasizing language development through manipulation of concrete materials, the teaching of mathematical concepts, language arts, reading readiness, and science-social studies.
Direct verbal	23	Bereiter-Engelmann academic skills approach which uses pattern drills for teaching language and arithmetic and a modified initial teaching alphabet (i/t/a) approach for teaching reading.

[1]Spicker (1971).
[2]Programs are listed in order from the least structured to the most structured.

cantly greater I.Q. and language gains than had the Community Integrated and Montessori Groups'' (Spicker, 1971, p. 632). A one-year intervention program, however, as noted earlier, may be an inadequate basis for evaluating gains. Spaulding (1972) pointed out in his report of a five-year compensatory education program that one-year intervention programs were less effective than two- to four-year treatment programs. He cited evidence to support the success of remedying learning disadvantages when the children were enrolled at a younger age, continued in the program for two or more years, and participated in a program designed to maximize their problem-solving and self-management skills—that is, their capacities for competence and power.

It must be remembered, however, that compensatory programs work with children whose learning development has already been slowed because of their lack of opportunities prior to entrance into the nursery school level program. Active stimulation and increased attention are bound to bring some improvements in intellectual functioning, no matter which of the formats in Table 12-1 is used. Even the existing ''follow-through'' apparently is inadequate to the task of maintaining such improvements. It is, as we are finding out, harder to undo than to prevent damage.

Training: Programs and Problem Areas

For children in institutions, we need to pay greater attention to the training of their caretakers and to the nature of expenditures on their behalf. The Scandinavian model—trained pediatric nurses and early childhood teachers in their day-care and residential centers—gives some clue as to what is needed. Instead of hiring attendants at low wages, a common practice that leads to poorly qualified staffs, we should be willing to train and pay adequately para-professionals who can provide the institutionalized child with more than the bare necessities of life. Foster grandparent programs, whether or not they are volunteer, offer an opportunity for the personal interaction so acutely necessary to the development of infants and toddlers. The foster grandparent can help slightly older children learn various skills. These programs give both parties a feeling of significance, an opportunity to build up the self-esteem that is so essential to later learning.

The Child Development Associate Consortium is working to improve the preparation of day-care workers and thereby enhance preschool learning experiences. The Consortium supports a number of new training programs, competency-based, that will lead to certification of the trainee as a Child Development Associate. Competence in six broad areas, rather than the accumulation of traditional academic credits, is the desired goal, with many separate behaviors specified in each area:

1. Set up and maintain a safe and healthy learning environment
2. Advance physical and intellectual competence
3. Build positive self-concept and individual strength
4. Organize and sustain the positive group functioning of children and adults in a learning environment
5. Bring about optimal coordination of home and center child-rearing practices and expectations
6. Carry out supplementary responsibilities related to the children's programs

Although it seems inconceivable in an age of mass communication, there are communities that teachers avoid because of the isolation, living conditions, and poverty. Such a community is described by Conroy (1972). The children he taught, already school-aged, lacked even the most fundamental information that we would expect of a preschooler, although they functioned quite adequately in nonacademic areas. The usual compensatory education techniques are not appropriate for most 6- to 15-year-olds, although in many academic areas this pre-skill, or readiness, training is precisely what is needed. The teacher in this situation must adapt readiness and other available materials to the students' ages, be resourceful, perceptive, warm, and definitely uncondescending. The children's previous experiences and skills can be used as a basis for further instruction. Quantities of audio (battery-operated if necessary) and visual materials will help bring the outside world to these isolated children.

A slightly different situation exists in Alaska. Here, the children speak fairly standard English but have spent their childhood in what is to us a nonstandard environment. As educators at the Northwest Regional Educational Laboratory have discovered, the Alaskan child frequently cannot relate to traditional basal readers or other elementary texts because she has not had experience with many of the objects or concepts they include. The family unit is different; she's never seen a car; she doesn't know what the "office" in which other parents work might be; and, in general, she is bewildered by the themes typical of readers published for children in the other forty-nine states. When this child moves into a non-Alaskan school, she can only be considered learning disadvantaged. Gradual exposure to these "civilized" concepts, however, should remedy the disadvantage in fairly short order for most of these children.

Large quantities of research data suggest the directions to follow in working with the learning disadvantaged. It makes considerably more sense to invest in preventive programs rather than to try to undo or remedy longstanding problems; the price of a single inoculation is far less than the cost of curing an illness. There is general agreement among psychologists that the first years of childhood are the most significant for future learning and performance. The pattern of personality development is also set in infancy and early childhood, as Erickson and others have stated in their theories of developmental stages.

Parenthood, however, is a profession for which virtually no training is offered. This being the case, it seems prudent to invest our efforts and our funds in improving maternal attitudes and practices and increasing the opportunities for infants and toddlers to develop and learn normally. There should be no excuse for a child to be learning disadvantaged simply because she was born to a poorly functioning or inadequately prepared set of parents. With changing attitudes toward day care, an increasing need for mothers as well as fathers to work, and a recognition that motherhood does not automatically make a person the best possible caretaker, more and more children will experience time away from mother in the preschool years. These experiences will more often be stimulating than in the past.

Implementation of intervention projects will require extensive reorientation and reeducation. After identification of the target population is completed, parental cooperation can be established through outpatient pediatric clinics and welfare agencies. (Middle-class parents should be informed by their pediatricians.) Ideally, mothers could be required to attend weekly sessions on child care and development in order to receive Aid to Dependent Children benefits. Realistically, however, course attendance, even if required, cannot guarantee a true modification of attitudes and practices. Concerted efforts by other community resource agencies could develop additional effective intervention and preventive programs for current and future parents. When these children move into the schools, these agencies can offer after-school programs that will continue to provide a supportive environment in which children can obtain a snack, tutoring assistance, and a learning atmosphere free of home difficulties.

13 Cultural Minorities

Group Characteristics

We tend to think fondly of the United States as the great melting pot in which ethnic and racial heritages are submerged (except on holidays) to enrich the population stew as flavors assimilate. The "average American" is thought to emerge finally, melted down to a white, English-speaking, middle-class person. With this point of view, it's often been expedient to ignore cultural differences, particularly in the schools.

As Kobrick points out, however, in his discussion of children from cultural minority groups: "One reason schools are failing in their responsibility to these children is that they offer only one curriculum, only one way of doing things, designed to meet the needs of only one group of children. If a child does not fit the mold, so much the worse for [her]. It is the child who is different, hence deficient; it is the child who must change to meet the needs of the school" (1972, p. 56).

Cultural minorities include a wide variety of immigrant and native-born children. Among those *considered* immigrant groups are the Mexican-Americans, Cubans, Puerto Ricans (despite the fact that they have held American citizenship for more than half a century), French-Canadians in New England, and Asian-Americans. The native-born include the American Indian, Eskimos, blacks, residents of Appalachia, and children of migrant workers, as well as the ghettoized third- and fourth-generation descendants of European immigrants.

It is not the difference in heritage alone that creates problems for the child in school. It is this plus economic disadvantage, plus geographic isolation (even within a large city), plus social isolation. The children's families are deeply enmeshed in a neighborhood or local cultural subgroup, attending to "outsiders" only when they must. As I have indicated elsewhere (Schwartz, 1977), many of these parents, if they wished to locate helpful resources for their children, would have no idea where to begin their search. Charnofsky (1971) has pointed out that the culturally different tend to remain different partly because they perceive themselves as powerless and partly because they are basically oriented to a rural lifestyle that serves them poorly in an urban setting.

The child from a cultural minority group may or may not fit the stereotype of the average American in some or all aspects of her appearance. But she has other differences that set her apart in the classroom and are among the sources of her difficulties with teachers, classmates, and the learning process.

For a more exhaustive discussion of the culturally different, you are referred to Charnofsky's sensitive and sensible book, *Educating the Powerless* (1971). Many of the psychological discomforts that were discussed in Chapter 2, the importance of feelings of competence and power particularly, are amplified in this work, which also includes recommendations for changing the current school situation.

Group Goals

A basic conflict must be kept in mind when discussing goals. Do we want to so "Americanize" the child that he loses identification with his heritage, or do we want to preserve that identification at the risk of leaving the child on the fringes of the larger society? There is a point of balance between these extremes, but we remain at some distance from it.

One essential goal for the child from a minority culture is the establishment of her self-respect and pride. If she thinks little of herself, she will have less reason to move forward. To build pride and self-respect, teachers must respect both the child and her heritage. This may require considerable teacher reeducation, an almost heretical notion, although it has been tried.

A second goal is to take the child from the point at which she enters school to another point that represents progress, not regression. Too many research studies of Indians, blacks, and Spanish-Americans indicate that the longer the child stays in school, the less progress she makes. This in itself is a strong indictment of our educational institutions. Continuing growth at a steady or accelerating pace is a legitimate educational goal for all children.

A third goal for the child from a minority culture is to provide her with appropriate opportunities and techniques for self-advancement. Although the number of black and Spanish-surnamed students in junior college and other higher-education institutions is increasing due to open enrollment and special programs, too often the public schools have not equipped these youth to take advantage of these opportunities. The net result is a mixed bag of frustration, anger, rejection, recurrent failure, and finally withdrawal and return to the security of the cultural group. This is the sort of gratuitous gesture—a false "generosity"—that humiliates, degrades, and alienates.

Finally, a fourth goal is to supply the child with options and the information needed to choose among them. That is, does she wish to move into a different social and economic situation or does she want to continue her parents' lifestyle? If she never learns the positive and negative aspects of other life-styles, she is in no position to choose. Perhaps she will choose to learn more in order to return to

---

Case in Point

Dr. Peggy Sanday, a mathematical anthropologist at the University of Pennsylvania, found that the socioeconomic class of the child's school appears to make a difference in her I.Q. test scores and, consequently, her academic progress. As a result of her eight-year longitudinal study in the Pittsburgh schools, she recommended that racial integration begin in the early grades. Dr. Sanday found specifically that patterns for test score gain or loss are set by the fourth grade and that both black and white children attending schools in low socioeconomic areas lose points on I.Q. tests as the years pass.

From *The Philadelphia Inquirer*, January 20, 1974, p. 4B

---

her culture and help its members. For this, too, she needs information. Not every minority culture youth wants to reject her background completely (evidence of which we see daily). If she prefers to return as a useful member of the group, she will have to be encouraged to set higher goals for herself. Economic advancement, a predominantly middle-class goal, is not the only goal toward which she can aim. If she decides to move out of her cultural sphere, she has already set other goals for herself, but will need support in coping with the emotional upheaval that frequently accompanies such a decision.

Modification of Education and Facilities

There is some question whether money alone will reduce the educational problems of the culturally different child. Can new paint and carpets reduce failure? Can new textbooks change the fact that the child's unique background is looked down upon by his teachers and peers? Can higher teacher salaries alter their attitudes toward the culturally different? (There are people who, for a fee, will change their behavior, but children, perceptive as they are, see through them quite easily.) Money can contribute to some of the necessary modifications in education for the child from a cultural minority, but it is not the most essential contribution.

The primary need is a new orientation in education. Education, as an institution, has regarded children in much the same way as some psychiatrists regard their patients: Fit the patient's problem to the therapeutic technique. We should, as educators, be like the tailor, instead, cutting the cloth and fitting the garment to the wearer.

Suggestions for adapting instruction to the many students who do not speak standard English were made in Chapter 11. If the child is already at school, reasonably ready and willing to learn what you have to offer, the first task is to determine what she knows and take her as and where she is. The fact that the teacher isn't familiar with the child's language makes the teacher as "ignorant" in the child's eyes as the child is in the teacher's. Lack of respect for the teacher hardly promotes learning. Suggestions for remedying this situation follow in the section on teacher preparation.

The relation between teacher expectation and student performance is another area in which money has little influence. Despite questions raised about the methodology of the Rosenthal and Jacobsen study (1968), their *Pygmalion in the Classroom* made a very clear point. Children tend to perform as they are expected to perform and behave by their teachers. The expectations come through in tone of voice, gestures, the way in which a child's paper is handled, smiles or lack of them, and so many other nonverbal ways. How does the teacher develop these negative expectations? They are rooted in stereotypes and prejudices, perhaps deeply buried within the individual. The teacher, middle-class oriented, abhors dirt, dislikes the casual attitude toward routines and rules, and does not want to understand another lifestyle. Children from cultural minority groups frequently bring to school with them characteristics that make some teachers uncomfortable. This is especially true when the child lives in poverty. Even if the child and the clothing are well-scrubbed, the teacher perceives poverty, and therefore difference, and consequently has low expectations for the child's success in learning. Some teachers' aversion to poverty may reflect anxiety about finding themselves in that condition or remind them of their "escape" from a similar background. Male and female teachers may also differ in their attitudes toward cleanliness, their associations of cleanliness with other characteristics, and their expectations of children from cultural minorities.

Not only do these children suffer from their low expectations, but the curriculum has little relationship to their past learning experiences and present home environment. If middle-class suburban high school students question the relevance of plane geometry to their lives, how much more valid is the culturally different child's unasked question about the relevance of the traditional curriculum to her life.

Most of the poor have few of the appliances and accessories taken for granted and pictured in their textbooks. They can't conceive of buying 3 pounds of steak at any price or a dozen oranges at one time, so that what are supposed to be practical arithmetic examples are really meaningless to them. The niceties of syntax in standard English contribute little to the child's functional language. History texts, even today, rarely mention the downtrodden and poor, unless negatively or with a simple statement that they existed in the nineteenth century and during depressions. The theoretical basis of science similarly offers little to a youngster who can't read or pronounce the terms, is aware of chemicals only as explosives or drugs, knows the "facts of life" from direct observation, and connects electricity and gas to hard-earned money.

School personnel must create ways to build up the child's self-esteem. Most of the children of cultural minorities are aware by school age that other people see them as lazy, incompetent, and inadequate. Accustomed to receiving the leftovers and hand-me-downs of society, they can hardly believe they have much significance in that society. Manipulated by the unscrupulous, even as preschoolers, they also perceive themselves as powerless. Given that sordid assortment of feelings, it is no wonder that they have low expectations of any positive experiences in school. The first step in the classroom, then, is for the teacher to accept the child as she is, shy or aggressive, with or without a standard English vocabulary, clean or dirty. Reinforce all the desirable behaviors, pay and mean a compliment (on a pretty smile, a sweet singing voice, a helpful hand), respond to the child's questions whether or not they relate to the topic of discussion, ask the children in the class how they are and what's important to them today, recognize each child as an individual. In other words, discover each child's strong points, help her see their significance, and encourage her at every turn to do her best.

Encouraging competence is a difficult task, however, unless the child has some motivation. She can match colors or shapes or sizes, then two of these at the same time, then count them, and finally use the objects to solve arithmetic questions. But she needs to be given a reason for this activity. What good will it do her? In the areas of reading and language arts, the "experience story" approach will be more meaningful than the basal readers. High-interest, low-vocabulary-level books are also useful.

When studying the community, it is more profitable to ask the children about their experiences with policemen and firemen than to present the usual middle-class talk on these "community helpers." The children of the urban poor learn that these are powerful authority figures and that they are not as altruistic in the ghetto as they are in the better neighborhoods. Children of migrant laborers have had similarly negative experiences with these authority figures. The opportunity to share and describe experiences also encourages verbal expression and the development of recall. With delicate handling by the teacher, the narrations become lessons in some sociological truths (on both sides of the desk) and permit the release of hostility and feelings of rejection in a constructive manner.

Bilingual education is now mandated for non-English-speaking children. As was pointed out in opinions regarding the *Lau* v. *Nichols* case (1974), it is hardly fair to expect these children to learn at the same rate, or indeed to have the same degree of learning readiness in first grade, as their English-speaking peers. In programs designed for non-English speakers, the children receive language instruction in their native tongue as well as English, and subject matter instruction in the native language until they are fluent enough to learn content in English. Projects and field trips relevant to both the minority and the dominant cultures makes the minority culture respectable and a positive factor in the child's self-concept. Such programs can be continued in more detail at the secondary school level with, for example, comparative studies of myths and legends in two or more cultures, the history of different groups of people, and common or unique social problems. These studies not only enhance respect for cultural diversity, but also increase classmates' understanding of one another's cultural behaviors and values. It is urged that studies in cultural pluralism be an integral part of the curriculum rather than an "add-on" in an artificial setting.

A number of documentary films and filmstrips are useful when field trips are impractical. These, too, help to suggest to the "culturally similar" that there is a quality and substance to minority cultures worthy of their attention. If the student feels that she and her culture are respected, there is less likelihood that she will feel so alienated from the school that she will drop out at the first opportunity. In the case of migrant children, it might be appropriate to point out the real contribution that they and their families make to the population by picking crops. Explanations of why they have to move about so much would also help to reduce rejection by increasing understanding.

Music, art, and physical education offer ample opportunities to integrate diverse cultural patterns into school life. Songs and crafts usually reflect cultural values, materials, style of life, and even history, thus providing a basis for more extensive study of the culture. The rhythms and dances are appropriate to physical education classes and extracurricular activities and, with the crafts and other studies, may be used to enrich and support school plays or pageants. Through concerts, art exhibits, and dance performances, the entire community can gain an appreciation of the ways in which people from other cultural backgrounds traditionally express their emotions and their views of events. What needs to be stressed here is an appreciation of differences. Cultural differences and similarities can be pointed out and explained, but the teacher should never imply that the traditions and values of one culture are superior. Today, psychologists and educators are making a strong effort to locate the gifted and creative among minority students.

Visits to the school by minority culture members who have "made it" in the larger society tend to increase pride in group identification and serve as a vivid illustration that one need not always be among the poor or powerless. This type of activity was one of the basic principles of the Higher Horizons program begun in the New York City schools several years ago.

Much of the attention paid to the culturally different centers on the drop-out rate. If we believe that it is important to educate every individual to her fullest potential, we must reduce this rate. Students stay in school only when they believe it holds positive consequences for them and when continued education is the most desirable option open to them. What is learned in the classroom must be coordinated with the student's life, which is often antithetical to the middle-class, urban, money-oriented system. If the student is capable of further studies, she should be made aware of this, given conscientious counseling and guidance, and encouraged to follow this path. Others should be encouraged to pursue one of the skilled trades. (Adolescents from cultural minorities should *not* be routinely placed in vocational schools, however. Are all middle-class white students equally successful in college?) The point is that whenever the student leaves school, it should be with a sense of having profited from the years of school attendance and knowing either how to do something well or how to accomplish the next education or career goal.

Teacher Preparation

As pride in our cultural diversity grows, teacher preparation programs must increase the teacher's exposure to different styles of life. Subject matter and teaching techniques continue to be important, but the prospective teacher will also need to have a greater understanding of the urban poor, the realities of socioeconomic disadvantage, the bureaucratic and legislative intricacies of dealing with social problems, and the cultural mores of the children she will meet in the classroom. A comparative study of nonstandard English dialects or one of the prevailing foreign languages in the areas where the student expects to teach would make classroom life a little easier, too, for both teacher and student. (Bilingual teachers are "in demand" in many school districts. Prospective teachers are urged to acquire this asset if they wish to increase the probability of obtaining a position.) Most colleges of education now have courses to meet these needs, frequently combined with field work experiences. It would be highly desirable for prospective teachers to live among the people whose children they will teach, but in many situations this experience must be foregone for very practical reasons.

There is no way to prepare the teacher for every possible classroom contingency aside from emphasizing problem-solving techniques, adaptability, flexibility, and seeking and using a wide variety of resources. Most important, teachers must be taught to respect individuals and their unique qualities. Any prospective teacher who cannot demonstrate respect, not merely tolerance, will save herself and her pupils much unhappiness by seeking another profession. Particularly with children from cultural minorities, who confront their difference from the larger society most forcefully when they enter the school system, the teacher's respect and encouragement are essential for learning.

Six

The Psychosocially Different

If a child is troubled and anxious, it is very difficult for her to learn. If she's in trouble with society, she may not be given an opportunity to learn, particularly not socially acceptable ideas and skills. The education of such children involves, first, the attempt to make learning positive and palatable, so that the child can function more successfully in and out of school.

The emotionally disturbed child tends to have problems in expressing or managing his feelings, thereby creating difficulties for himself alone and in interpersonal situations. The socially maladjusted youth, who may also have emotional problems, tends to have difficulties primarily with society and its laws. Both groups of children and youths are found in the schools in greater profusion than statistics indicate, for many cases go unreported.

The teacher is not the only person involved with these learners. Psychologists and psychiatrists try to reduce the individual's problems to a manageable level, social workers frequently intervene in the home situation, and other personnel (probation officers, art or occupational therapists, and others) are called upon as needed. Ideally, all of these people, teachers included, coordinate their efforts to maximize educational opportunities for the child with psychosocial problems. It is essential to their success that youngsters classified as psychosocially different be regarded not as problem children but as children with problems. It is from this perspective that the next two chapters are presented.

14 Emotionally Troubled Children

Group Characteristics

How can one begin to characterize so diverse a group as the emotionally disturbed when frequently the disturbance, like beauty, lies in the eye of the beholder? What one teacher or principal or parent perceives as emotional disturbance may be perceived by another as "normal" behavior—merely excess energy, shyness, or exuberance. Indeed, the validity of most statistics involving the emotionally disturbed must be questioned. One must remember that for each child erroneously diagnosed as emotionally disturbed there is probably another child who has been erroneously excluded from this diagnosis.

The causes of emotional disturbance are many. At one extreme are those mental health problems that *may* have a physical basis. It is thought that schizophrenia, for example, may be the result of a biochemical imbalance predisposing the individual to the condition, plus an environment that nourishes the imbalance. Other difficulties result principally from the child's environment—abuse by parents, inadequate parenting, ineffective parenting.

With these diagnostic difficulties in mind, let us consider the behavior traits usually exhibited by emotionally disturbed children. There are, first, the children who are hostile to everyone and everything. Perhaps they learned distrust in infancy, were rejected or mistreated by their families in their early years, had negative experiences with authority figures, or simply imitated someone who seemed to accomplish a great deal by being negative in attitude and behavior. They snarl and growl responses to questions, take a defiant or "try me" attitude, reject friendly overtures, and may be physically aggressive or destructive as well. Sometimes their hostility is a front for anxiety about whether or not they will be accepted by others; in other cases, the negativism is genuine. Where the wall of hostility does reduce acceptance, the hostile youngster becomes more negative, using the rejection as justification for her increased unpleasantness. The youngster who limits her hostility to verbal behavior can be unpleasant to have around, but she is mostly self-defeating. If physically aggressive, however, she hurts others and thus becomes a threat to their emotional and physical health as well as her own.

Another type of emotionally disturbed child is often perceived by teachers and parents as a "model child." The child sits quietly, does as she is told, never talks when she's not supposed to, and may be regarded as "a little shy, but so well-behaved." The timidity and docile behavior often reflect general anxiety, feelings of rejection, lack of "virtue," or excessive guilt feelings for real or imagined actions.

In other cases, the child suffers from depression stemming from abuse at home or parental illness, death, or divorce and the child's belief that she is responsible for the situation. She may withdraw, cry easily and excessively, and have some difficulty in handling her aggressive impulses.

Some of the children in the two groups just mentioned are overanxious to please authority figures for fear of punishment or rejection. Frequently the child has been punished for any autonomous behavior—for example, for speaking when not spoken to. She has resolved the conflicts of Erikson's second and third stages on the negative side.

If the child also seems to daydream a great deal, living in a world of her own even when spoken to directly, she may have found the real world so unpleasant and painful that she finds comfort only in the world of fantasy. At the extreme, children who live in a world of their own making, who either refuse to communicate at all or use their own idiom as language, and who exhibit other bizarre gestures and behaviors, are diagnosed as *autistic*. They seem to have rejected the world completely. Most psychologists believe that autistic behavior is caused by a combination of genetic and experiential factors. Although autism may be observed in a nursery-school child, it is less commonly found in the public schools after age 6, principally because the autistic child is rarely permitted to continue in the public schools unless a class for the emotionally disturbed is available. If the autistic child can be taught to respond to people, and to communicate (as has been done—slowly—by I. Lovaas and others), then there is a possibility for further development.

Many children exhibit less serious behavior problems, in terms of a continuum of problems. Finding it difficult to control their own behavior, they may indulge in temper tantrums, excessive crying, or other immature and excessive reactions. In some cases, they have never learned more mature and acceptable responses, while in other instances they have learned that such behavior is a very effective means of getting what they want. Although lack of self-control initially poses problems for the teacher, there are techniques by which the behavior can be changed with the cooperation of the child's parents. Many children have emotional problems, but should not be categorized by their teachers as emotionally disturbed. Often the disturbing behavior is a bid for the teacher's attention, especially when the teacher rarely reinforces the child's desirable behavior. Attention-seeking behavior may also reflect an attempt to be noticed, if not accepted, by classmates.

Case in Point

An extreme case of parental rejection and neglect was reported by the
Associated Press in 1970. Susan, a 13-year-old girl, was kept in diapers all her
life, was never taught to talk, and, when found, had the intellectual level of an
infant.

Placed at Children's Hospital in Los Angeles, Susan began special treatment with speech therapists and other experts. The county juvenile officer
stated that she uttered noises but no words, could understand some words and
directions, and looked "frightened" but did not cry. He added, "The doctors
say she is just beginning to realize that there are other people in the world."

The first five years of rehabilitative therapy have enabled the girl to acquire some normal speech patterns, although pronouns are a source of continuing confusion. From the published report in 1978, she is aware of her
father's behavior toward her earlier, and its effects on her.

Associated Press, November 17, 1970, and *New York Times*,
May 14, 1978

The child who holds herself in low esteem also has an emotional problem,
even if her perception is inaccurate. The child who suffers chronic frustration
because of being "low person" in comparison with her classmates has an emotional problem. The child who is left out of group activities—that is, rejected by
her classmates—has an emotional problem. The child who is frequently absent
from school without legitimate cause, or who complains frequently of headaches or stomach upsets, or who frequently seeks adjustments in her school
program, may also be communicating an emotional problem. The effectiveness of her signals depends upon who is receiving and interpreting them. The
child suffering from school phobia, who often exhibits these symptoms, may
have separation anxiety or may be attempting to withdraw from a threatening
situation or may have other problems. Each school-phobic child has different
reasons for this behavior.

All of these children can be challenges to the teacher's patience. But all of
them can be helped to reduce their problems so that instead of being emotionally,
and therefore educationally, handicapped, they can function more acceptably and
effectively in learning and other situations.

Group Goals

One of my former professors used to say that the normal person exhibited
adaptive, adequate, and appropriate behavior and was neither a threat, a

nuisance, nor a liability to herself or others. If we accept that definition, we would have to admit that few of us are normal on all occasions throughout our lives. Although normality may be too broad and vague a goal when working with the emotionally disturbed child, we can stipulate that her behavior should be more adequate, more adaptive, and more appropriate in whatever situation she finds herself. This is not to be construed as demanding or expecting uniform behavior from all children. Rather, it is a goal based on the recognition of individual differences in age, maturity, and temperament. (Even in the new-borns' nursery, such differences are readily apparent as one lies placidly, while another moves about actively even though well-fed, rested, and dry.)

A second goal (without which the first can hardly be realized) is to help the child reduce her problems to a magnitude with which she can cope. Putting problem situations in perspective, distinguishing reality from fantasy, understanding why other people behave toward the child in certain ways, ascertaining why the child feels the need for her teacher's and peers' constant attention, and recognizing that problems change in importance with maturity are all techniques of problem-reduction.

In the case of battered children, there is obvious concern for the physical as well as the psychological well-being of the youngsters. The teacher, counselor, or principal who becomes aware of a case of child abuse is advised to be certain of the facts in the case before seeking judicial or welfare agency intervention. It is a legal obligation in some states, however, such as New Hampshire, to report suspected instances of child abuse. Hospital networks have been established in many cities to identify children who are frequently brought in with broken bones, burns, and/or severe bruises, because these are often abused children.

Although prevention of further abuse is the aim of reporting child abuse cases, and "the best interests of the child" is an increasingly common judicial guideline, it is still difficult to remove a child from his parents' custody. There is a long history of "traditional family rights" that have been upheld and cited by the courts. Historically and legally, parents have been entitled to raise their children as they saw fit, including using discipline techniques of their choice. These conflicting legal views make remediation of child abuse situations a difficult task.

Since helping the child to learn is a primary function of the schools, the third goal, closely related to the second, is to help the child maintain an emotional state in which she can profit from instruction. A certain amount of test anxiety, anger in response to frustration, and withdrawal where there is negative inter-personal interaction can be expected. It is the excessive use of such behaviors that needs to be modified if the child is to learn. Many research studies indicate that emotionally disturbed children begin to build up feelings of incompetence and nonacceptance during the elementary school years and then progress at slower rates until they give up and leave school in their early or middle teens. Attainment of the third goal, therefore, implies a need for early intervention in the child's problems.

Modification of Education
and Facilities

The nature of modifications in education for the emotionally disturbed child varies with the seriousness of her problem and the availability of special resources. In a large school district or in the pooled efforts of several small districts, there are usually a few classes for emotionally disturbed students at both the elementary and secondary levels. In a less cosmopolitan, less populated, and/or less affluent district, the disturbed child either may not be allowed to remain in the public schools or may be placed in a catch-all special education class that includes, among others, the retarded and the learning disabled. Neither of these alternatives is satisfactory.

School placement should be based on student needs, not administrative convenience. There are a few elements essential to successful placement: small classes (from eight to twelve elementary and ten to fifteen secondary students); a teacher who is skilled in remedial techniques and has a sincere interest in working with the emotionally disturbed learner; and consultation and coordination with mental health specialists, social workers, and curriculum and guidance personnel. As the child exhibits more acceptable behavior, her program can be adjusted so that she takes academic content work with the special class and less ego-threatening activities with a regular class. The Madison Plan, suggested for the child with learning disabilities, is also appropriate for the child with emotional problems.

As with several other types of exceptional children, the emotionally troubled child needs to have the curriculum presented in a way that can be meaningful to her. For the older students particularly, life-experience units, human relations discussions, and consideration of future employment and recreation opportunities should be incorporated into the curriculum.

There are a number of ways to include academic content in seemingly nonacademic learning situations. For example, math is easily incorporated into sewing, cooking, and industrial arts courses. Reading ability is also necessary, of course, in order to follow directions. Most students are capable of following simple instructions and gain not only a feeling of competence but also considerable pride in their achievement. Instructions are given in an informal, linear, programmed format, so that the learner immediately recognizes the results of her efforts. Teachers need to be alert to the potential danger of boiling water, knives, scissors, or carpentry tools should one of the disturbed youngsters lose control of her behavior. For this reason, too, classes should be small and the staff adequate.

Music has both diagnostic and therapeutic value in working with disturbed children. Nordoff and Robins (1965) reported success in breaking through the barriers of autism with percussion instruments, rhythms, and special songs. As the child moved from unstable and disordered drum beating to a variety of ordered rhythms and singing, the authors could observe some connection between the changing musical self-portrait and the child's personality and problems. These connections were then utilized in therapy sessions. In other instances, music has been used to relax the angry and stimulate the withdrawn child. As behavior becomes more acceptable, the disturbed child may be integrated into regular music classes.

In both music and art classes, the disturbed child should be encouraged to express herself freely (but not to the extent of throwing the instruments or paints around the room). Limited self-control is encouraged when these activities are conducted in appropriate locations and in confined physical space.

Library privileges should be extended to those children capable of using books without destroying them. Bookshelves should be bolted to the floor in case of explosive behavior.

Basic to any instruction of the emotionally disturbed is the need to teach the child how to handle frustration in constructive ways. Emphasis should be on successes, no matter how small, and calm guidance should be given in correcting errors. The child needs to learn that she can be accepted even if her performance is imperfect. She also needs to learn that she can benefit more from making an effort than she can from constantly withdrawing from activities to avoid the frustrations of failure. She must also acquire patience, accepting the fact that the teacher cannot respond to her instantly every time she wants attention. Toleration may have to be developed very gradually, with positive reinforcement given as it is appropriate.

Since psychotherapy is needed by most of these children, scheduling adjustments may be necessary to permit visits to the therapist. The therapist and the teacher should be in contact with each other on a regular basis, exchanging information on the child's behavior and progress or changes in treatment. In some cases, the therapist may prescribe drugs to help modify the child's behavior, a fact to which the teacher should be alerted. (Several researchers have reported that certain stimulant drugs have good effects on emotionally disturbed children, reducing aggression and improving both class performance and inter-personal relationships. Two cups of coffee a day are also reported to have a calming effect, and there is less concern about possible drug addiction.) A social worker, to coordinate the school's efforts with the family situation, should also be part of the professional team.

In the case of school-phobic children, there is a need to reintroduce the youngster to school gradually. Most therapists use what is often called a "desensitization" procedure, having the child approach the school neighbor-hood, then the school building without entering, then walking up to the front door, and so on until he or she is integrated once again into the normal school routine. At each step, the anxiety is faced and conquered (Gordon and Young, 1976). If the root of the problem is within the school, as, for example, with a very sarcastic or hostile teacher, there are two alternatives: transfer to another school or transfer to another teacher. The anxiety-reduction process and any placement decisions should be worked out by the therapist, parents, and school personnel (and the child, if old enough) on a mutually cooperative and supportive basis.

Three areas in which the therapist and the teacher can cooperate are: bringing the child into greater touch with the real world; increasing her understanding of herself and others; and encouraging her to acquire the social skills needed for acceptance by others.

Some high schools have tried small group counseling sessions with disturbed adolescents. Here, with guidance, they can discuss common problems, release pent-up feelings, and exchange suggestions for handling various situations. With younger children, there is a trend in the area of prevention toward Glasser's proposal (1971) that class meetings be used to discuss feelings and ideas without evaluative judgments.

Everyone sits in a circle, listening to and interacting with each other. They become involved in sharing experiences, reduce tensions, and discover that, although each child is unique, her problems often are not. Knowing this helps to reduce the magnitude of the problem and place it in proper perspective. The child who creates problems in the classroom may be asked by another child to evaluate her behavior. (The same question—"Is what you are doing helping you?"—can be asked by the teacher in a private conference.) Mutual airing of feelings, without recrimination, can help the child to see herself as others see her now and would prefer to see her. Such sessions, however, demand the skillful, tactful, and experienced guidance of the teacher or psychologist.

Assuming that there is a special class available, the teacher does have some practical concerns. Bill is 12, reads at a primer level, and tends to throw things when frustrated. Suzy, also 12, is so fearful of failure that she cannot write down an answer to a simple question and virtually hides under the desk whenever someone speaks to her. Johnny speaks to no one but nevertheless radiates hostility toward everyone. Karla whimpers whenever someone raises her voice. Ned daydreams constantly. Wilma tears up her work as soon as she completes it. Group instruction is obviously inappropriate, if not impossible, in this classroom.

However, assignments with individualized written and signed contracts have been found effective in this type of situation. The youngster is not in competition with anyone else, and the onus of failure is removed because his assignment is one that he has agreed he can complete in a reasonable amount of time. Contracts can be written for behavior as well as for academic work. In addition to the individualized instruction in this approach, similar in some ways to the "open classroom," there is less potential for viewing the teacher as an authoritarian figure and greater potential for building a positive relationship with an adult who cares.

Related to such behavior modification practices as contracts, reinforcement, and so on is the use of a "time-out room" when the student cannot control her impulses. This is not used as a punitive measure (in the sense that teachers years ago told a child to "go stand in the closet because you're so naughty"), but puts the responsibility on the child for pulling herself together. The time-out room usually has a chair and a light, but is otherwise bare. The child takes nothing into the room. The first few times she enters it may take her an hour or more to calm down, but she gradually learns to come around in a matter of minutes, returning to her work area as if nothing had happened. Nothing *has* happened, except that she is coming to terms with herself and others. Some children learn that having something to do, even lessons, is more desirable than twiddling their thumbs in a stimulus-barren room. For a few children, of course, the time-out room is not a successful or constructive alternative.

Placing the youngster in a one-to-one situation is another alternative, but the disadvantage is that it may become an effective reinforcer for undesirable behavior. The entire attention of the teacher may be just what the child desires. On the other hand, some children are threatened by the presence of other children from time to time, and the one-to-one setting may be just what such children need. Deciding which is the case in a specific instance is the teacher's delicate task.

Teacher Preparation

Like teachers of other exceptional children, the prospective teacher of emotionally disturbed children should have a solid background in general and professional education, coursework in the psychology and educational needs of exceptional children, and extensive opportunities to work directly with exceptional children. The practical experience ideally should be with emotionally disturbed children and should include not only interaction with the special teacher and class but also with other professionals working with these children. Several colleges offer an undergraduate curriculum for preparing to teach emotionally disturbed children. This curriculum includes courses related to the special psychological and educational problems of the emotionally disturbed. In other colleges, the curriculum is offered at a graduate level only and may be appropriate either for those who have completed a general program in special education or for inservice teachers who wish to specialize in this field. Familiarity with the literature and research is also important to both the education student and the practicing teacher.

Where specially prepared teachers are not available when a special class is being established, it has been found that home economics, physical education, and other special teachers may, with additional instruction and the help of other members of the professional staff, be good teachers for the emotionally disturbed. These teachers may have a more general approach and are often more aware of the need for individual help than teachers who are prepared in a particular content subject. Experience with this kind of emergency measure in the Philadelphia and surrounding school districts has indicated that, depending upon individual personal qualities, such special teachers often have a knack for reaching emotionally disturbed students. Naturally, this is to be regarded as an emergency step, not a common practice, that demands careful selection by administrative personnel.

A few studies emphasize the competencies needed by the teacher of the emotionally disturbed. Hewett (1965), in particular, described a hierarchy of these competencies. In descending order of importance they are: objectivity, flexibility, structure (that is, the ability to set consistent and reasonable behavior limits that are maintained even when adapted to individual needs), resourcefulness, social reinforcement, curriculum expertise, and the ability to serve as an intellectual model. These are in addition to the personal characteristics of sensitivity, warmth without sentimentality, and dedication.

15 Socially Maladjusted Children

Group Characteristics

Socially maladjusted students have characteristics in common with many of the other groups of exceptional children. Intellectually, some are gifted, but more function at a retarded level. Physically, illnesses or disabilities may have contributed to their handicapped social functioning. Culturally, they may share some of the problems of minority children, but the socially maladjusted are found increasingly among middle-class, suburban families. Psychosocially, they have many of the difficulties of the emotionally disturbed—feelings of hostility. rejection, and unresolved anxiety—but their response to these difficulties is negative involvement with the laws and customs of our society.

Headlines almost daily inform us of shoplifters and pickpockets, some of whom, shockingly, aren't even old enough to attend school. Shoplifting, particularly, is not limited to the poor, but is an increasing source of thrills and kicks for youngsters from affluent, "respectable" families. These shoplifters are not sociopathic personalities; they are immoral, but not amoral, and are not products of a criminal environment or unable to learn from their own or others' experiences. They are socially maladjusted, however, as they put personal impulse above all other considerations—familial, legal, and rational. Some of the more affluent shoplifters see their activity as "ripping off" a society to which they cannot or choose not to adjust, for whatever reason. The shoplifter from the poverty-stricken family, on the other hand, may feel that she has been deprived of some of life's necessities. She wants to have a share in some of the "goodies" she sees daily but cannot afford. Still other shoplifters are conforming to the demands of that microcosm of society, the peer group.

Prominent in the news, too, is the violence of gang warfare. Looked at objectively, the gang is a miniature and highly authoritarian society. The gang leader is often a youngster with good intellectual potential that has been ignored, submerged in the welter of emotional problems common to his environment or otherwise gone astray. He has to be fairly bright to plan the activities of the gang and a strong leader to maintain group cohesion and see that his plans are carried out. His followers are in the developmental pattern of seeking peer-group acceptance in the dominant group available to them. In this sense, they are "normal," but their goals don't conform to those of the larger society. They take opportunity—legal or not—where they find it.

Also among the socially maladjusted (and frequently the disturbed) are arsonists, looters, muggers, rapists, terrorists, extortionists, and burglars. Many of these are also drug addicts whose motivation is obtaining the money to support their addiction. Whatever the initial underlying emotional conflicts, and there were some such conflicts, these youngsters' antisocial acts eventually are performed almost autonomously. That is, they are performed for the thrill obtained, rather than for the original motive, regardless of risk or negative consequences.

Depending on the community, a youngster may also be considered a social misfit if she runs away from home, is chronically truant from school, or is an unwed mother. Frequently, of course, what is considered delinquent behavior in youth is not even mentioned in most adult felony codes. Nevertheless, when children or teenagers act in certain ways that upset the status quo, the public and school authorities view these behaviors as signs of social maladjustment. Increasing concern for the rights of children should lead to greater justice in handling these particular problems.

Among practically all of the socially maladjusted, there is a disregard for, almost an obliviousness to, what is accepted by society at large. There is little concern for the long-range future or for the consequences, other than immediate gratification, of asocial behavior. The youngster may feel little remorse or guilt even when apprehended and jailed. Because members of this group tend toward poor academic performance (although they may have good learning potential), they also tend to be retarded in grade placement. This further reduces any possibility of a favorable attitude toward education and authority. Even if they lack a sense of competence, a feeling of being significant to others, and a sense of virtue, many of the socially maladjusted do have more self-esteem than some other exceptional children because they focus on their power. Probably because they felt powerless in nearly every sense during their early childhood, a sense of power assumes enormous importance in the minds of the socially maladjusted. Similarly, exaggerated significance may be attached to the source of power, whether it be physical strength, a weapon, or the peer group. Whatever it is, it will be used as long as it satisfies the need for even the most temporary and superficial dominance.

Group Goals

It is desirable, of course, that the individual turn his energies and capabilities to constructive, socially acceptable pursuits. To do this, he will need to learn skills or their applications that differ from those he is now using. As an example, the child who can dismantle and steal parts of an automobile engine can, with training, become a skilled auto mechanic. The ability to read the appropriate manuals is, of course, helpful. In order to read manuals, she needs to learn how to read words. Thus, working backward from a desirable goal, we return to a basic educational aim.

There is more to reaching the goal of socially acceptable behavior than simply learning the three R's, however. There must be a basic alteration in the individual's attitude toward society. Considering that many of the socially maladjusted come to first grade already out of tune with the larger society, early intervention and very powerful techniques are necessary to turn the child to a different path. This means finding ways to make legal or acceptable behavior infinitely more attractive than asocial behavior. For example, it must be demonstrated to older youths, who seek peer-group acceptance through socially deviant behavior, that social acceptability is more rewarding than peer-rejection—a difficult task indeed. It is important, as part of this task, that the youth learn to care about other people. If he can see others as significant to himself, perhaps he will gain a sense of his own significance to them, providing another avenue to self-esteem. Further, caring about other people will cause him to consider the consequences of his behavior in terms of his relationship with them, possibly deterring him from asocial actions.

For many, if not all, of the socially maladjusted, a major goal is to develop the ability to substitute recognition and acceptance of long-range goals for immediate gratification. In an increasingly hedonistic society, this, too, is a difficult task. Some public service "commercials" in the mass media take this long-range approach, however, when they highlight a 17-year-old shoplifter who can't be admitted to college or a chosen profession because of her police record.

Another goal is to enable the socially maladjusted youngster to function appropriately and adequately in a regular classroom. We want her to be able to learn skills that will help her contribute to, not destroy, society. We want her to learn social as well as academic skills that will help her to be a mature adult who can respect herself and be respected by others in the larger society. (She may have respect from others in the socially deviant group because of her power, but respect from other deviants only reinforces her destructive behavior.)

Modification of Education and Facilities

Socially maladjusted children and youths are usually in one of three settings: regular classes, special classes or schools, and correctional institutions.

By this point in the twentieth century, we should have come to realize that the moralistic approach to the socially maladjusted does not produce remediation and contrition. Further, the youthful offender who is institutionalized as punishment for his asocial behavior frequently learns new techniques of extortion, sadism, and thievery from instruction by his fellow inmates and his treatment by the attendants. Juvenile detention centers are, therefore, generally not sources for constructive reeducation or rehabilitation. The effectiveness of half-way houses, which seek to provide a supportive environment within the larger community (Vachon, 1972), remains to be seen. Half-way houses, too, are controversial, partly because no one in the community wants a group of delinquents living on *his* street.

The socially maladjusted child in the classroom poses a number of problems for the teacher. Any pupil's actual or alleged asocial classroom or schoolground behavior is commonly referred to the building principal or the disciplinarian. (How many of the latter appreciate this title? If they do like it, what does this say about such individuals?) Depending on the nature of the offense and/or the number of times the student has been referred to the office, she may be expelled or suspended from school, sent to a detention room during or after school hours, or warned of future penalties in the event of recurrence. Most of these practices at least temporarily reduce the pressure on the teacher but do little to assist the student's academic learning. It should be noted that suspension and expulsion require due process hearings at which the student's civil rights must be protected. Referral to mental health personnel for diagnostic testing or for therapy similarly must be respectful of student and parental rights.

Once in the classroom, the socially maladjusted pupil tends to resist learning. Often the pupil has reading disabilities which increase her frustration in the learning situation and the likelihood of classroom misbehavior. One obvious modification in the education of the socially maladjusted, then, is to provide a remedial reading program that will lessen their frustrations in learning. Concurrently, through careful selection of materials and teachers, the reading program can be combined with therapy to alleviate emotional problems.

Truancy also creates learning gaps that cause frustration and subsequent aggression. In this case, school attendance must somehow be more attractive than the reasons for truancy. Behavior modification techniques have been used successfully for this purpose. Group therapy sessions also offer an opportunity to air anxieties, grievances, and other problems. These sessions require the guidance of skilled and sensitive psychologists, of whom there is a shortage in the public schools.

In many of our urban schools, some classes seem to be made up almost entirely of youths who are hostile to authority, rebellious, and anti- or asocial. It is pointless for a teacher to try to instruct them in algebra, literature, or American history in a traditional way. Creativity and flexibility are mandatory if anything is to be learned. Some of these students' abundant energy can be turned to acting out scenes in the text, either as the author wrote them or as the students imagine they should have occurred. Discussion after the role-playing is then based on more than wisecracks and can result in real learning. Math can be taught in applied fashion or integrated into other subject matter. Here, too, behavior modification techniques can produce a gradual extension of attention span and increasing competence. Field trips of interest *to the students* should gradually be worked into their program. These should be carefully planned on every level: duration of the trip, definition of acceptable (and unacceptable) behavior, and so on. The teacher needs to establish reasonable limits for behavior, despite the students' antiauthoritarian attitudes. It may be the first time anyone has ever expressed enough concern for these youths to set limits, and the novelty can be very effective. As each field trip occurs without untoward incident, the students can be encouraged to help plan more ambitious projects.

A "crisis teacher" is an additional means of dealing with behavior problems. This is a special resource teacher to whom the student can go when she cannot control her behavior acceptably. The crisis teacher is not a disciplinarian; she uses problem-solving techniques with the student who has a problem with which she cannot cope or is in a situation in which she feels powerless. Working with the classroom teachers and other school personnel, the crisis specialist can suggest and develop a number of ways to reduce the tensions and conflicts that plague the socially maladjusted.

A similar program can help the disruptive elementary school student and her teacher. The disruptive student who fights, throws things in the classroom, and verbally attacks the teacher or his classmates frequently needs to be taken out of the room both as a relief to others and to obtain remedial instruction. Principal and teachers can work together to choose the twenty to thirty most disruptive students in the school for the program. A special teacher with two aides can work with five or six students each hour. If the hour is divided into three 20-minute periods, each child can have both remedial help in reading and arithmetic and affective education to help her improve her relationships with others. The remedial instruction will reduce the frustration that undoubtedly contributes to the child's disruptive classroom behavior, while the affective instruction will help to change his emotional behavior and attitudes. When a student improves enough to function satisfactorily in the classroom without the educational and emotional support of the special teacher, another child can enter the daily program.

Regular class placement is not appropriate for all of the children. Nor is academic learning the only concern. If we are to expect students to learn honesty and fairness, it is imperative that the educators' behavior demonstrate these characteristics. There may be little or no consistency between expected and real behavior in the home. On all socioeconomic levels, parents preach one behavior and practice another. As the parent condemns stealing, she brags of her own achievement in out-foxing the traffic officer. Lack of consistency and subtle condoning of asocial behavior (as long as it goes uncaught) are not overlooked by the child.

A major consideration is whether the socially maladjusted pupil's behavior is primarily self-damaging or whether it affects the well-being or rights of other students. The pregnant, unmarried 15-year-old generally complicates primarily her own life, while the arsonist or thief affects the rights and well-being of others. Even in this sexually permissive era, however, the evidence of the pregnant girl's behavior is perceived by some as a psychological threat to her (supposedly) sexually naive peers, and she is removed from the class. Although there can be some justification for this treatment, she should not be forever banned from education but offered an opportunity to continue in special academic and preparation-for-motherhood classes. On the other hand, a 9- or 10-year-old who has already learned how to extort his classmates' lunch money poses a real threat to the physical and psychological well-being of his peers. He, too, may need a special class, on a part- or full-time basis, plus counseling. Challenges to his physical strength and attention to his emotional needs will also help to modify his behavior.

Special classes or schools for the socially maladjusted are found in many school districts. Too often these represent the last-ditch effort to cope with these pupils. They are the only public facilities where such students can be sent on an "out-patient" basis, but they do not necessarily provide constructive education. In fact, frequently, they are schools or classes in which the power goes to the strongest and biggest youths, and more crime than reading is learned. Attempts at counseling and therapy are rarely successful because, as noted earlier, there are seldom enough skilled counselors in a school district to perform this monumental task. The special classes in a regular school should be rehabilitative "half-way" sections, not detention rooms. Such special schools as Philadelphia's orthogenic disciplinary schools and New York's "600" schools should also be rehabilitative rather than punitive. Rigid rules and frequent demerits have not solved the problems of dealing with the socially maladjusted. What *can* be done?

Small units rather than large special schools reduce anonymity and increase the probability of staff-student contacts. Classes of eight to ten students with a variety of teachers and activities are more desirable than a highly academic, passive curriculum with a single teacher. The changes of activity, however, should be within a routine structure, for many of these students have difficulty dealing with the unexpected. Planning should be on an individual basis, taking into consideration the age, attention span, abilities, interests, and level of control of each pupil. Alternation between active and passive tasks and the assignment of individual and group work should be balanced. Some children need almost constant support from the teacher in their efforts to accomplish anything, while others can function within a small group adequately or work on their own for reasonable periods of time.

When class assignments are made, thought should be given to placing the student with those teachers most likely to establish rapport with her. Evaluation of the placement, sometimes ignored or occurring only as the result of a crisis, should continue regularly. It is important that the student have confidence in the teacher, as far as possible, and that the teacher have a sympathetic interest in the student and his problems. The selection of personnel to work with the socially maladjusted youngster is a critical factor in the success or failure of any program.

Some of these children will respond well to a highly authoritarian teacher, since they cannot respect anyone who does not demonstrate a sense of power. Others need a warmer, softer figure who supplies the nurturing they have not received from parents. Such matching, to be realistic, may not be possible in all school or therapeutic situations. However, there should be an alternative to an initial placement, if at all possible.

For most of the socially maladjusted, establishing a positive relationship with any adult, especially an authority figure, is a difficult and lengthy process achieved only when confidence and trust have been tested many times. This means that limits must be set (within which some deviant behavior will be tolerated) in terms of age, types of maladjustment, facilities, and staff-student ratio. Older socially maladjusted students may be guided toward more socially acceptable behavior if they are allowed to participate in setting the limits and dealing with violators. This also helps them to perceive why rules or laws are necessary for society to function.

In many cases, the socially maladjusted students in special classes or schools are already involved with the courts. Whenever this is true, teachers, probation officers, social workers, and psychologists working with the individual student must coordinate their efforts and aims to plan a consistent program. A consistent approach is a primary aim with these students, many of whom adopt socially deviant behavior in an effort to handle their chaotic environment.

Among the special classes available in some school districts are those for unwed mothers-to-be. The special class should offer the girl an opportunity to continue her usual school studies so that she can eventually graduate from high school. It should supplement these with classes in nutrition, infant and child care, and health (including sex education) so that she will be better prepared to care for herself and her baby. Again, professional mental health personnel should work with the teaching staff and the girls to provide counseling and emotional support. Some school districts continue classes after childbirth for the benefit of both mother and child (see Chapter 12).

The principles of behavior modification have been applied quite effectively in classes for the socially maladjusted. Reinforcement for doing something right is a unique experience for most of these students. So is success. The use of a time-out room, often combined with behavior modification practices, is also effective with the socially maladjusted. When the pressures mount, the student can withdraw while she wrestles with her problems, or she can meet with the crisis teacher. Small group discussions, too, can help to relieve building tensions as each group member expresses her views. Skillful application of group-dynamics techniques also encourages the feeling of belonging that these students heretofore have found in the gang. Skilled therapists can use this group cohesiveness to lead individuals and the group as a whole in new and constructive directions.

The third setting in which the socially maladjusted are found is the residential institution: juvenile detention centers, reformatories (which rarely reform anyone), and prisons (by any other name) for youths. As presently operated, these institutions offer little in the way of positive educational opportunities and not too much in the line of marketable vocational skills.

Case in Point

An experimental program at the Federal Detention Center in Washington, D.C. in the 1960s used behavior modification techniques quite effectively to induce the youths there to participate in learning sessions, do homework, and abide by the less stringent rules that were put into effect. Briefly, where there had been ready access to recreation facilities, the youths now had to earn the privilege of using these facilities by completing study contracts. The reinforcements, incidentally, were dispensed by the guard who had been the most disliked in the Center. The youths became very active learners, especially improving their extremely weak reading and math skills.

For example, withdrawal programs for drug addicts may offer some counseling so that the addict can handle her problems without drugs, but unless her emotional and practical capabilities are also improved, she will still lack adequate means of coping with her environment when released.

Because many studies have indicated the relationship between poor educational performance and social maladjustment, improvement in educational achievement is seen as one way to improve behavior as well. Institutional courses should emphasize basic skills and occupational training (with modern equipment). Those capable of pursuing high school courses should have the opportunity to do so. If there are too few students to warrant hiring a teacher, correspondence or programmed materials should be provided, with, if possible, assistance from a volunteer tutor. In addition, there should be extensive occupational counseling to increase the probability of the youth's acceptance and success when she returns to society. The occupational counselor should also be in contact with local businessmen to develop job opportunities for youths.

As in other settings, cooperative and coordinated efforts of all personnel who work with the socially maladjusted are very important. The teacher and the psychologist contribute their knowledge of the youth's academic and personal strengths and weaknesses, the social worker brings information about his home environment, the parole officer and community worker add knowledge of the community, and the occupational/educational counselor provides information about future options. Together they can develop a reeducation and rehabilitation program that offers several alternatives. The alternatives are then presented to the young people for their reactions and subsequent participation.

Obviously, psychotherapy is an essential part of such a program, whether on an individual or group basis and whether for the institutionalized arsonist or the pregnant adolescent. The absence of such help says to the socially maladjusted youth that he is perceived as both insignificant and incorrigible. The results of such perceptions are highly predictable.

Teacher Preparation

Few undergraduate professional preparation programs are geared toward the socially maladjusted alone. They are generally focused on the emotionally disturbed, however, with whom the socially maladjusted have much in common. To supplement this type of program, the prospective teacher of the socially maladjusted should take courses dealing with delinquency and urban youth. Experience as a volunteer in the numerous tutoring programs, anti-gang projects, inner city recreation programs, and court-sponsored rehabilitation efforts provides a vital dimension to the academic work and is strongly urged.

Teachers of the socially maladjusted should generally have some experience with regular classes before attempting to work in this special field. They should have familiarity with remedial techniques and materials as well as an understanding of group dynamics. Sensitivity to the psychological needs of the socially maladjusted, imagination, a sense of humor, and the ability to be firm and consistent without rigidity or harshness are important personal attributes. Finally, the teacher of the socially maladjusted needs to be a positive thinker.

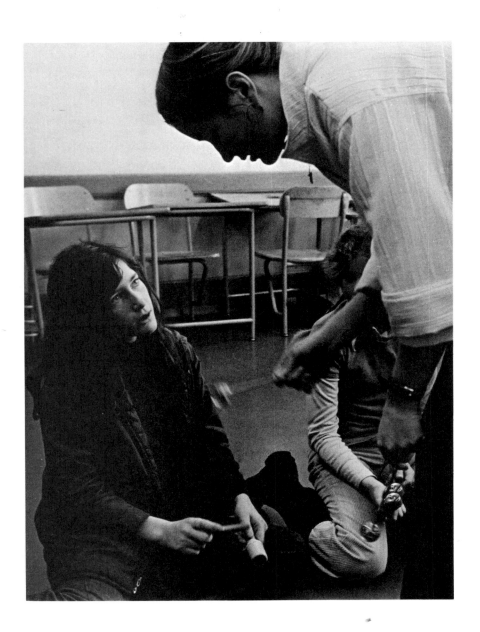

Seven

Afterviews

Each of the thirteen preceding chapters has focused on a different group of exceptional children and their educational needs. Although the approach generally has been pragmatic and practical, little has been said about the administration of special education in the public school or, indeed, what administrative details must be handled. In Chapter 16, these matters are discussed in relation to a variety of administrative functions and personnel.

The concluding chapter deals with a number of special concerns within the broad field of special education: the family of the exceptional child; guidelines and practices established by recent legislation and judicial decisions; and home-school relationships. In one way or another, these are important to each of the special groups previously discussed.

In these final chapters, the subdivisions of special education are brought together to provide an overview of the field. Like the introductory chapters, they are integral to an understanding of special education.

16

Administration and Special Education

We have considered, through this book, a number of modifications in the education of exceptional children. These have varied from segregated classes to placement in a regular classroom, with or without the support of resource centers and itinerant teachers—the whole range of "least restrictive environments." In any of these settings, there are administrative details that have to be worked out for scheduling, teacher selection, student selection and assignment, curriculum, supplies, equipment, facilities, and interpersonal relationships within the school. To whom do these tasks belong as a responsibility? What factors need to be considered when making decisions in these areas?

School System Organization

The organizational chart of a school system shows who has authority over whom and who serves as an adviser to whom. The special education coordinator. or supervisor or director, can be placed either in a "line" position, as shown in Figure 16-1, or in a "staff" position, as shown in Figure 16-2. In the line position, the coordinator has responsibility for and authority over both the special education teachers and the special education program. Since the teachers are located in different buildings, the coordinator becomes a kind of principal without a building. In the staff position, on the other hand, the coordinator of special education is an adviser or consultant to building principals and the special education teachers but has little direct authority over the teachers and pupils assigned to a particular school building.

The administrative functions in special education can include:

1. Personnel selection
2. Personnel evaluation
3. Budget preparation for special education programs
4. Curriculum design
5. Selection of students for admission to special classes

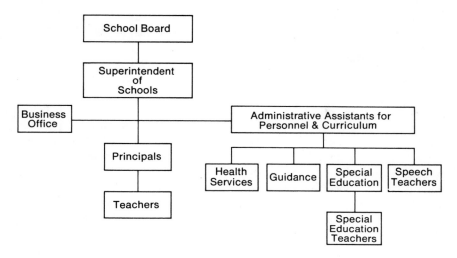

Figure 16-1.   **Special Education as a Line Position**

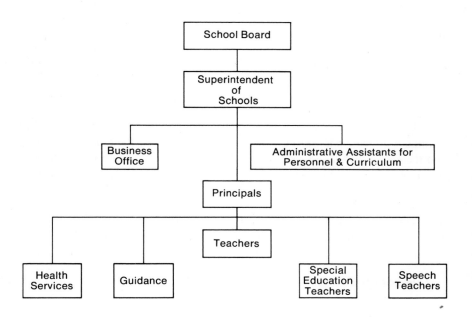

Figure 16-2.   **Special Education as a Staff Position**

6. Interaction with parents of students in special classes
7. Providing a supportive climate for innovation and research by special education teachers
8. Selection of materials for special education programs
9. Coordination of efforts with ancillary personnel

A number of advantages and disadvantages must be considered before deciding who has the responsibility for these and related tasks. In a line position, the coordinator has primary responsibility for all of these functions. This poses some problems in terms of the range of necessary competencies and the amount of time required for effective supervision of each function. In a staff position, there is greater division of labor, with more specialists available for dealing with specific problems. Each school district ultimately bases its organization on its particular situation and the considerations presented in the following pages.

Personnel Selection

The school board (board of directors) is the legally constituted body responsible for the selection, employment, and dismissal of all school personnel. As a practical matter, the board generally follows the recommendations of the superintendent of schools, hired by the board. The superintendent, in turn, tends to follow the recommendations of his assistant in charge of personnel. In the area of special education, one would expect that the assistant would consult with the special education coordinator about the teacher-applicant's professional qualifications and with the building principal about the applicant's ability to fit into the school staff and program.

If the coordinator is in a line position, the building principal *may* participate minimally in personnel selection, but the coordinator has the primary authority, and the teacher's assignment to a specific school building is perceived only as a physical placement. On the other hand, if the coordinator is in a staff position, the building principal has greater responsibility for and authority in teacher selection and, therefore, participates more actively. In this case, the special education teacher is perceived as an integral part of the staff of a particular school, not as someone with primary ties to the central administration.

Personnel Evaluation

Teachers, tenured or not, usually are subject to a formal (written) annual evaluation. This practice seems destined to be continued as demands for performance-based criteria and teacher accountability increase.

If the coordinator is in a line position, it is her responsibility to evaluate the special education teacher's performance. If the coordinator is in a staff position, the responsibility goes to the building principal. Who should be responsible? Logically, the evaluator should be the person who has the best opportunity to observe and interact with the special education teacher. Since special education teachers are placed in several schools, the coordinator can observe a given teacher only periodically, while the school principal has this opportunity daily. The decision then has to be made on which set of observations and interactions provides the more valid evaluation: periodic lengthy stays or brief but frequent visits.

Budget Preparation

The usual pattern for transmission of budget requests is from the special education coordinator (after consultation with the teachers) to the administrative assistant in charge of budgets to the superintendent and then to the school board. Modifications in the budget can, and usually do, occur anywhere along the way.

There should be little question that the entire special education staff knows, better than most other school system personnel, which materials are best suited to the needs of exceptional children. On the basis of their information and experience, they should be able to recommend necessary and appropriate instructional and supporting materials, whether for short-term or long-term investment. The question then is whether such costs as custodial service for the special education classrooms, chalk, paper, audiovisual materials, texts, films, and records should be included in the special education or building principal's budget.

Curriculum Design

Planning the curriculum for exceptional children must be a team effort. The development of individualized education programs (IEPs), in keeping with the regulations of PL 94-142, requires the participation of the child's classroom teacher, a second academically qualified person, the child's parents (unless they adamantly refuse), and the child himself, whenever possible. Other appropriate staff members to include in the planning sessions may be ophthalmologists, audiologists, psychologists, school counselors, psychiatrists, speech therapists, social workers, and orthopedists, to name a few. A critical reason for the existence of IEPs is to enforce a view of the exceptional child as an individual rather than as a faceless member of one of the categories we have considered. The attention given by staff members and one or more of the specialists contributes to such a view. To reach the goal of planning for the individual, however, teachers and administrators alike will probably need in service training in the needs and abilities of exceptional children as well as in the preparation of IEPs.

All IEPs must include "statements of the child's present levels of educational performance, annual goals, short-term instructional objectives, the extent to which the child will participate in regular programs, the dates during which the IEP will be applicable, and the criteria and procedures that will be used in evaluating the program's effectiveness" (National Advisory Commission on the Handicapped, 1977, pp. 7–8). In creating the IEP, consultations might appropriately be held with the special education coordinator and the building principal for possible suggestions regarding such practical matters as space, equipment, and transportation needs. The effective implementation of the IEP will require the active support of these personnel.

Selection of Students

There is no question that certain children need to be placed in a special education class. The trainable mentally retarded and the deaf-blind are two examples. In other situations, however—for example, the gifted, learning disabled, or psychosocially different child—someone has to decide whether the child will profit from special placement and, if so, whether this should be a short-term or long-term assignment.

Before a decision is reached, the special education teacher should have an opportunity both to observe the child and to review records of her past school performance, if she has attended school. The psychologist should have the responsibility for testing the child to determine her functional intellectual and emotional levels and to diagnose, if possible, her particular strengths and weaknesses. Depending on the nature of the child's alleged exceptionality, the school counselor, a consulting psychiatrist, a reading specialist, and other personnel may also need to participate in the case study. If there are several children under consideration for a limited number of spaces in special classes, the coordinator, in consultation with the reviewing team of teachers and specialists, will have to establish a placement priority list. The list would be based on a combination of entrance criteria for special education, the constellation of individual children's needs, and each family's willingness for and support of the new placement.

In selecting students, it is necessary to be careful to avoid labeling them. It is much too easy to test children, using tests that may be biased, and to place them in "pigeonholes" on the basis of narrow assessment procedures. The "pigeonholes" are frequently classes for the mentally retarded. The victims of such inadequate and/or inappropriate assessments are often minority-group children or economically disadvantaged children for whom the tests and other measures used are unrealistic. If the language and item content of a test are unfamiliar to the child, it is unfair to expect him to perform at an "average" level. Similarly, if values of the school and home conflict, it is unfair to judge the child on erroneous norms, let alone assign him to a class for the retarded. The placement in such classes of disproportionate numbers of minority children usually sets them on to an educational path from which they cannot easily escape.

These practices are in violation of the *Standards for Educational and Psychological Tests* (1972); the law, as defined in the Civil Rights Act of 1964 and various state acts; and court decisions, such as *Griggs et al.* v. *Duke Power Co.* (1971), *Diana* v. *California State Board of Education* (1970), and *Larry P.* v. *Riles* (1972) (Oakland, 1977). Accordingly, efforts are being made to design tests that are appropriate in language and content to the minority or poor children's background. The test results, together with other means of assessment, are then evaluated before proceeding with the development of an IEP, placing the child on a list for special education services, and seeking the least restrictive environment in which the child can profit from instruction.

Interaction with Parents

When the average school child has a problem, or if her parents have questions, concerns, or complaints about the classroom situation, the parents usually request an appointment with the school principal. It is no different with the parents of exceptional children. If, however, the special education coordinator is in a line position, the parents must go to him. This may pose practical problems for both parties. It may be difficult for the parents to get to the coordinator's office in the central administration building. They may feel uncomfortable going there rather than to the more familiar school building. On the coordinator's part, travel to different locations for conferences with different sets of parents takes up time that the busy coordinator can ill afford.

If the person responsible for all students in the school is the principal, there are fewer problems. It would be expected, however, that once the problem is presented by the parents, the principal would consult with the child's teacher and, if warranted, with the special education coordinator. It should be noted here that it is difficult to divide a child into parts. Classroom performance and classroom behavior are two expressions of the same child. It is difficult for parents, particularly, to understand that one person is chiefly concerned with the child's learning and another with whether or not she is a disciplinary problem. Parental confusion on this point is justified: most of the time, the two are intertwined.

Supporting the Teacher's Efforts

A classroom teacher may need several kinds of support: guidance in finding alternative instructional or classroom management techniques, information on new materials, resources for research, and opportunities to develop and test original ideas. In most cases, these can be supplied effectively by a competent and flexible special education coordinator. When a special class teacher becomes too involved with a child's problem or overwhelmed by difficulties in the classroom, to whom should she turn?

When the coordinator is in a line position, she will be responsible for both emotional and academic support. This creates a practical problem. If the coordinator and the special education teacher are 5 miles apart, can the crisis be handled or even reduced by a phone call? (This assumes that the teacher feels psychologically free to make the call and that the coordinator can be reached immediately.) On the other hand, the school principal tends to be ''on the spot,'' so to speak, and the teacher may feel more comfortable and secure about taking a short walk to the office than about making a phone call. Even if the principal knows relatively little about special education itself, the teacher can expect an understanding of both teacher-pupil relationships and classroom problems.

Selection of Materials

Since the special education coordinator is assumed to be a specialist, one would expect that locating, evaluating, and selecting instructional materials for special classes would be properly in her domain. Such selection must be done in consultation with the special education teachers, psychologist, guidance personnel, and other appropriate resource people. Competence and expertise in this area are more common among special education coordinators than building principals.

Coordination

It seems fairly clear that the administrative aspects of special education require considerable interaction among the special teachers, the coordinator, the principal, and other specialists in the school system. It is also clear that the geographical dispersion of special education teachers creates possibilities for jurisdictional conflicts.

Scholl (1958), Calovini (1969), and Roe and Drake (1974) maintain that the building principal has the final responsibility for all programs, students, and staff in her school. The feasibility of renewing a special class teacher's perspective, integrating both students and teacher into the total school picture, coordinating the programs of special and regular class teachers with respect to a particular student, insuring acceptance of the special classes by others in the school, and working with the parents of exceptional children is greatest when the coordinator of these activities is on the premises. This is especially true when special education is provided by either an itinerant or a resource teacher. The principal is then the liaison between the special and regular teachers. Together, they work out the best program for the child and allocate space and facilities for the special teacher.

The principal also must decide whether the special class will be isolated from or integrated with the rest of the school; must decide how student and teacher schedules can be arranged to accommodate class sessions and therapy sessions, lunch periods, and transportation; and, if necessary, must interpret the special education program to parents of other children in the school. First, of course, the principal has to be willing to accept the special education program, the special teacher, and exceptional children into the school. Calovini states that "the building principal has the same responsibility for supervision of the special classes that he has for the total school program" (1969, p.33). Further, to a large extent, "the success of the special program depends upon the degree of leadership exercised by the principal" (Scholl, 1958, p. 25).

Does this leave the special education coordinator with nothing to coordinate? Hardly. The coordinator is the key resource person in instructional matters, providing information to the special education teachers and other school personnel. She must coordinate the work of the teams involved in student selection and placement. This activity may be done appropriately by the coordinator. Her presence—in order to present and clarify the specalists' recommendation—may be appropriate at interviews with parents of children who are being recommended for special class placement. She has important consulting responsibilities to the principals and the central administration and is the logical person to develop proposals for programs funded under the Education of the Handicapped Act.

Summary

Special education programs reach into almost every part of the school system and necessitate a great deal of administrative work. The advantages in having one person primarily responsible for all phases of the program are outweighed by a range of skills and an expenditure of time that is too great for one person. It is suggested, therefore, that pupil selection and program development be the primary responsibilities of the special education coordinator and that all other matters involving special teachers and their students, including supervision and evaluation, be the responsibility of the building principal. The coordinator would be a key consultant to the principal, in all special education matters in her jurisdiction, and to the special education teachers.

To increase the integration of special education with the total school program, the principal should arrange for the special teachers to participate in the professional activities of the school and to share in the usual faculty responsibilities and duties as much as possible. Such integration is personally and professionally valuable to the teacher, and encourages acceptance of the program and its students by the entire school population.

The complexities of school organization and the expansion of information in special education are such that the special education coordinator is best viewed as a specialist in a staff position in the administrative hierarchy. The principal, a generalist in a line position, utilizes the expertise of the coordinator and other specialists in her decisions affecting the education of exceptional children.

17 Special Considerations

This final chapter brings us full circle to the underlying assumption of this book and a basic principle of special education: The exceptional child is first a child and second, exceptional. The first part of the chapter focuses on the child as part of his family and the problems this may pose. This is followed by discussion of the parent-teacher relationship. The chapter closes with a brief review of current concerns in special education.

The Family of the Exceptional Child

Two tasks are particularly urgent in the educator's work with parents of exceptional children. First, he must familiarize the parents with the general field of exceptionality relevant to their child, and its implications for them and their child. Second, they must understand their child's special placement and what it means in terms of progress and development.

Parents who are willing to communicate to the school personnel their anxieties, experiences, and hopes make the teacher's task easier. Some will be willing to discuss the difficulties or rewarding experiences they have had inside and outside the home. Others will be reticent. Informal conferences and home visits, where appropriate, can reduce the reticence, minimize the resistance, and reveal some of the family relationships and sources of stress. This sort of communication benefits the child both at home and at school.

From the time of identification and diagnosis of the child's exceptionality, which may be shortly after his birth, the family faces a new challenge. What does having an exceptional child at home mean to the parents? His siblings? His grandparents? How does having an exceptional child affect relationships with friends and neighbors? How do the parents respond to their child and his needs? How do they view special education—as an opportunity or as a disgrace?

A child with either a gift or a handicap obviously demands more time, attention, and financial expenditure than the average child. In some cases, the demands may be so overwhelming as to interfere with normal family interaction, possibly resulting in (especially) the mother's neglect of her other children and her husband. This can lead to emotional problems in the other children and a very strained relationship with the husband, possibly even a divorce. Professionals involved with a family in this situation should recommend relief for the mother, even for an hour a day. She should be made aware that her preoccupation with the exceptional child is unfair to herself, the child, and others in the family. The brief daily respite may help her to regain some perspective.

A second possible parental reaction to the exceptional child is denial of any exceptionality. This, of course, impedes the child's development and reduces the probability that special education will be beneficial. When the child is in a special program, the denying parents frequently undo at home any progress made in the program. To mention a few examples, they deny learning opportunities to the gifted child, omit recommended exercises in the orthopedically handicapped child's daily routine, do too much for the blind child, and reinforce the undesirable behavior of the emotionally disturbed child. As a result, every Monday the special class teacher has to begin anew, attempting to compensate for the lack of parental cooperation over the weekend.

There is, of course, a third parental response: realistic acceptance of the child's differences and constructive efforts to work with her and the professionals. These parents make special care and special education easier for everyone concerned, particularly the child.

For all the parents who are trying to help their exceptional child, there are tormenting questions. At what point do the mother's and family's sacrifices become too high a price to pay for keeping the child at home? Where is the money to come from for special education and other care? What will happen to the physically or mentally dependent child when the parents die? Is it fair to place a lifelong burden on any siblings? Is the handicap inherited? Should the retarded child *or* her siblings marry? If they marry, should they have children? Is there any prospect of social interaction for the child? Although most of these questions face the parents of all but the gifted and creative, even they must be concerned about the quality of their child's education, financial sacrifices, time commitments, and emotional involvement.

Siblings, grandparents, friends, and neighbors often take their cues from the parents' behaviors and attitudes, although there are always some people who feel personally threatened by anything different from the "normal" or "average."

Siblings may either resent or accept the exceptional child. Overindulgence of the exceptional child by one or both parents can cause resentment by the other children. Realistic acceptance and participation in caring for the exceptional child, with responsibilities geared to the abilities and maturity of the sibling, creates a happier family situation. Siblings cannot and should not be expected to devote all of their spare time to the exceptional child, but they can play with her, teach her, accompany her outside the home, baby-sit occasionally, and help with therapy. They should not always have to include the exceptional child in their peer-group activities, any more than an older sister should have to include a younger sister in her activities. Siblings may have to face taunts from other children, and this can be difficult at any age. How they handle this and other situations depends largely on the parents' attitudes and degree of support. Brothers and sisters, like parents, can reassure the exceptional child and those with whom she comes in contact by conveying their own acceptance and positive responses.

Grandparents, like some parents, may perceive the exceptional child as a negative reflection on themselves. Or, on the other hand, they may be a source of strong emotional support for the parents and willing to help with the child's care. Much of their influence on the child and her family depends, of course, on their physical proximity.

Neighbors vary in their reactions to exceptional children. Some will shun the child and keep their own children at a distance. They may even avoid the parents. This can be understood to some extent if the child is in trouble with the law or a threat to another person's safety. Avoidance is far less justifiable in other cases. Often, however, children with learning disabilities, speech difficulties, emotional problems, and reduced motor coordination are accepted by neighborhood children, included in their after-school activities, and so on. Adults can be supportive, too, by occasionally relieving the mother, assisting in therapeutic exercises, or just being friendly and sensitive.

The effects of an accepting environment are certainly helpful to the child. And it is interesting that many siblings, cousins, and neighborhood children, as a result of their interaction with an exceptional child, frequently enroll in college as special education majors.

Parents and Special Education

Not only do parents and teachers need to communicate with each other about the child's initial placement and subsequent progress, but they also must understand the other's problems. Parents too often are perceived by teachers as neglectful when they are not. There is no need for teachers or other school personnel to create or increase parental guilt feelings when the parents are doing all they can within their own resources and capabilities, however limited, to help the child. Excellent discussions of the need for mutual communication and respect between parents and teachers, indeed between parents and all the professionals with whom they deal, are to be found in Turnbull and Turnbull (1978).

Understanding is needed especially when the child is identified after school entrance as in need of special education. The child who appears to be bright and quick at home and who is found to need special placement at school is a case in point. The selection committee, homeroom teacher, or principal can explain to the parents that the classroom demands skills different from those expected or observed at home. Behaviors that the parents may have tolerated or become accustomed to, such as head-banging or perseveration, may, with other behavioral indicators, point to previously unsuspected minimal brain damage. Parents, of course, should inform school personnel if the child spoke or walked unusually late for no apparent reason or has exhibited other problems that can interfere with learning.

Rather than condemn culturally different parents for their seeming unwillingness to cooperate with the school, teachers should try to understand and respect their reluctance. Frequently these parents have had negative experiences with other government agencies or personnel, or with authority figures, and have strong anxiety feelings as a result. They may feel psychologically uncomfortable, perhaps inadequate, in the presence of the better-educated teacher. These feelings, the result of negative experiences, are unfortunately common, particularly to the culturally different. Their reluctance to confront, let alone cooperate with, school authorities need not mean lack of interest in their child's welfare.

Even when the child is gifted or creative, the parents may resist emphasizing this difference from the other children. Perhaps the father is afraid that artistic talent, encouraged in the special class placement, will make his son a "sissy." Or the parents of a very intelligent girl may believe that encouragement of her scientific curiosity and abilities will somehow defeminize her. Sometimes, too, parents anticipate that a brilliant or talented child will reject them. These anxieties must be dealt with skillfully and sensitively by school personnel.

Selection of exceptional children for admission to special education programs rests in anticipated parental support. The teacher's cooperation and support are necessary, too, and may be increased by her understanding of what it can mean to live with a retarded or deaf or crippled child day after day and year after year.

Parent Organizations

After a child's problem has been identified, the parents may be called, either at the instigation of the family physician or a mutual friend, by someone whose child shares a similar exceptionality. This can provide needed reassurance that the parents are neither alone nor unique in their situation. As this initially informal contact recurred in recent years, parents of children with a common condition formed formal organizations to sponsor related research, give each other moral support, provide recreation for their children, and serve additional related needs.

As the organizations have become more sophisticated, and as society has become more attuned to the needs of minority groups, the united parents have, in some instances, become action groups. A notable example was the suit brought by the Pennsylvania Association for Retarded Children to have their children educated at public expense under the "right-to-education" principle. In Colorado, a similar suit was filed by a parent organization on behalf of children who were retarded, perceptually handicapped, physically handicapped, autistic, and emotionally disturbed. In other instances, parent groups have found sponsors for legislation that would provide needed services and benefits for their exceptional children. Annual national conventions bring together special educators, clinical specialists, and parents to exchange information and to learn from each other. Similar meetings are held at local and state levels.

Special educators must recognize the concern and dedication of these parents and acknowledge the contributions and progress their organizations have brought about. They should also realize that more and more parents of exceptional children, through their experiences in these organizations, gain sufficient expertise to qualify them as valuable resource persons.

Right-to-Education Laws

The previously mentioned Pennsylvania suit on behalf of the mentally retarded, and the subsequent court decision in the spring of 1972 have guaranteed the public school education of all retarded children in that state. Similar suits resulted, by 1973, in the passage of comprehensive laws affecting special education in fifteen states. Passage of the Education for All Handicapped Children Act in 1975 made free public special education services available to these children in every state. The gifted, who are not included in this law, have similar rights to education and due process under laws in some states, such as one passed in Pennsylvania, also in 1975.

What difficulties do these rulings and laws create for the schools? Since most exceptional children should be in small classes of eight to fifteen children, there is a need for a large number of special education teachers and classrooms. The truth is that there are not nearly enough properly prepared teachers, even in the large urban areas. Nor is there enough classroom space. Nor are the funds generally available to pay so many specialists or to build additional physical facilities. Some school districts have had special education classes for many years (for example, BOCES in New York State). However, even they can provide education for only part of the exceptional student population. Present needs greatly exceed available resources.

Parents of exceptional children pay taxes to the school district whether their children are average, bright, retarded, blind, or emotionally disturbed. Relatively few of them can afford the tuition of private special schools, even with state subsidies and scholarship aid. They feel that their children deserve an education regardless of the family income. What does the worker with a retarded child, two or three other children, and an annual income of $8,000—$10,000 do for her child if the public schools refuse to admit her? What about the family with a learning disabled child who is referred for psychotherapy at $25−$35 per session plus special tutoring at $10 or more an hour? Must they go into debt, or should they expect that public education is the right of their child, too? The answer, of course, is to be found in the 1975 law, which extends that right to their child.

There is a problem inherent in the right-to-education decisions, however. How much can the child be expected to gain even from special education? Will the profoundly retarded child profit at all, or is it more practical to exempt these from the court's ruling? Furthermore, who will determine the point at which a child will not profit? And, for that matter, what are the indicators of "profit"? Where will we find enough teachers for the homebound? How quickly can the school districts meet the requirements of the court decisions?

Bilingual Education

A related problem is education for the non-English-speaking child. As noted in Chapter 11, some state laws require special instruction where there are twenty or more children in a school district who speak a common language other than English. Designed in part to meet the needs of growing immigrant populations in various urban areas, the laws create difficulties in other situations.

As one example, consider the increasing number of adoptions of Korean and Vietnamese children by English-speaking adults. Perhaps there are five or even ten of these children in a given school district. Under the law, the district is not required to provide special education unless it contains twenty such children. Even if the district, or a group of districts, is willing to sponsor special classes, where will it find enough Korean- or Vietnamese-speaking teachers of English as a second language? Is it also necessary to provide courses in the social studies and literature of the child's native country in order to reinforce her cultural background? Should she, perhaps, be taught entirely in her native language for the same reason? To some extent, answers are to be found in the *Lau* v. *Nichols* decision (1974) which mandates some form of instruction in the native language for non-English speaking children. For a full discussion of the varying points of view on these questions, you are referred to the federal Civil Rights Commission volume, *A Better Chance to Learn: Bilingual-Bicultural Education* (1975).

Other difficulties may be encountered if the parents cannot or will not try to speak English. These would include both communication problems between home and school and the inner conflicts for the child mentioned in an earlier chapter. Some means of gaining the parents' support is necessary if the child is to benefit from special classes.

In planning special education to carry out legal mandates, the child's age, English-speaking ability, language environment, and previous educational experiences must be considered. If the goal of the special program is to have the child think, speak, and read in English so that she will function more capably in society at large, the program should focus on teaching her English, with supplementary subject matter instruction in her native language until she has learned English fairly well. If the goal is simply to teach her subject matter, the language of instruction is of secondary importance. Legislators and school directors need to determine their philosophy in these matters before, not after, developing guidelines for a program.

An Afterword or Two

Whether or not to provide special education for exceptional children is no longer the question. It is, instead, a question of how best to provide for the varied needs of unique individuals within the limitations of financial and personnel resources and in keeping with the desires of a rapidly changing and highly mobile society. Too much may be attempted and too little accomplished when we try to please everyone. Too little may be attempted and nothing accomplished when we try to offend no one. Between these extremes is a vast area in which much can be accomplished if there is cooperation and understanding among school directors, administrators, special educators, legislators, parents, and the children themselves.

References

Of General Interest

Books of general interest are sometimes listed here rather than under the chapter in which they are cited.

Abeson, A., and J. Blacklow, *Environmental Design: New Relevance for Special Education*, Arlington, Va.: Council for Exceptional Children, 1971.

———, E. Trudeau, and F. Weintraub, "Law review: Legal opportunities and considerations for early childhood education," *Exceptional Children*, 37 (1971), 697–701.

Aiello, B., ed., *Making It Work: Practical Ideas for Integrating Exceptional Children into Regular Classes*, Reston, Va.: Council for Exceptional Children, 1975.

"Airline transportation for the handicapped and disabled," Chicago: National Easter Seal Society for Crippled Children and Adults, n.d.

Alexander, M., "Let me learn with the other kids," *Learning*, 1, No. 5 (1973), 18–21.

"American standard guide for school lighting," Washington: American Institute of Architects, 1962. (ED–019–868)

Ayrault, E. W., *Helping the Handicapped Teenager Mature*, New York Association Press, 1971.

Barrier-Free School Facilities for Handicapped Students, Arlington, Va.: Educational Research Service, 1977.

Blumenfeld, J., P. E. Thompson, and B. S. Vogel, *Help Them Grow: A Pictorial Handbook for Parents of Handicapped Children*, New York: Abingdon Press, 1971.

Bower, E., *The Handicapped in Literature and Life*, Belmont, Calif.: Wadsworth, 1979.

Bransford, L., and B. Brooks, "Early exposure experiences with exceptional children," *TED Newsletter*, 8, No. 2 (1972), 9–12.

"Breakthrough in early education of handicapped children," *American Education*, 6, No. 1 (1970).

Careers in Special Education, Arlington, Va.: Council for Exceptional Children, 1968.

Combs, R. H., and J. L. Harper, "Effects of labels on attitudes of educators toward handicapped children," *Exceptional Children*, 33 (1967), 339−403.

Deno, E. N., ed., *Instructional Alternatives for Exceptional Children*, Reston, Va.: Council for Exceptional Children, 1973.

Dolinar, L., "Public education for the ∴ ˙ ∷ ∴˙ ⋯ ˙ ⁝ ⁝ ˙. ∷ , " *Learning*, 1, No. 5 (1973), 14−17.

Ellingson, C., and J. Cass, *Directory of Facilities for the Learning-Disabled and Handicapped*, New York: Harper & Row, 1972.

Friedlander, B. Z., G. M. Sterritt, and G. E. Kirk, *Exceptional Infant: Assessment and Intervention*, vol. 3, New York: Brunner/Mazel, 1975.

Gardner, O. S., "The birth and infancy of the Resource Center at Hauula," *Exceptional Children*, 38 (1971), 53−58.

Gilhool, T. K., "Education: an inalienable right," *Exceptional Children*, 39 (1973), 597−609.

Glassman, L., "Directory of resources on early childhood education," *Exceptional Children*, 37 (1971), 703−712.

Harmonay, M., ed., *Promise and Performance: Children with Specific Needs: ACT's Guide to TV Programming for Children*, vol. 1, Cambridge, Mass.: Ballinger, 1977.

Heffernan, V., ed., "Exceptional child and the library," *Top of the News*, (April 1969), 259−290. (American Library Association)

Heisler, V., *A Handicapped Child in the Family*, New York: Grune & Stratton, 1972.

Hewett, S., *The Family and the Handicapped Child*, Chicago: Aldine, 1970.

Hobbs, N., *The Futures of Children*, San Francisco: Jossey-Bass, 1976.

Hughes, M. C., R. B. Smith and F. Benitz, "Travel training for exceptional children: Public transportation is a classroom, too," *Teaching Exceptional Children*, 9 (1977), 90−91.

Ingold, J., "Where handicaps are forgotten," *American Education*, 8, No. 2 (1972), 25−28.

Janicki, M. P., "Attitudes of health professionals toward twelve disabilities," *Perceptual and Motor Skills*, 30 (1970), 77−78.

Karnes, M. B., and R. R. Zehrbach, "Flexibility in getting parents involved in the school," *Teaching Exceptional Children*, 5, No. 1 (1972), 6−19.

Krauch, V., "Fitting the handicapped for jobs," *American Education*, 8, No. 5 (1972), 28−32.

Lake, T. P., ed., *Career Education: Exemplary Programs for the Handicapped*, Reston, Va.: Council for Exceptional Children, 1974.

Landau, E., S. Epstein and A. Stone, *The Exceptional Child through Literature*, Englewood Cliffs, N.J.: Prentice-Hall, 1977.

Lutz, R. J., and L. A. Phelps, *Career Exploration and Preparation for the Special Needs Learner*, Boston: Allyn & Bacon, 1977.

Maddock, J., "Sex education for the exceptional person: A rationale," *Exceptional Children*, 40 (1974), 273–278.

Meyen, E. L., G. A. Vergason, and R. J. Whelan, *Strategies for Teaching Exceptional Children*, Denver: Love, 1972.

Murphy, P., *A Special Way for the Special Child in the Regular Classroom*, San Rafael, Calif: Academic Therapy Publications, 1971.

"Music in special education," *Music Educators Journal*, (April 1972).

National Advisory Committee on the Handicapped, "The Unfinished Revolution: Education for the Handicapped," *1976 Annual Report*, Washington: NACH, Bureau of Education for the Handicapped, USOE, 1976.

———, *1977 Annual Report*, Washington: NACH, Bureau of Education for the Handicapped, USOE, 1977.

Nazzaro, J. N., *Exceptional Timetables: Historic Events Affecting the Handicapped and Gifted*, Reston, Va.: Council for Exceptional Children, 1977.

Nordoff, P., and C. Robins, *Music Therapy in Special Education*, New York: John Day, 1971.

Olshin, G. M., "Model centers for preschool handicapped children—year II," *Exceptional Children*, 37 (1971), 665–669.

Orem, R. C., *Montessori and the Special Child*, New York: Capricorn, 1970.

Peter, L. J., *The Peter Prescription*, New York: William Morrow, 1972.

Reynolds, M. C., and J. W. Birch, "The interface between regular and special education," *Teacher Education and Special Education*, 1 (1977), 12–27.

Richardson, S. A., and J. Royce, "Race and physical handicap in children's preference for other children," *Child Development*, 39 (1968), 467–480.

Robins, F., and J. Robins, *Educational Rhythmics for Mentally and Physically Handicapped Children*, New York: Association Press, 1968.

Rogow, S., and C. David, "Special education, perspectives, trends, and issues," *Phi Delta Kappan*, 55 (1974), 514–515.

Ross, A. O., *The Exceptional Child in the Family*, New York: Grune & Stratton, 1964.

Rouse, B. M., and J. Farb, "Training adolescents to use behavior modification with the severely handicapped," *Exceptional Children*, 40 (1974), 286–288.

Rousseau, J., and K. Schmidt, "28,000 special ed jobs created," *Learning*, 2, No. 8 (1974), 58–59.

Schwartz, L. L., *Educational Psychology: Focus on the Learner*, 2nd ed., Boston: Holbrook Press, 1977.

Shotel, J. R., R. P. Iano, and J. F. McGettigan, "Teacher attitudes associated with the integration of handicapped children," *Exceptional Children*, 38 (1972), 677–683.

Smith, J. O., and J. R. Arkans, "Now more than ever: A case for the special class," *Exceptional Children*, 40 (1974), 497−502.

Spock, B., and M. O. Lerrigo, *Caring for Your Disabled Child*, New York: Macmillan, 1965.

Stahl, D. K., and P. Anzalone, *Individualized Teaching in Elementary Schools*, West Nyack, N.Y.: Parker, 1970.

Standards for Educators of Exceptional Children in Canada, Downsview, Ont: National Institute on Mental Retardation, York University Campus, (n.d.).

Telford, C. W., and J. M. Sawrey, *The Exceptional Individual*, 3rd ed., Englewood Cliffs, N.J.: Prentice-Hall, 1977.

Thiagarajan, S., D. S. Semmel, and M. I. Semmel, *Instructional Development for Training Teachers of Exceptional Children: A Sourcebook*, Bloomington, Ind.: Center for Innovation in Teaching the Handicapped, Indiana University, 1974.

Thursby, D. D., "Everyone's a star: Music therapy for young handicapped children," *Teaching Exceptional Children*, 9 (1977), 77−78.

Tractenberg, P. L., and E. Jacoby, "Pupil testing: A legal view." *Phi Delta Kappan*, 59 (1977), 249−254.

Trudeau, E., ed., *Digest of State and Federal Laws: Education of Handicapped Children*, Arlington, Va.: Council for Exceptional Children, 1971.

Uhlin, D. M., *Art for Exceptional Children*, Dubuque, Iowa: Wm. C. Brown, 1972.

Wedemeyer, A., and J. Cejka, *Creative Ideas for Teaching Exceptional Children*, Denver: Love, 1970.

———, *Learning Games for Exceptional Children*, Denver: Love, 1971.

Weyman, J., *The Dental Care of Handicapped Children*, Baltimore: Williams and Wilkins, 1971.

Wilkinson, C. E., *Educational Media and You*, Toronto: GLC Educational Materials and Services Ltd., 1971.

Zifferblatt, S. M., "Architecture and human behavior: Toward increased understanding of a functional relationship," *Educational Technology*, 12, No. 8 (1972), 54−57.

Chapter 1

Abeson, A., and J. Zettel, "The end of the quiet revolution: The Education for All Handicapped Children Act of 1975," *Exceptional Children*, 44 (1977), 114−128.

Collins, J. F., and J. A. Mercurio, eds., *Meeting the Special Needs of Students in Regular Classrooms*, Syracuse: National Consortium of Competency Based Education Centers and Syracuse University School of Education, n.d. (c. 1976).

Gearheart, B. R., and M. W. Weishahn, *The Handicapped Child in the Regular Classroom*, St. Louis: C. V. Mosby, 1976.

"Implementing the IEP concept," *American Education*, 13, No. 7 (1977), 6−8.

"The IEP and nonacademic services," *American Education*, 13, No. 9 (1977), 23–25.

"The IEP and personnel preparation," *American Education*, 13, No. 8 (1977), 6–8.

Milofsky, D., "Schooling the kids no one wants," *New York Times Magazine*, (January 2), 1977, 24–28, 33.

Paul, J. L., A. P. Turnbull, and W. M. Cruickshank, *Mainstreaming: A Practical Guide*, Syracuse: Syracue University Press, 1977.

Reynolds, M. C., and J. W. Birch, *Teaching Exceptional Children in All America's Schools*, Reston, Va.: Council for Exceptional Children, 1977.

Chapter 2

Brookover, W. B., and T. Shailer, "Self-concept and school achievement," *Sociology of Education*, 37, No. 2 (1964), 38.

Burke, D. A., and D. F. Sellin, "Measuring the self-concept of ability as a worker," *Exceptional Children*, 39 (1972), 126–132, 145–151.

Coopersmith, S., *The Antecedents of Self-Esteem*, San Francisco: W. H. Freeman, 1967.

Dimitroff, L., "Concept of self and teaching culturally different people," in *Children, Psychology and the Schools*, B. Feather and W. S. Olsen, eds., Glenview, Ill.: Scott, Foresman, 1969.

Elkind, D., "Piaget's theory of perceptual development; its application to reading and special education," *Journal of Special Education*, 1, No. 4 (1967), 357–361.

Elkind, D., *A Sympathetic Understanding of the Child Six to Sixteen*, Boston: Allyn & Bacon, 1971.

Erikson, E., *Childhood and Society*, New York: W. W. Norton, 1950.

Hogan, E. O., and R. L. Green, "Can teachers modify children's self-concepts?" *Teachers College Record*, 72 (1971), 423–426.

Lawrence, E. A., and J. F. Winschel, "Self-concept and the retarded: Research and issues," *Exceptional Children*, 39 (1973), 310–319.

Lippitt, R., R. Fox, and R. Schmuck, "Innovating classroom practices to support achievement motivation and ego-development," in *Behavioral Science Frontiers in Education*, E. M. Bower and W. J. Hollister, eds., New York: John Wiley & Sons, 1967.

MacMillan, D. L., and B. L. Keogh, "Normal and retarded children's expectancy for failure," *Developmental Psychology*, 4 (1971), 343–348.

Maier, H. W., *Three Theories of Child Development*, New York: Harper & Row, 1969.

Mussen, P. H., J. Langer, and M. Covington, eds., *Trends and Issues in Developmental Psychology*, New York: Holt, Rinehart and Winston, 1969.

Norton, D. L., "The rites of passage from dependence to autonomy," *School Review*, 79 (1970), 19–41.

Piaget, J., and B. Inhelder, *The Psychology of the Child*, New York: Basic Books, 1969.

Sullivan, H. S., *The Interpersonal Theory of Psychiatry*, New York: W. W. Norton, 1953.

Chapter 3

Alamshah, W. H., "Blockages to creativity," *Journal of Creative Behavior*, 6 (1972), 105–113.

Boston, B. O., ed., *Gifted and Talented: Developing Elementary and Secondary School Programs*, Reston, Va.: Council for Exceptional Children, 1975.

———, ed., *A Resource Manual of Information on Educating the Gifted and Talented*, Reston, Va.: Council for Exceptional Children, 1975.

Bruch, C., "Degree programs in gifted education," *Gifted Child Quarterly*, 21 (1977), 141–154.

Chen, J., and S. W. Goon, "Recognition of the gifted from among disadvantaged Asian children," *Gifted Child Quarterly*, 20 (1976), 157–164.

Clark, B. M., and N. Trowbridge, "Encouraging creativity through in-service teacher education," *Journal of Research and Development in Education*, 4, No. 3 (1971), 87–94.

Davis, G., *Psychology of Problem-Solving*, New York: Basic Books, 1973.

Dennis, W., and M. Dennis, eds., *The Intellectually Gifted: An Overview*, New York: Grune & Stratton, 1976.

Dentler, R. A., and B. Mackler, "Originality: Some social and personal determinants," *Behavioral Science*, 9 (1964), 1–7.

Dunn, H. C., "Gifted children find research can be fun," *Gifted Child Quarterly*, 12 (1968), 10–13.

Engle, J. D., Jr., "Giftedness and writing: Creativity in the classroom," *Gifted Child Quarterly*, 14 (1970), 220–229.

Evans, B., "What is erovinrac spelled backwards?" *Gifted Child Quarterly*, 21 (1977), 47–53.

Feldhusen, J. F., and D. J. Treffinger, "Design and evaluation of a workshop on creativity and problem-solving for teachers," *Journal of Creative Behavior*, 10 (1976), 12–14.

———, *Teaching Creative Thinking and Problem Solving*, Dubuque: Kendall/Hunt, 1977.

Gallagher, J. J., *Teaching the Gifted Child*, 2nd ed., Boston: Allyn & Bacon, 1975.

Getzels, J. W., and J. T. Dillon, "The nature of giftedness and the education of the gifted," in *Second Handbook of Research on Teaching*. R. M. W. Travers, ed. Chicago: Rand McNally, 1973, 689–731.

Goodale, R. A., "Methods for encouraging creativity in the classroom," *Journal of Creative Behavior*, 4 (1970), 94.

Gowan, J. C., and E. P. Torrance, eds., *Educating the Ablest: A Book of Readings on the Education of Gifted Children*, Itasca, Ill.: F. E. Peacock, 1971.

Haddon, F. A., and H. Lytton, "Primary education and divergent thinking abilities—four years on," *British Journal of Educational Psychology*, 41 (1971), 136–147.

Hahn, R., *Creative Teachers: Who Wants Them?* New York: John Wiley & Sons, 1973.

Halpin, G., R. Goldenberg, and G. Halpin, "Are creative teachers more humanistic in their pupil control ideologies?" *Journal of Creative Behavior*, 7 (1973), 282–286.

Halpin, G., D. A. Payne, and C. D. Ellett, "Biographical correlates of the creative personality: Gifted adolescents," *Exceptional Children*, 39 (1973), 652–653.

Heist, P., ed., *The Creative College Student: An Unmet Challenge*. San Francisco: Jossey-Bass, 1968.

Holman, E. R., "A Master of Education degree in elementary education with an emphasis on creative teaching-learning," *Journal of Creative Behavior*, 11 (1977), 98–100.

Hooper, P. P., and E. R. Powell, "Influence of musical variables on pictorial connotations," *Journal of Psychology*, 76 (1970), 125–128.

Iarusso, M. B., "Creative children: Children as filmmakers," *Top of the News*, 28, No. 1 (1971), 60–67. (American Library Assoc.)

Kanigher, H., *Everyday Enrichment for Gifted Children at Home and School*, Ventura, Calif.: Ventura County Superintendent of Schools, 1977.

Kaplan, S. N., *Providing Programs for the Gifted and Talented: A Handbook*, Reston, Va.: Council for Exceptional Children, 1975.

Karnes, F. A., and E. Collins, "Teacher certification in gifted education: A national survey," *Gifted Child Quarterly*, 21 (1977), 204–207.

Korth, V. A. "The gifted in children's fiction," *Gifted Child Quarterly*, 21 (1977), 246–260.

Laird, A. W., "The fifty states' educational provisions for gifted children," *Gifted Child Quarterly*, 15 (1971), 205–216.

Learning: The Magazine for Creative Teaching, Palo Alto, Calif.: Education Today.

Lee, R. E., and T. E. Newland, "A small community and its gifted school children," *Educational Forum*, 30 (1966), 363–368.

Lyon, H. C., Jr., "The other minority," *Learning*, 2, No. 5 (1974), 64–66.

Maeroff, G. I., "The unfavored gifted few," *The New York Times Magazine*, August 21, 1977, 30–32, 72–76.

Maker, C. J., *Training Teachers for the Gifted and Talented: A Comparison of Models*, Reston, Va.: Council for Exceptional Children, 1975.

Mancini, P. M., "School for whiz kids," *New York*, November 14, 1977, 73–87.

Marland, S. P., Jr., "The gifted child and the library," *Top of the News*, 28, No. 1 (1971), 27–28. (American Library Assoc.)

Martinson, R., D. Hermanson, and G. Banks, "An independent study-seminar program for the gifted," *Exceptional Children*, 38 (1972), 421–426.

Maw, W. H., and E. W. Maw, "Children's curiosity and parental attitudes," *Journal of Marriage and the Family*, 28 (1966), 343–345.

McCurdy, H. G., "The childhood pattern of genius," *Horizon*, 2 (1960), 33–38.

Mednick, S. A., "The associative basis of the creative process," *Psychological Review*, 69 (1962), 220–232.

Meeker, M., "Creative experiences for the educationally and neurologically handicapped who are gifted," *Gifted Child Quarterly*, 11, No. 3 (1967), 160–164.

Moustakas, C., "Creativity and conformity in education," in *Explorations in Creativity*, R. Mooney and T. Razik, eds., New York: Harper, 1967.

Pang, H., "Undistinguished school experiences of distinguished persons," *Adolescence*, 3 (1968), 319–326.

Parnes, S. J., "Idea-stimulation techniques," *Journal of Creative Behavior*, 10 (1976), 126–129.

Renzulli, J. S., and L. H. Smith, "Two approaches to identification of gifted students," *Exceptional Children*, 43 (1977), 512–518.

Rogers, W., and S. Ryan, "Extending reading skills into today's world," *Teaching Exceptional Children*, 5 (1973), 58–65.

Ryder, V. P., "A docent program in science for gifted elementary pupils," *Exceptional Children*, 38 (1972), 629–631.

Sanderlin, O., *Teaching Gifted Children*. New York: A. S. Barnes, 1973.

Schaefer, C. E., "The self-concept of creative adolescents," *Journal of Psychology*, 72 (1969), 233–242.

Schwartz, L. L., "Can we stimulate creativity in women?" *Journal of Creative Behavior*, 11 (1977), 264–267.

Sebasta, S. L., "Language arts programs for the gifted," *Gifted Child Quarterly*, 20 (1976), 18–23.

Sisk, D. A., "What if your child is gifted?" *American Education*, 13, No. 8 (1977), 23–26.

"Smorgasbord for an IQ of 150," *Time*, June 6, 1977, 64.

South, J. A., "Gifted children among minority groups: A crying need for recognition," *Top of the News*, 28, No. 1 (1971), 43–46. (American Library Assoc.)

Stanley, J. C., "Accelerating the educational progress of intellectually gifted youths," *Educational Psychologist*, 10 (1973), 133–146.

———, "The case for extreme acceleration," *Gifted Child Quarterly*, 20 (1976), 66–75.

Syphers, D. F., *Gifted and Talented Children: Practical Programming for Teachers and Principals*, Arlington, Va.: Council for Exceptional Children, 1972.

Taylor, C. W., "Multiple-talent approach: A teaching scheme in which most students can be above average," *Instructor*, 77, No. 8 (1968), 27, 142–146.

Torrance, E. P., "Achieving socialization without sacrificing creativity," *Journal of Creative Behavior*, 4 (1970), 183–189.

———, "Can we teach children to think creatively?" *Journal of Creative Behavior*, 6 (1972), 114–143.

———, "Creative young women in today's world," *Exceptional Children*, 38 (1972), 597–603.

———, "Curiosity of gifted children and performance on timed and untimed tests of creativity," *Gifted Child Quarterly*, 13, No. 3 (1969), 155–158.

———, "Future careers for gifted and talented students," *Gifted Child Quarterly*, 20 (1976), 142–156.

———, "Guidelines for creative teaching," *High School Journal*, 48 (1965), 459–464.

———, "Helping gifted children read creatively," *Gifted Child Quarterly*, 7 (1963), 3–8.

Uhler, S., "A confederacy against the gifted," *Phi Delta Kappan*, 59 (1977), 285–286.

Weininger, O., "Some thoughts on creativity and the classroom," *Journal of Creative Behavior*, 11 (1977), 109–118.

Welsh, G. S., "Perspectives in the study of creativity," *Journal of Creative Behavior*, 7 (1973), 231–246.

Witty, P., et al., "Recognizing gifted children: A symposium," *Top of the News*, 28, No. 1 (1971), 34–42. (American Library Assoc.)

Woodliffe, H. M., *Teaching Gifted Learners: A Handbook for Teachers*, Toronto: Ontario Institute for the Study of Education, 1978.

Zaffrann, R. T., and N. Colangelo, "Counseling with gifted and talented students," *Gifted Child Quarterly*, 20 (1977), 305–321.

Chapter 4

Baker, J. G., B. Stanish, and B. Fraser, "Comparative effects of a token economy in nursery school," *MR/Mental Retardation*, 10, No. 4 (1972), 16–19.

Baller, W. R., "A study of the present social status of a group of adults who, when they were in elementary schools, were classified as mentally deficient," *Genetic Psychology Monographs*, 18 (1936), 165–244.

———, D. C. Charles, and E. L. Miller, "Mid-life attainment of the mentally retarded: A longitudinal study," *Genetic Psychology Monographs*, 75 (1967), 235–329.

Bensberg, G. J., C. N. Colwell, and R. H. Cassel, "Teaching the profoundly retarded self-help activities by behavior shaping techniques," *American Journal of Mental Deficiency*, 69 (1965), 674–679.

Bialac, V., *The Severely and Profoundly Retarded: A Bibliography*, Olympia, Wash.: Institutional Library Services, Washington State Library, 1970.

Bijou, S. W., et al., "Programmed instruction as an approach to teaching of reading, writing, and arithmetic to retarded children," *Psychological Record*, 16 (1966), 505−522.

Blatt, B., and F. Garfunkel, "Teaching the mentally retarded," in *Second Handbook of Research on Teaching*, R. M. W. Travers, ed., Chicago: Rand McNally, 1973, 632−656.

Blum, E. R., "The Madison Plan as an alternative to special class placement: An interview with Frank Hewett," *Education and Training of the Mentally Retarded*, 6, No. 1 (1971), 29−42.

Bortner, M., and H. G. Birch, "Cognitive capacity and cognitive competence," *American Journal of Mental Deficiency*, 74 (1970), 735−744.

Brace, D. K., "Physical education and recreation for mentally retarded pupils in public schools," *MR/Mental Retardation*, 6, No. 6 (1968), 18−20.

Bradfield, R. H., et al., "The special child in the regular classroom," *Exceptional Children*, 39 (1973), 384−390.

Brick, J. W., *Retarded Pupils in the Mainstream: The Special Education of Educable Mentally Retarded Pupils in Regular Classes*, Arlington, Va.: Council for Exceptional Children, 1974.

Brolin, D., "Value of rehabilitation services and correlates of vocational success with the mentally retarded," *American Journal of Mental Deficiency*, 76 (1972), 644−651.

Bruininks, R. H., J. E. Rynders, and J. C. Gross, "Social acceptance of mildly retarded pupils in resource rooms and regular classes," *American Journal of Mental Deficiency*, 78 (1974), 377−383.

Chaffin, J. D., "Production rate as a variable in the job success or failure of educable mentally retarded adolescents," *Exceptional Children*, 35 (1959), 533−538.

Chandler, C. R., " 'Babysitting' for houseplants," *Teaching Exceptional Children*, 9 (1977), 61−63.

Condell, J. F., "Parental attitudes toward mental retardation," *American Journal of Mental Deficiency*, 71 (1966), 85−92.

D'Amelio, D., *Severely Retarded Children: Wider Horizons*, Columbus, O.: Charles E. Merrill, 1971.

Dicks-Mireaux, M. J., "Mental development of infants with Down's syndrome," *American Journal of Mental Deficiency*, 77 (1972), 28−32.

Drowatzky, J. N., *Physical Education for the Mentally Retarded*, Philadelphia: Lea and Febiger, 1971.

Dunham, P., Jr., "Teaching motor skills to the mentally retarded," *Exceptional Children*, 35 (1969), 739−744.

Edgerton, R. B., *The Cloak of Competency*, Berkeley: University of California Press, 1967.

Fowle, C. M., "The effect of the severely mentally retarded child on his family," *American Journal of Mental Deficiency*, 73 (1968), 468–473.

Gardner, W. I., *Behavior Modification in Mental Retardation: The Education and Rehabilitation of Mentally Retarded Adolescent and Adult*, Chicago: Aldine/Atherton, 1971.

Geursen, T. A., "Architectural planning and mental retardation," in *Proceedings of the First Congress of the International Association for the Scientific Study of Mental Deficiency*, B. W. Richards, ed., Surrey, England: Michael Jackson Publishing, 1968, 692–694.

Gordon, M. L., D. H. Ryan, and T. Shilo, *Helping the Trainable Mentally Retarded Child Develop Speech and Language: A Guidebook for Parents, Teachers, and Paraprofessionals*, Springfield, Ill.: Charles C Thomas, 1972.

Gozali, J., and E. L. Meyen, "The influence of the teacher expectancy phenomenon on the academic performance of educable mentally retarded pupils in special classes," *Journal of Special Education*, 4 (1970), 417–424.

Hannen, R. W., "A program for developing self-concept in retarded children," *MR/Mental Retardation*, 6 (1968), 33–37.

Hislop, M. W., C. Moore, and B. Stanish, "Remedial classroom programming: Long-term transfer effects from a token economy system," *MR/Mental Retardation*, 11, No. 2 (1973), 18–20.

Hollander, H. C., *Creative Opportunities for the Retarded Child*, New York: Doubleday, 1971. (6 booklets)

Iano, R. P., et al., "Sociometric status of retarded children in an integrative program," *Exceptional Children*, 40 (1974), 267–271.

Jones, R. L., "Preferences for teaching intellectually exceptional children," *Education and Training of the Mentally Retarded*, 6, No. 1 (1971), 43–48.

Kaplan, F., and E. Fox, "Siblings of the retardate: An adolescent group experience," *Community Mental Health Journal*, 4 (1968), 499–508.

Kaplan, S., "Toward teaching and counseling excellence: A student profile," *Teaching Exceptional Children*, 10 (1977), 18–23.

Keane, V. E., "The incidence of speech and language problems in the mentally retarded," *MR/Mental Retardation*, 10, No. 2 (1972), 3–8.

Koch, R., and J. C. Dobson, eds., *The Mentally Retarded Child and His Family: A Multidisciplinary Handbook*, New York: Brunner/Mazel, 1971.

Kokaska, S. M., and C. J. Kokaska, "Individualized work centers: An approach for the elementary retarded child," *Education and Training of the Mentally Retarded*, 6, No. 1 (1971), 25–27.

Krishef, C. H., "State laws on marriage and sterilization of the mentally retarded," *MR/Mental Retardation*, 10, No. 3 (1972), 36–38.

Leff, R. B., "Teaching the TMR to dial the telephone," *Mental Retardation*, 12, No. 2 (1974), 12–13.

Levine, B., "Readying retarded adolescents for work through volunteer service," *Children*, 15 (1968), 131–134.

"Library services for the mentally retarded," *AHIL Quarterly*, (Spring 1971). (Association of Hospital and Institution Libraries)

Lindsay, Z., *Art Is for All: Arts and Crafts for Less Able Children*, New York: Taplinger, 1968.

Lynch, J., and W. A Bricker, "Linguistic theory and operant procedures: Toward an integrated approach to language training for the mentally retarded," *MR/Mental Retardation*, 10, No. 2 (1972), 12–17.

MacMillan, D. L., *Mental Retardation in School and Society*, Boston: Little, Brown, 1977.

McVey, G. F., "Learning experiences via educational technology for the EMR," *Mental Retardation*, 11, No. 6 (1973), 49–53.

Meyen, E. L., ed., *Planning Community Services for the Mentally Retarded*, Scranton, Pa.: International Textbook Co., 1967.

Miller, J. F., and D. E. Yoder, "On developing the content for a language teaching program," *MR/Mental Retardation*, 10, No. 2 (1972), 9–11.

Mitchell, A. C., and V. Smeriglio, "Growth in social competence in institutionalized mentally retarded children," *American Journal of Mental Deficiency*, 74, No. 5 (1970).

Monroe, J. D., and C. E. Howe, "The effects of integration and social class on the acceptance of retarded adolescents," *Education and Training of the Mentally Retarded*, 6, No. 1 (1971), 20–24.

Nawas, M. M., and S. H. Braun, "The use of operant techniques for modifying the behavior of the severely and profoundly retarded: Part II, the techniques," *MR/Mental Retardation*, 8 (1970), 18–24.

Ogland, V. S., "Language behavior of EMR children," *MR/Mental Retardation*, 10, No. 3 (1973), 30–32.

Perske, R., "About sexual development: An attempt to be human with the mentally retarded," *Mental Retardation*, 11, No. 1 (1973), 6–8.

Rapp, J., E. A. Lemka, and J. Landis, "Incentives affecting behavior changes in the retarded," *Exceptional Children*, 38 (1971), 229–232.

Roberts, N., and B. Roberts, "Patience and expectation," *Saturday Review*, September 18, 1971, 70–71, 75.

Rouse, S. T., "Effects of a training program on the productive thinking of educable mental retardates," *American Journal of Mental Deficiency*, 69 (1965), 666–673.

Schien, J. O., and J. A. Salvia, "Color blindness in mentally retarded children," *Exceptional Children*, 35 (1969), 609–613.

Sluyter, G. V., "Puppetry for the retarded learner: An instructional goldmine," *Journal for Special Education of the Retarded*, 8, No. 1 (1971), 29–34.

Smith, R. M., *An Introduction to Mental Retardation*, New York: McGraw-Hill, 1971.

Solomon, A., and R. Pangle, "Demonstrating physical fitness improvement in the EMR," *Exceptional Children*, 34 (1967), 177–181.

Stanfield, J. S., "Graduation: What happens to the retarded child when he grows up?" *Exceptional Children*, 39 (1973), 548–552.

State of Ohio, *Curriculum Guide for Moderately Mentally Retarded Learners*, Columbus: Ohio Department of Mental Health and Mental Retardation, 1977.

Swadron, B. B., and D. R. Sullivan, *Mental Retardation—the Law—Guardianship*, Toronto: National Institute on Mental Retardation, 1972.

Taylor, A. S., "A reading scheme for moderately to mildly retarded children," *The Slow Learning Child*, 15, No. 2 (1968), 85–88.

Taylor, G. R., "Special education at the crossroad: Class placement for the EMR," *MR/Mental Retardation*, 11, No. 2 (1973), 30–33.

Walker, V. S., "The efficacy of the resource room for educating retarded children," *Exceptional Children*, 40 (1974), 288–289.

Webb, R. C., "Sensory-motor training of the profoundly retarded," *American Journal of Mental Deficiency*, 74 (1969), 283–295.

"When retarded children grow up," *Transaction*, 5, No. 2 (1967), 6–7.

Younie, W. J., *Instructional Approaches to Slow Learning: Practical Suggestions for Teaching Series*, New York: Teachers College Press (Columbia University), 1968.

Zeiler, M. D., and S. S. Jervey, "Development of behavior: Self-feeding," *Journal of Consulting and Clinical Psychology*, 32 (1968), 164–168.

Chapter 5

Abrams, N., and W. Pieper, "Experiences in developing a pre-school program for neurologically handicapped children; a preliminary report," *Journal of Learning Disabilities*, 1 (1968), 394–402.

Adelman, H. S., "Graduate training in the 'specialty' of learning disabilities: Some thoughts," *Journal of Learning Disabilities*, 3 (1970), 66–72.

Anderson, C., *Society Pays: The High Costs of Minimal Brain Damage in America*, New York: Walker, 1972.

Bateman, B., "Learning diabilities—yesterday, today, and tomorrow," *Exceptional Children*, 31 (1964), 156–169.

Bolen, J. E., "Toward a taxonomy of curricular experiences," *Journal of Learning Disabilities*, 3 (1970), 247–251.

Bone, J., "Peotone fights school failure," *American Education*, 13, No. 1 (1977), 32–35.

Bosco, J. J., and S. S. Robin, eds., *The Hyperactive Child and Stimulant Drugs*, Chicago: University of Chicago Press, 1976.

Christoplos, F., "Programming for children with learning disabilities," *Journal of Learning Disabilities*, 2 (1969), 43–48.

Cruickshank, W. M., ed., *The Teacher of Brain-Injured Children: A Discussion of the Bases for Competency*, Syracuse: Syracuse University Press, 1966.

———, et al., *A Teaching Method for Brain Injured and Hyperactive Children*, Syracuse: Syracuse University Press, 1961.

Edwards, J. S., "Self-management in children labeled learning disabled," *Psychonomic Society Bulletin*, 8, No. 1 (1976), 51–53.

Ekwell, E. E., *Diagnosis and Remediation of the Disabled Reader*, Boston: Allyn & Bacon, 1976.

Farley, G., and L. Goodard, "Sex education for emotionally disturbed children with learning disorders," *Journal of Special Education*, 4 (1970), 445–450.

Frierson, E. C., and W. B. Barbe, *Educating Children with Learning Disabilities: Selected Readings*, New York: Appleton-Century-Crofts, 1967.

Gardner, H., "Developmental dyslexia: The forgotten lesson of Monsieur C," *Psychology Today*, 7, No. 3 (1973), 62–67.

Gordon, S., *Facts about Sex for Exceptional Children*, East Orange, N.J.: New Jersey Association for Brain Injured Children, 1969.

Graham, C., "Labels for Timmy," *Human Behavior*, 2, No. 7 (1973), 25–28.

Harvat, R. W., *Physical Education for Children with Perceptual-Motor Learning Disabilities*, Columbus, O.: Charles E. Merrill, 1971.

Hecherl, J. R., and S. M. Webb, "An educational approach to the treatment of children with learning disabilities," *Journal of Learning Disabilities*, 2 (1969), 199–204.

Kaslow, F., "A therapeutic creative arts unit for children with learning disabilities," *Academic Therapy Quarterly*, 7 (1972), 297–306.

Kronick, D., "Regular and special camp, or no camp," *Academic Therapy Quarterly*, 4 (1969), 207–211.

Landreth, G. L., W. S. Jacquot, and L. Allen, "A team approach to learning disabilities," *Journal of Learning Disabilities*, 2 (1969), 82–87.

Lev, J. L., "Organization and design of a learning center's approach for children with specific learning disabilities," *Slow Learning Child*, 16, No. 1 (1969), 33–36.

McCarthy, J. J., and J. F. McCarthy, *Learning Disabilities*, Boston: Allyn & Bacon, 1969.

McWhirter, J. J., *The Learning Disabled Child: A School and Family Concern*, Champaign, Ill.: Research Press, 1977.

Peter, L. J., *The Peter Principle*, New York: Morrow, 1968.

Reger, R., W. Schroeder, and K. Uschold, *Special Education: Children with Learning Problems*, New York: Oxford University Press, 1968.

Richardson, S. O., "Learning disorders and the preschool child," *New Jersey Education Association Review*, 41, No. 6 (1968), 1–4. (New Jersey Education Assoc.)

Ross, A. O., *Psychological Aspects of Learning Disabilities and Reading Disorders*, New York: McGraw-Hill, 1976.

Schwartz, L. L., "Survey of certification requirements for teachers of children with learning disabilities," paper presented at Association for Children with Learning Disabilities Convention, Fort Worth, Texas, 1969.

Sharpe, L. W., "The effects of a creative thinking skills program on intermediate grade educationally handicapped children," *Journal of Creative Behavior*, 10 (1976), 138−145.

Smith, B. K., "Free to learn," *American Education*, 8, No. 5 (1972), 11−16.

Strauss, A. A., and N. C. Kephart, *Psychopathology and Education of Brain-Injured Children*, Vol. 2, New York: Grune & Stratton, 1955.

Towne, R. C., and L. M. Joiner, "Some negative implications of special placement for children with learning disabilities," *Journal of Special Education*, 2 (1968), 217−222.

Wagner, R. F., *Dyslexia and Your Child*, New York: Harper & Row, 1971.

Wender, P. H., *Minimal Brain Dysfunction in Children*, New York: Wiley Interscience, 1971.

Wetter, J., "Parent attitudes toward learning disability," *Exceptional Children*, 38 (1972), 490−491.

Chapter 6

Bare, C., E. Boettke, and N. Waggoner, *Self-Help Clothing for Handicapped Children*, Chicago: National Society for Crippled Children and Adults, 1962.

Caniff, C. E., "Architectual barriers—a personal problem," *Rehabilitation Literature*, 23, No. 1 (1962), 13−14.

Cogen, V., and W. F. Ohrtmann, "A comprehensive plan for services to the handicapped," *Journal of Special Education*, 5, No. 1 (1971), 73−79.

Conine, T., and W. T. Brennan, "Orthopedically handicapped children in regular classrooms," *Journal of School Health*, 29, No. 1 (1969), 59−63.

Connor, F. P., J. R. Wald, and M. J. Cohen, eds., *Professional Preparation for Educators of Crippled Children*, New York: Teachers College Press, 1971.

Cratty, B. J., and J. E. Breen, *Educational Games for Physically Handicapped Children*, Denver: Love, 1972.

Creer, T. L., and W. P. Christian, *Chronically Ill and Handicapped Children: Their Management and Rehabilitation*, Champaign, Ill.: Research Press, 1976.

Dykes, M. K., "Competency needs of special educators of crippled and other health-impaired children," *Journal of Special Education*, 9 (1975), 367−374.

Freeman, R. D., "Psychiatric problems in adolescents with cerebral palsy," *Developmental Medicine and Child Neurology*, 12, No. 1 (1970), 64−69.

Gellman, W., "Helping the crippled child reach attainable occupational goals." Chicago: National Easter Seal Society for Crippled Children and Adults, n.d.

Gertenreich, R., "A simple mouth-held writing device for use with cerebral palsy patients," *MR/Mental Retardation*, 4 (Aug. 1966), 13–14.

Goodman, E. M., "Vocational education for the handicapped: A cooperative approach," *Rehabilitation Literature*, 30 (1969), 199–202.

Hallenbeck, P. N., "Special clothing for the handicapped: Review of research and resources," *Rehabilitation Literature*, 27, No. 2 (1966), 34–40.

Hetherington, E. M., "Humor preferences in normal and physically handicapped children," *Journal of Abnormal and Social Psychology*, 69 (1964), 694–696.

Jones, R., "The acorn people: What I learned at summer camp," *Psychology Today*, 11, No. 1 (1977), 70–81.

Kniest, J. H., "The therapeutic value of toys in a training center for handicapped children," *Rehabilitation Literature*, 23, No. 1 (1962), 2–7, 30.

Kogan, K. L., and N. Tyler, "Mother-child interaction in young physically handicapped children," *American Journal of Mental Deficiency*, 77 (1973), 492–497.

Lynch, D. J., and C. Arndt, "Developmental changes in response to frustration among handicapped children," *Journal of Personality Assessment*, 37 (1973), 130–135.

Molloy, L., "The handicapped child in the everyday classroom," *Phi Delta Kappan*, 56 (1975), 337–340.

Moss, J. W., "Resource centers for teachers of handicapped children," *Journal of Special Education*, 5, No. 1 (1971), 67–71.

Nugent, T. J., "Opportunities unreachable," *Safety*, 5, No. 4 (1969), 14–17. (EC–500–797)

Robbins, J., and J. Robbins, "The boy who found the sun," *Redbook*, December, 1966.

Schiller, E. J., "Creative habilitation of the cerebral palsy child," in *The Guidance of Exceptional Children: A Book of Readings*, J. C. Gowan and G. D. Demos, ed., New York: David McKay, 1965, 381–386.

Schwartz, A., "Recreation for the handicapped child," *Rehabilitation Record*, (Nov.-Dec. 1971), 7–11.

Sinclair, M., "On campus in a wheelchair," *American Education*, 8, No. 2 (1972), back cover.

Swack, M., "Therapeutic role of the teacher of physically handicapped children," *Exceptional Children*, 35 (1969), 371–374.

Velleman, R. A., "The school library in the education of handicapped children," *Rehabilitation Literature*, (May 1971), 138–140.

Weininger, O., G. Rotenberg, and A. Henry, "Body image of handicapped children," *Journal of Personality Assessment*, 36 (1972), 248–253.

Chapter 7

Altschuler, D., "Use of videotape in programs for the deaf," *Volta Review*, 72 (1970), 102–106.

Bellugi, U., and E. S. Klima, "The roots of language in the sign talk of the deaf," *Psychology Today*, 6, No. 1 (1972), 60–64, 76.

Bender, R. E., *The Conquest of Deafness*, Cleveland: Case Western Reserve University Press, 1970.

Berges, S. A., "The deaf student in physical education: Programs for the handicapped," *Journal of Health, Physical Education, and Recreation*, 40, No. 3 (1969), 69–70.

Cohen, S., D. C. Glass, and J. E. Singer, "Apartment noise, auditory discrimination, and reading ability in children," *Journal of Experimental Social Psychology*, 9 (1973), 407–421.

Connor, L. E., "Mainstreaming a special school: Lexington School for the Deaf, N.Y.," *Teaching Exceptional Children*, 8 (1976), 76–80.

———, L. E., "Secondary education of deaf children," *Volta Review*, 67 (Feb. 1965), 126–132, 165.

———, ed., *Speech for the Deaf Child: Knowledge and Use*. Washington: Alexander Graham Bell Association for the Deaf, 1971.

Craig, W. N., and J. M. Salem, "Partial integration of deaf with other hearing students," *American Annals of the Deaf*, 121 (1976), 63–68.

Dale, D. M. C., *Deaf Children at Home and at School*, London: University of London Press, 1967.

Fitch, J. L., and D. A. Sachs, "Strengthening the visual perception of deaf children," Southeastern Psychological Association meeting, Atlanta (Ga.), 1972.

Frey, R. M., and I. B. Krause, "The incidence of color blindness among deaf children," *Exceptional Children*, 37 (1971), 373–394.

Furth, H. G., *Deafness and Learning: A Psychosocial Approach*, Belmont, Calif.: Wadsworth, 1973.

Hehir, R. G., "Integrating deaf students for career education," *Exceptional Children*, 39 (1973), 611–618.

Hoag, R. L., and Stelle, R. M., "Teachers of the deaf: Artisans to professionals," *Volta Review*, 78, No. 4 (1976), 47–51.

Jeffers, J., and M. Barley, *Speechreading (Lipreading)*, Springfield, Ill.: Charles C Thomas, 1971.

Kennedy, P., and R. H. Bruininks, "Social status of hearing impaired children in regular classrooms," *Exceptional Children*, 40 (1974), 336–342.

Kindred, E. M., "Integration at the secondary school level," *Volta Review*, 78, No. 1 (1976), 35–43.

Kreamer, R. S., "New ways to educate deaf children successfully," *Pennsylvania Education*, 3, No. 2 (1971), 38ff.

Leitman, A., *Science for Deaf Children*. Washington: Alexander Graham Bell Association for the Deaf, 1968.

Leshin, G., *Speech for the Hearing-Impaired Child*, Tucson: University of Arizona Press, 1975.

Meadow, K. P., "Early manual communication in relation to the deaf child's intellectual, social, and communicative functioning," *American Annals of the Deaf*, 113 (1968), 29—41.

Mindel, E. D., and V. McCay, *They Grow in Silence: The Deaf Child and His Family*. Silver Springs, Md.: National Association of the Deaf, 1971.

Moorefield, S., "Opening a new door for the deaf," *American Education*, 10, No. 3 (1974), 30—33.

Moores, D. F., *Educating the Deaf: Psychology, Principles, and Practices*, Boston: Houghton Mifflin, 1978.

Myklebust, H. R., *The Psychology of Deafness*, New York: Appleton-Century-Crofts, 1964.

Neuhas, M., "Parental attitudes and the emotional adjustment of deaf children," *Exceptional Children*, 35 (1969), 721—727.

Nix, G. W., ed., *Mainstream Education for Hearing Impaired Children and Youth*, New York: Grune & Stratton, 1976.

Northcott, W. N., "The integration of young deaf children into ordinary educational programs," *Exceptional Children*, 38 (1971), 29—32.

Polis, J. E., Observation at the school for the deaf in Luxembourg, private communication, 1973.

Reid, W. R., "Action verb materials developed for deaf children," *Exceptional Children*, 34 (1971), 203—205.

Roach, R. E., and C. J. Rosecrans, "Verbal deficit in children with hearing loss," *Exceptional Children*, 38 (1972), 395—399.

Schiff, W., "Social perception in deaf and hearing adolescents," *Exceptional Children*, 39 (1973), 289—297.

Schlesinger, H. S., and K. P. Meadow, "Development of maturity in deaf children," *Exceptional Children*, 38 (1972), 461—467.

Streng, A. H., *Syntax, Speech, and Hearing: Applied Linguistics for Teachers of Children with Language and Hearing Disabilities*, New York: Grune & Stratton, 1972.

Vernon, McC., "Rh factor and deafness: The problem, its psychological, physical, and educational manifestations," *Exceptional Children*, 34 (1967), 5—12.

Wood, W., "By the deaf, for the deaf," *American Education*, 10, No. 1 (1974), 18—24.

Youniss, J., H. G. Furth, and B. M. Ross, "Logical symbol use in deaf and hearing children and adolescents," *Developmental Psychology*, 5 (1971), 511—517.

Chapter 8

Abel, G. L., "The blind adolescent and his needs," *Exceptional Children*, 27 (1961), 309–310, 325–334.

Barraga, N., *Visual Handicaps and Learning: A Developmental Approach*, Belmont, Calif.: Wadsworth, 1976.

Bischoff, R. W., "Improvement of listening comprehension in partially sighted students," *Sight-Saving Review*, 37, No. 3 (1967), 161–165.

Bishop, V. E., *Teaching the Visually Limited Child*, Springfield, Ill.: Charles C Thomas, 1971.

Bommarito, J. W., "Implications of severe visual handicaps," *The Record* (also known as *Teachers College Record*), 70 (1969), 523–534.

Buell, C. E., *Physical Education for Blind Children*. Springfield, Ill.: Charles C Thomas, 1966.

Chase, J. C., "A retrospective study of retrolental fibroplasia," *New Outlook for the Blind*, 68 (1974), 61–71.

Clark, L. L., ed., *International Catalog: Aids and Appliances for Blind and Visually Impaired Persons*, New York: American Foundation for the Blind, 1973.

Coveny, T. E., "Standardized tests for visually handicapped children: A review of research," *New Outlook for the Blind*, 70 (1976), 232–236.

Cratty, B. J., *Movement and Spatial Awareness in Blind Children and Youth*, Springfield, Ill.: Charles C Thomas, 1971.

Davidson, I., *Handbook for Parents of Preschool Blind Children*, Toronto: Ontario Ministry of Education, 1977. (also available in French)

Duggar, M. P., "What can dance be to someone who cannot see?" *Journal of Health, Physical Education, and Recreation*, 39, No. 5 (1968), 28–30.

Eaglestein, A. S., "The social acceptance of blind high school students in an integrated school," *New Outlook for the Blind*, 69 (1975), 447–451.

Fraiberg, S., "Intervention in infancy: A program for blind infants," in *Exceptional Infant: Assessment and Intervention*, vol. 3, B. Z. Friedlander, G. M. Sterritt, and G. E. Kirk, eds., New York: Brunner/Mazel, 1975, 40–62.

Franks, F. L., and R. M. Baird, "Geographical concepts and the visually handicapped," *Exceptional Children*, 38 (1971), 321–324.

Hanninen, K. A., *Teaching the Visually Handicapped*, Columbus, O.: Charles E. Merrill, 1975.

Hill, E., and P. Ponder, *Orientation and Mobility Techniques*, New York: American Foundation for the Blind, 1976.

Hulsey, S., "Liberating the blind student," *American Education*, 9, No. 6 (1973), 18–22.

Kephart, J. G., C. P. Kephart, and G. C. Schwarz, "A journey into the world of the blind child," *Exceptional Children*, 40 (1974), 421–427.

Krents, H., *To Race the Wind*, New York: G. P. Putnam's Sons, 1972.

Lappin, C. W., "At your service—the Instructional Materials Reference Center for the Visually Handicapped," *Teaching Exceptional Children*, 5 (1973), 74−76.

Linn, M. C., "An experiential science curriculum for the visually impaired," *Exceptional Children*, 39 (1972), 37−43.

———, *Our Blind Children (Growing and Learning with Them)*, Springfield, Ill.: Charles C. Thomas, 1971.

Lowenfeld, B., G. L. Abel, and P. H. Hatlen, *Blind Children Learn to Read*, Springfield, Ill.: Charles C Thomas, 1969.

Marsh, V., and R. Friedman, "Changing public attitudes toward blindness," *Exceptional Children*, 38 (1972), 426−428.

Moore, D. D., "Sex education for blind high school students," *Education of the Visually Handicapped*, 1, No. 1 (1969), 22−25.

Myers, W. A., "Color discriminability for partially-seeing children," *Exceptional Children*, 38 (1971), 223−228.

Napier, G., D. L. Kappan, D. W. Tuttle, W. L. Schrotberger, and A. L. Dennison, *Handbook for Teachers of the Visually Handicapped*, Louisville, Ky.: American Printing House for the Blind, 1975.

Nezol, A. J., "A pilot course to assist blind potential teachers," *New Outlook for the Blind*, 69 (1975), 317−319.

Parten, C. B., "Encouragement of sensory motor development in the preschool blind," *Exceptional Children*, 37 (1971), 739−741.

Paul, R., and P. W. Gioine, "Composition, through typing: Instruction in communication for the blind," *Exceptional Children*, 35 (1968), 154−158.

Scholl, G., and R. Schnur, *Measures of Psychological, Vocational, and Educational Functioning in the Blind and Visually Handicapped*, New York: American Foundation for the Blind, 1976.

Scouting for the Visually Handicapped, New Brunswick, N.J.: Boy Scouts of America, 1968.

Step-by-Step Guide to Personal Management for Blind Persons, New York: American Foundation for the Blind, 1970.

Tisdall, W. J., A. E. Blackhurst, and C. H. Marks, "Divergent thinking in blind children," *Journal of Educational Psychology*, 62 (1971), 468−473.

Woodcock, C. C., "A sensory stimulation center for blind children," *Phi Delta Kappan*, 55 (1974), 541.

Chapter 9

Anderson, R. M., and G. D. Stevens, "Practices and problems in educating deaf retarded children in residential schools," *Exceptional Children*, 35 (1969), 687−694.

Bolkestein, G., "Teaching blind retarded children in the Netherlands," *Phi Delta Kappan*, 55 (1974), 559–560.

Calvert, D. R., and others, "Experiences with preschool deaf-blind children," *Exceptional Children*, 38 (1972), 415–421.

Dinsmore, A., "Unmet needs of deaf-blind children," *New Outlook for the Blind*, 61, No. 8 (1967), 262–266.

Doob, D., "An intensive speech and language program in the rehabilitation process of multihandicapped children," *Rehabilitation Literature*, 29 (1968), 8–10.

Frampton, M. E., E. Kerney, and R. Schattner, *Forgotten Children: A Program for the Multihandicapped*, Boston: Porter Sargent, 1969.

Frey, R. M., and I. B. Krause, "The incidence of color-blindness among deaf children," *Exceptional Children*, 37 (1971), 373–394.

Gold, M. W., and R. K. Rittenhouse, "Task analysis for teaching eight practical signs to deaf-blind individuals," *Teaching Exceptional Children*, 10 (1978), 34–37.

Green, A., "A preventive care guide for multihandicapped children: Dental care begins at home," *Rehabilitation Literature*, 31, No. 1 (1970), 10–12.

Guess, D., "Mental retardation and blindness: A complex and relatively unexplored dyad," *Exceptional Children*, 33 (1967), 472–473.

Hall, S. M., and L. W. Talkington, "Trends in programming for deaf mentally retarded in public residential facilities," *MR/Mental Retardation*, 10, No. 2 (1972), 50–52.

Hedrick, V., "Applying technology to special education," *American Education*, 8, No. 1 (1972), 22–25.

Hurwitz, S. N., and S. DiFrancesca, "Behavioral modification of the emotionally retarded deaf," *Rehabilitation Literature*, 29 (1968), 258–264.

Lawson, J. L., Jr., and H. R. Myklebust, "Ophthalmological deficiences in deaf children," *Exceptional Children*, 37 (1970), 17–20.

Leach, F., "Multiply handicapped visually impaired children: Instructional materials needs," *Exceptional Children*, 38 (1971), 153–156.

Michal-Smith, H., "Rehabilitation of the mentally retarded blind," *Rehabilitation Literature*, 30 (1969), 194–198.

Mira, M., and S. Hoffman, "Educational programming for multihandicapped deaf-blind children," *Exceptional Children*, 40 (1974), 513–514.

"New centers to serve deaf-blind children," *Hearing and Speech News*, (Nov.-Dec. 1968), 17.

Schattner, R., *An Early Childhood Curriculum for Multiply Handicapped Children*, New York: John Day, 1971.

Stein, L. K., and M. B. Green, "Problems in managing the young deaf-blind child," *Exceptional Children*, 38 (1972), 481–484.

Vernon, McC., *Multiply Handicapped Deaf Children: Medical, Educational and Psychological Considerations*, Washington: Council for Exceptional Children, 1969.

Zimmerman, J., and others, "Effects of token reinforcement on productivity in multiple handicapped clients in a sheltered workshop," *Rehabilitation Literature*, 30 (1969), 34–41.

Chapter 10

Ahr, E. A., *Speech Therapy: Objectives, Methods, and Evaluation Techniques*. Skokie, Ill.: Priority Innovations, 1970.

Alvord, D. J., "Innovation in speech therapy: A cost effective program," *Exceptional Children*, 43 (1977), 520–525.

Boone, D., *The Voice and Voice Therapy*, Englewood Cliffs, N.J.: Prentice-Hall, 1971.

Falk, M. L., ed., *A Cleft Palate Team Addresses the Speech Clinician*, Springfield, Ill.: Charles C Thomas, 1971.

Goldiamond, I., "Stuttering and fluency as manipulable operant response classes," in *Research in Behavior Modification*, L. Krasner and L. P. Ullman, eds. New York: Holt, Rinehart and Winston, 1965, 106–156.

Gottsleben, R. H., et al., "Developmental language programs for aphasic children," *Academic Therapy Quarterly*, 3 (1968), 278–282.

Greenberg, J. B., "The effect of the metronome on the speech of young stutterers." *Behavior Therapy*, 1 (1970), 240–244.

Hainfield, H., "Using sound films for speech analysis," *Academic Therapy Quarterly*, 4 (1969), 213–214.

Johnson, W., *Toward Understanding Stuttering*. Chicago: National Society for Crippled Children and Adults, 1958.

Lloyd, M., "Say it right and they will too," *American Education*, 7, No. 1 (1971), 5–7.

Martyn, M. M., J. Sheehan, and K. Slutz, "Incidence of stuttering and other speech disorders among the retarded," *American Journal of Mental Deficiency*, 74 (1969), 206–211.

Mowrer, D., "Speech problems: What you should do and shouldn't do," *Learning*, 6, No. 5 (1978), 34–37.

Panagos, J. M., and S. J. Hanna, "A speech and hearing program in Appalachia," *Rehabilitation Literature*, 29 (1968), 2–7.

Perry, B. F., "The liberation of Johnny," *Teaching Exceptional Children*, 6, No. 3 (1974), 154–161.

Phillips, P. P., "Variables affecting classroom teachers' understanding of speech disorders," *Language, Speech, and Hearing Services in Schools*, 7 (1976), 142–149.

Rosenthal, R., and L. Jacobsen, *Pygmalion in the Classroom*, New York: Holt, Rinehart and Winston, 1968.

Sailor, W., D. Guess, and D. M. Baer, "Functional language for verbally deficient children: An experimental program," *MR/Mental Retardation*, 11 No. 3 (1973), 27–35.

Sloane, H. N., Jr., and B. D. MacAulay, eds., *Operant Procedures and Remedial Speech and Language Training*, Boston: Houghton Mifflin, 1968.

Sullivan, H. S. *The Interpersonal Theory of Personality*, New York: Norton, 1953.

Wingate, M. E., *Stuttering: Theory and Treatment*, New York: Irvington (Halsted Press), 1976.

Wriner, P. S., "The emotionally disturbed child in the speech clinic: Some considerations," *Journal of Speech and Hearing Disorders*, 33 (1968), 158–166.

Chapter 11

Adler, S., "Dialectical differences: Professional and clinical implications," *Journal of Speech and Hearing Disorders*, 36, No. 1 (1971), 90–100.

Anastasi, A., and F. A. Cordova, "Some effects of bilingualism upon the intelligence test performance of Puerto Rican children in New York City," *Journal of Educational Psychology*, 44 (1953), 1–19.

Anderson, J. D., *Language in Education: The Coordinated Helps in Language Development (CHILD) Program*, Portland, Ore.: Northwest Regional Educational Laboratory: Program Report, Intercultural Programs, 1971.

Bernstein, B., "Special structure, language, and learning," *Educational Research*, 3 (1961), 163–173.

Bricker, W. A., and D. D. Bricker, "A program of language training for the severely language handicapped child," *Exceptional Children*, 37 (1970), 101–111.

Carpenter, I., "Babel reversed," *American Education*, 13, No. 7 (1977), 27–30.

Carroll, J. B., "Language and cognition: Current perspectives from linguistics and psychology," in *The Causes of Behavior*, J. F. Rosenblith, W. Allinsmith, and J. P. Williams, eds., Boston: Allyn & Bacon, 1972.

Chapline, E. B., and W. G. Oxman, "Relationships among language dominance, language preference, and achievement in a bilingual education program," paper presented at American Educational Research Association meeting, Chicago, 1974.

Cohen, A. D., "The Culver City Spanish immersion program: The first two years," *The Modern Language Journal*, 58 (1974), 95–103.

Genesee, F., G. R. Tucker, and W. E. Lambert, "Communication skills of bilingual children," *Child Development*, 46 (1975), 1010–1014.

Hornby, P. A., ed., *Bilingualism: Psychological, Social, and Educational Implications*, New York: Academic Press, 1977.

Howes, E. R., "Twin speech: A language of their own," *The New York Times*, September 11, 1977.

Knapp, M. O., "Black dialect and reading: What teachers need to know," *Journal of Reading*, 19 (1975): 231–236.

Kobrick, J. W., "The compelling case for bilingual education," *Saturday Review*, (April 29, 1972), 54–58.

Marwit, S. J., K. L. Marwit, and J. J. Boswell, "Negro children's use of nonstandard grammar," *Journal of Educational Psychology*, 63 (1972), 218–224.

McConnell, F., K. B. Horton, and B. R. Smith, "Language development and cultural disadvantagement," *Exceptional Children*, 35 (1969), 597–606.

Northwest Regional Education Laboratory, *The Alaskan Readers: A Reading and Language Development System for an Intercultural Setting*, Portland, Ore.: May, 1970.

Ovando, C. J., "School implications of the peaceful Latino invasion," *Phi Delta Kappan*, 59 (1977), 230–234.

Palmer, M. B., "Effects of categorization, degree of bilingualism, and language upon recall of select monolinguals and bilinguals," *Journal of Educational Psychology*, 63 (1972), 160–164.

Quay, L. C., "Negro dialect and Binet performance in severely disadvantaged black four-year-olds," *Child Development*, 43 (1972), 245–250.

Report of the Royal Commission on Bilingualism and Biculturalism, *Book II: Education*, Ottawa: Queen's Printer, 1968.

Saudargas, R. A., C. H. Madsen, Jr., and F. Thompson, "Prescriptive teaching in language arts remediation for black rural elementary school children," *Journal of Learning Disabilities*, 3 (1970), 364–370.

Segalowitz, N., "Communicative incompetence and the non-fluent bilingual," *Canadian Journal of Behavioural Science*, 8 (1976), 122–131.

Sloane, H. N., and B. D. MacAulay, eds., *Operant Procedures in Remedial Speech and Language Training*, Boston: Houghton Mifflin, 1968.

Spencer, M. G., "B.O.L.D. Bicultural orientation and language development," ERIC Document, 1968. (ED–030–342)

Torrance, E. P., and P. Torrance, "Combining creative problem solving with creative expressive activities with disadvantaged children," *Journal of Creative Behavior*, 6 (1972), 1–10.

Wright, L., "The bilingual education at the crossroads," *Phi Delta Kappan*, 55 (1973), 183–186.

Chapter 12

Baratz, S. S., and J. C. Baratz, "Early childhood intervention: The social science base of institutional racism," *Harvard Educational Review*, 40 (1970), 29–50.

Bereiter, C., "Instructional planning in early compensatory education," *Phi Delta Kappan*, 48 (1967), 355–356.

Blank, M., "Implicit assumptions underlying preschool intervention programs," *Journal of Social Issues*, 26, No. 2 (1970).

Brody, J. E., "Coping with life: Preschoolers—generation of 5-year-old failures?" *Philadelphia Evening Bulletin*, January 31, 1974, p. 22.

Brooks, R. E., "Homework center," *Vassar Alumnae Magazine*, 53, No. 4 (1968), 23.

Busse, T. V., et al., "Environmentally enriched classrooms and the cognitive and perceptual development of Negro preschool children," *Journal of Educational Psychology*, 63 (1972), 15–21.

Caldwell, B. M., "The effects of psychosocial deprivation on human development in infancy," *Merrill-Palmer Quarterly*, 16, No. 3 (1970).

———, "The rationale for early intervention," *Exceptional Children*, 36 (1970), 717– 726.

Calvert, D. R., "Dimensions of family involvement in early childhood education," *Exceptional Children*, 37 (1971), 655–659.

Cartwright, C. A., and G. P. Cartwright, "Competencies for prevention of learning problems in early childhood education," *Educational Horizons*, 53 (1975), 151– 157.

Conroy, P., *The Water Is Wide*, Boston: Houghton Mifflin, 1972.

Day Care and Early Education, Behavioral Publications. (bimonthly)

Diamond, F., "A play center for developmentally handicapped infants," *Children*, 18, No. 5 (1971).

Eckerson, L. O. "Following Through with Follow Through," *American Education*, 9, No. 10 (1973), 10–16.

"Environmental design for young children," *Children in Contemporary Society*, 11 (1977), whole issue.

Fein, G. G., and A. Clarke-Stewart, *Day Care in Context*, New York: Wiley-Inter-science, 1973.

Foster, F. P., "Cooking to learn," *Day Care and Early Education*, 1, No. 2 (1973), 26–30.

Hamblin, J. A., and R. L. Hamblin, "On teaching disadvantaged preschoolers to read: A successful experiment," *American Educational Research Journal*, 9 (1972), 209–216.

Hunt, J. McV., *The Challenge of Incompetence and Poverty: Papers on the Role of Early Education*, Urbana: University of Illinois Press, 1971.

Jensen, A. R., "How much can we boost I.Q. and scholastic achievement," *Harvard Educational Review*, 39 (1969), 1–123.

Klaus, R. A., and S. W. Gray, "The early training project for disadvantaged children: A report after five years," *Monographs of the Society for Research in Child Development*, 33, No. 4, Whole No. 120 (1968).

Kohlberg, L., "Early education: A cognitive developmental view," *Child Development*, 39 (1968), 1013–1062.

McDonald, P. L., and M. Soeffing, "Prevention of learning problems: Capsule summaries of research studies in early childhood education," *Exceptional Children*, 37 (1971), 681–686.

Marmorale, A. M., and F. Brown, *Mental Health Intervention in the Primary Grades,* New York: Behavioral Publications, Inc., 1974.

Norman, M., "Update/Substitutes for mother," *Human Behavior,* 7, No. 2 (1978), 18–22.

Spaulding, R. L., "Effects of a five-year compensatory education program on social, intellectual, linguistic, and academic development," paper presented at Eastern Psychological Association meeting, Boston, 1972.

Spicker, H. H., "Intellectual development through early childhood education," *Exceptional Children,* 37 (1971), 629–640.

Spicker, H. H., W. L. Hodges, and B. R. McCandless, "A diagnostically based curriculum for psycho-socially deprived preschool mentally retarded children," *Exceptional Children,* 33 (1966), 215–220.

Strickland, S. P., "Can slum children learn?" *American Education,* 7, No. 6 (1971), 3–7.

Tjossen, T. D. *Intervention Strategies for High Risk Infants and Young Children,* Baltimore: University Park Press, 1976.

Trotter, R., "Environment and behavior," *APA Monitor,* 7, Nos. 7, 10 (1976), 4–5, 19, 46.

Tulkin, S. R., and J. Kagan, "Mother-child interaction in the first year of life," *Child Development,* 43 (1972), 31–41.

Tymchuk, A. J., "Personality and sociocultural retardation," *Exceptional Children,* 38 (1972), 721–728.

Weikart, D. P., ed., *Preschool Intervention: A Preliminary Report of the Perry Preschool Project,* Ann Arbor, Mich.: Campus Publishers, 1967.

White, B. L., "High payoff likely on money invested in early childhood education," *Phi Delta Kappan,* 53 (1972), 610–612.

Yarbrough, W. V., "Preschool goes into the mountains," *American Education,* 9, No. 6 (1973), 27–31.

Zigler, E., "Project Head Start: Success or Failure?" *Learning,* 1, No. 7 (1973), 43–47.

Zigler, E., E. C. Butterfield, and F. Capobianco, "Institutionalization and the effectiveness of social reinforcement: A five- and eight-year follow-up study," *Developmental Psychology,* 3 (1970), 255–263.

Chapter 13

Baker, G. C., "Multicultural training for student teachers," *Journal of Teacher Education,* 24 (1973), 306–307.

Blank, M., and Solomon, F., "A tutorial language program to develop abstract thinking in socially disadvantaged preschool children," *Child Development,* 39 (1968), 379–390.

————, "How shall the disadvantaged child be taught?" *Child Development*, 40 (1969), 47–61.

Borowitz, G. H., J. G. Hirsch, and J. Costello, "Play behavior and competence in ghetto four-year-olds," *Journal of Special Education*, 4 (1970), 215–221.

Brazziel, W. E., "Quality education for minorities," *Phi Delta Kappan*, 53 (1972), 547.

Carter, T. P., *Mexican Americans in School: A History of Educational Neglect*, New York: College Entrance Examination Board, 1970.

Charnofsky, S., *Educating the Powerless*, Belmont, Calif.: Wadsworth, 1971.

Cohen, S. A., "Some learning disabilities of socially disadvantaged Puerto Rican and Negro children," *Academic Therapy Quarterly*, 2, No. 1 (1967), 37–41.

Coleman, J. S., et al., *Equality of Educational Opportunity*, Washington: U.S. Department of Health, Education, and Welfare, Office of Education, 1965.

Cuban, L., "Ethnic content and 'white' instruction," *Phi Delta Kappan*, 53 (1972), 270–273.

DiLorenzo, L. T., "Which way for pre-K: Wishes or reality?" *American Education*, 7, No. 1 (1971), 28–32.

Edington, E. D., "Disadvantaged rural youth," *Review of Educational Research*, 40 (1970) 69–85.

Elkind, D., and J. A. Deblinger, "Perceptual training and reading achievement in disadvantaged children," *Child Development*, 40 (1969), 11–20.

Elliott, J. L., ed., *Immigrant Groups*, Scarborough, Ont.: Prentice-Hall of Canada, 1971.

"Ethnic isolation of Mexican Americans in the public schools of the Southwest," Washington: U.S. Commission on Civil Rights, Reports I and II, (April) 1971.

Fersh, S., "Orientals and orientation," *Phi Delta Kappan*, 53 (1972), 315–318.

Frost, J. L., and G. B. Hawkes, eds., *The Disadvantaged Child: Issues and Innovations*, Boston: Houghton Mifflin, 1970.

Fuchs, E., "How teachers learn to help children fail," *Transaction*, 5, No. 9 (1968), 45–49.

Gold, A. R., and M. C. St. Ange, "Development of sex role stereotypes in black and white elementary school girls," *Developmental Psychology*, 10 (1974), 461.

Goldberg, M. L., "Adapting teacher style to pupil differences: Teachers for disadvantaged children," *Merrill-Palmer Quarterly*, 10 (1964), 161–178.

Goodman, M. E., *Race Awareness in Young Children*, New York: Collier Books, 1964.

Guerra, M. H., "Educating Chicano children," *Phi Delta Kappan*, 53 (1972), 313.

Hamilton, A., "Education and La Raza," *American Education*, 9, No. 6 (1973), 4–8.

Hernandez, N. G., "Variables affecting achievement of middle school Mexican-American students," *Review of Educational Research*, 43 (1973), 1–39.

Herzog, E., and H. Lewis, "Children in poor families: Myths and realities," *American Journal of Orthopsychiatry*, 40 (1970), 375–387.

Houston, D. E., "CUTE: A training program for inner-city teachers," *Journal of Teacher Education*, 24 (1973), 302–303.

Innis, H. R., *Bilingualism and Biculturalism* (An abridged version of the Royal Commission Report), Canada: McClelland and Stewart Limited, 1973.

Kaltsounis, T., "The need to Indianize Indian schools," *Phi Delta Kappan*, 53 (1972), 291.

Khatena, J., "Teaching disadvantaged preschool children to think creatively with pictures," *Journal of Educational Psychology*, 62 (1971), 384–386.

Kobrick, J. W., "The compelling case for bilingual education, *Saturday Review*, April 29, 1972, 54–58.

Looff, D. H., *Appalachia's Children: The Challenge of Mental Health*, Lexington: University of Kentucky Press, 1971.

Marjoribanks, K., "Environment, social class, and mental abilities," *Journal of Educational Psychology*, 63 (1972), 103–109.

Mingione, A. D., "Need for achievement in Negro, white, and Puerto Rican children," *Journal of Consulting and Clinical Psychology*, 32 (1968), 94–95.

Multiculturalism, Toronto: Guidance Centre, Faculty of Education, University of Toronto. (quarterly journal)

Murray, John, *Toronto Educational Governance/Multiculturalism Case Study*, Toronto: Ontario Ministry of Education, 1977.

Muskrat, J., "The need for cultural empathy," *School Review*, 79 (1970), 72–75.

Noar, G., "Sensitizing teachers to ethnic groups," *ADL Bulletin*, (March 1972). (Anti-Defamation League of B'nai Brith)

Ramirez, M., III, C. Taylor, Jr., and B. Petersen, "Mexican-American cultural membership and adjustment to school," *Developmental Psychology*, 4 (1971), 141–148.

Rosenthal, R., and L. Jacobsen, *Pygmalion in the Classroom*, New York: Holt, Rinehart and Winston, 1968.

Sabatino, D. A., K. Kelling, and D. L. Hayden, "Special education and the culturally different child: Implications for assessment and intervention," *Exceptional Children*, 39 (1973), 563–567.

Schwartz, A. J., "A comparative study of values and achievement: Mexican-American and Anglo youth," *Sociology of Education*, 44 (1971), 438–462.

Schwartz, L. L., and N. Isser, "Attitudes toward the Jewish minority in public education," *Jewish Education*, 45, No. 3 (1977), 33–39.

Seda Bouilla, E., "Cultural pluralism and the education of Puerto Rican youths," *Phi Delta Kappan*, 53 (1972), 294.

Shields, H., "Crossing the cultural gap," *American Education*, 8, No. 2 (1972), 32–36.

Smith, D. H., "Training teachers for ethnic minority youths," *Phi Delta Kappan*, 53 (1972), 285–287.

Stein, Z., and M. Susser, "Mutability of intelligence and epidemiology of mild mental retardation," *Review of Educational Research*, 40 (1970), 29–67.

Thomas, E., and K. Yamamoto, "Minority children and their school-related perceptions," *Journal of Experimental Education*, 40, No. 1 (1971), 89–96.

Wagner, N. N., and M. J. Haug, *Chicanos: Social and Psychological Perspectives*, St. Louis: C. V. Mosby, 1971.

Wahrhaftig, A. L., and R. K. Thomas, "Renaissance and repression: The Oklahoma Cherokee," *Transaction*, 6, No. 4 (1969), 42–48.

Walsh, R., "The children of Smith Street Projects," *Vassar Quarterly*, 58 (1971), 27–32.

Weller, J. E., *Yesterday's People, Life in Contemporary Appalachia*, Lexington: University of Kentucky Press, 1965.

World Educators Conference on Multi-cultural Education, *Official Proceedings*, Honolulu, 1976.

Chapter 14

Amos, R. T., and R. M. Washington, "A comparison of pupil and teacher perceptions of pupil problems," *Journal of Educational Psychology*, 51 (1960), 255–258.

Bettelheim, B., *Truants from Life: The Rehabilitation of Emotionally Disturbed Children*, Glencoe, Ill.: Free Press, 1955.

Bower, E. M., *Early Identification of Emotionally Handicapped Children in School*, Springfield, Ill.: Charles C Thomas, 1969.

Bullock, L. M., and R. K. Brown, "Behavioral dimensions of emotionally disturbed children," *Exceptional Children*, 38 (1972), 740–742.

Chamberlin, R. W., and P. R. Nader, "Relationships between nursery school behavior patterns and later school functioning," *American Journal of Orthopsychiatry*, 41 (1971), 597–601.

Clarizio, H. F., and J. F. McCoy, *Behavior Disorders in School-Aged Children*, Scranton, Pa.: Chandler, 1970.

D'Ambrosio, R., *No Language But a Cry*, New York: Doubleday, 1970.

DeCourcy, P., and J. DeCourcy, *A Silent Tragedy: Child Abuse in the Community*, Port Washington, N.Y.: Alfred, 1973.

Dorward, B., "A comparison of the competencies for regular classroom teachers and teachers of emotionally disturbed children," *Exceptional Children*, 29 (1963), 67–73.

Feldhusen, J. F., J. R. Thurston, and J. J. Benning, "Aggressive classroom behavior and school achievement," *Journal of Special Education*, 4 (1970), 431–439.

Gardner, J. E., et al., "Measurement, evaluation, and modification of selected social interaction between a schizophrenic child, his parents, and his therapist," *Journal of Consulting and Clinical Psychology*, 32 (1968), 537–542.

Giebink, J. W., D. O. Stover, and M. A. Fahl, "Teaching adaptive responses to frustration to emotionally disturbed boys," *Journal of Consulting and Clinical Psychology*, 32 (1968), 366–368.

Glasser, W., *The Effect of School Failure on the Life of a Child*, Washington: National Education Association, 1971.

Goldenberg, H., and I. Goldenberg, "School phobia: Childhood neurosis or learned maladaptive behavior?" *Exceptional Children*, 37 (1970), 220–226.

Gordon, D. A., and R. D. Young, "School phobia: A discussion of etiology, treatment, and evaluation," *Psychological Reports*, 39 (1976), 783–804. (Also in Chess, S., and A. Thomas, eds., *Annual Progress in Child Psychiatry and Child Development*, Vol. 10, New York: Brunner/Mazel, 1977, 409–433.)

Greenfeld, J., *A Child Called Noah: A Family Journey*, New York: Holt, Rinehart and Winston, 1972.

Grosenick, J., "Preparing undergraduates as teachers of emotionally disturbed: Ingenuity or insanity," *TED Newsletter*, 8, No. 2 (1972), 4–8. (Council for Exceptional Children)

Halpern, W. I., and S. Kissel, *Human Resources for Troubled Children*, New York: John Wiley & Sons, 1976.

Harris, I. D., *Emotional Blocks to Learning*, Glencoe, Ill.: Free Press, 1961.

Helfer, R. E., and C. H. Kempe, eds., *The Battered Child*, 2nd ed., Chicago: University of Chicago Press, 1974.

Henderson, R. A., "Special education for the emotionally disturbed," *Exceptional Children*, 38 (1971), 313–317.

Hewett, F. M., "A hierarchy of competencies for teachers of emotionally handicapped children," *Exceptional Children*, 33 (1966), 7–11.

————, *The Emotionally Disturbed Child in the Classroom*, Boston: Allyn & Bacon, 1968.

————, "Teaching speech to an autistic child through operant conditioning," *American Journal of Orthopsychiatry*, 35 (1965), 927–936.

————, F. D. Taylor, and A. A. Artuso, "The Santa Monica Project: Evaluation of an engineered classroom design with emotionally disturbed children," *Exceptional Children*, 35 (1969), 523–529.

Hoover, T., "A rural program for emotionally handicapped students: Democracy in action," *Teaching Exceptional Children*, 10 (1978), 30–32.

Kalman, R., *Child Abuse: Perspectives on Diagnosis, Treatment and Prevention*, Dubuque: Kendall/Hunt, 1977.

Knoblock, P., ed., *Intervention Approaches in Educating Emotionally Disturbed Children*, Syracuse: Syracuse University Press, 1966.

Long, N. J., W. C. Morse, and R. G. Newman, *Conflict in the Classroom*, 2nd ed., Belmont, Calif.: Wadsworth, 1976.

Martin, H. P., ed., *The Abused Child: A Multidisciplinary Approach to Developmental Issues and Treatment*, Cambridge, Mass.: Ballinger, 1976.

Morse, W. C., "Competency in teaching socio-emotional impaired," *Behavioral Disorders*, 1 (1976), 83–88.

Noland, R. L., ed., *Counseling Parents of the Emotionally Disturbed Child*. Springfield, Ill.: Charles C Thomas, 1972.

Pappanikou, A. J., and J. L. Paul, eds., *Mainstreaming Emotionally Disturbed Children*, Syracuse: Syracuse University Press, 1977.

Penningroth, P. W., *A Study of Programs for Emotionally Disturbed Children in Selected European Countries, 1963*, Bethesda, Md.: U.S. Department of Health, Education, and Welfare, National Institute of Mental Health, n.d.

Phillips, B. N., "Problem behavior in the elementary school," *Child Development*, 39 (1968), 895–903.

Poznanski, E., and J. P. Zrull, "Childhood depression: Clinical characteristics of overtly depressed children," *Archives of General Psychiatry*, 23 (1970).

Rickard, H. C., C. S. Serum, and W. Wilson, "Developing problem-solving attitudes in emotionally disturbed children," *Adolescence*, 6 (1971), 451–456.

Risley, T. R., and M. M. Wolf, "Establishing functional speech in echolalic children," *Behavior Research and Therapy*, 5 (1967), 73–88.

Rothman, E., *The Angel Inside Went Sour*, New York: David McKay, 1971.

Saunders, B. T., "The effect of the emotionally disturbed child in the public school classroom," *Psychology in the Schools*, 8 (1971), 23–26.

Scheuer, A. L., "The relationship between personal attributes and effectiveness in teachers of the emotionally disturbed," *Exceptional Children*, 37 (1971), 725–731.

Schopler, E., "Parents of psychotic children as scapegoats," *Journal of Contemporary Psychotherapy*, 4, No. 1 (1972), 17–22.

Schultz, E. W., et al., "Special educaton for the emotionally disturbed," *Exceptional Children*, 38 (1971), 313–319.

Thomas, R. M., *Aiding the Maladjusted Pupil: A Guide for Teachers*, New York: David McKay, 1967.

Toolan, J. M., "Depression in children and adolescents," *American Journal of Orthopsychiatry*, 32 (1962), 404–414.

Vacc, N. A., "A study of emotionally disturbed children in regular and special classes," *Exceptional Children*, 35 (1968), 197–204.

———, "Long term effects of special class intervention for emotionally disturbed children," *Exceptional Children*, 39 (1972), 15–22.

Vogel, E. F., and N. W. Bell, "The emotionally disturbed child as the family scapegoat,'' in *A Modern Introduction to the Family*, N. W. Bell and E. F. Vogel, eds., Glencoe, Ill.: Free Press, 1960, 382–397.

Weinstein, L., "The Zoomer Class: Initial Results," *Exceptional Children*, 38 (1971), 56–65.

Young, L., *Wednesday's Children*, New York: McGraw-Hill, 1964.

Chapter 15

Amos, W. E., and C. F. Welford, eds., *Delinquency Prevention: Theory and Practice*, Englewood Cliffs, N.J.: Prentice-Hall, 1967.

Benson, F. A. M., ed., *Modifying Deviant Social Behavior in Various Classroom Settings*, Eugene, Ore.: University of Oregon Press, 1969.

Clements, C. B., and J. M. McKee, "Programmed instruction for institutionalized offenders: Contingency management and performance contracts," *Psychological Report*, 22 (1968), 957–964.

Cohen, A. K., *Delinquent Boys: The Culture of the Gang*, Glencoe, Ill.: Free Press, 1955.

Engelhardt, G. M., "Increasing the efficacy of special class placement for the socially maladjusted," *Journal of Special Education*, 4 (1970), 441–444.

Freedman, A. M., and E. A. Wilson, "Addiction and alcoholism," in *The Child: His Psychological and Cultural Development*, Vol. II, A. M. Freedman and H. I. Kaplan, eds., New York: Atheneum, 1972, 193–200.

Freedman, M. K., "Sociological aspects of juvenile delinquency," in *The Child: His Psychological and Cultural Development*, Vol. II, A. M. Freedman and H. I. Kaplan, eds., New York: Atheneum, 1972, 180–184.

Glavin, J. P., et al., "An experimental resource room for behavior problem children," *Exceptional Children*, 38 (1971), 131–137.

Hetherington, E. M., R. J. Stouvic, and E. H. Ridberg, "Patterns of family interaction and child-rearing attitudes related to three dimensions of juvenile delinquency," *Journal of Abnormal Psychology*, 78 (1971), 160–176.

Holyoak, W. H., "Playing out family conflicts in a female homosexual 'family' group (Chick-Vot) among institutional juveniles: A case presentation," *Adolescence*, 7 (1972), 153–168.

Klerman, L. V., and J. F. Jekel, *School-Age Mothers: Problems, Programs, and Policy*, Hamden, Conn.: Archon & Linnet, 1973.

Kulik, J. A., T. R. Sarbin, and K. B. Stein, "Dimensions and patterns of adolescent antisocial behavior," *Journal of Consulting and Clinical Psychology*, 32 (1968), 375–382.

———, "Language, socialization, and delinquency," *Developmental Psychology*, 4 (1971), 434–439.

McCord, W., and J. McCord, *Psychopathy and Delinquency*, New York: Grune & Stratton, 1956.

Margolin, J. B., M. Roman, and C. Harari, "Reading disability in the delinquent child," *American Journal of Orthopsychiatry*, 25 (1955), 25—35.

Morse, W. C., "The crisis teacher," *Today's Education*, 61, No. 6 (1972), 52—54.

Niklason, L. V., "Factors affecting status within a group of delinquent girls," *Adolescence*, 2 (1967), 503—528.

Novak, D. F., "A comparison of delinquent and non-delinquent vocational interests," *Exceptional Children*, 28 (1961), 63—66.

Osofsky, H. J., and J. D. Osofsky, "Adolescents as mothers: Results of a program for low-income pregnant teen-agers with some emphasis upon infants' development," *American Journal of Orthopsychiatry*, 40 (1970), 825—834.

Pauker, J., "Fathers of children conceived out of wedlock: Prepregnancy, high school, psychological test results," *Developmental Psychology*, 4 (1971), 215—218.

Phillips, E. L., "Achievement Place: Token reinforcement procedures in a home-style rehabilitation setting for 'pre-delinquent' boys," *Journal of Applied Behavior Analysis*, 1 (1968), 213—223.

Redl, F., and D. Wineman, *The Aggressive Child*, New York: Free Press, 1957.

————, *Children Who Hate*, New York: Free Press, 1951.

Reinert, H. R., *Children in Conflict*, St. Louis: C. V. Mosby, 1976.

Schwitzgebel, R., and D. A. Kolb, "Inducing behavior change in adolescent delinquents," in *New Directions in Special Education*, R. L. Jones, ed., Boston: Allyn & Bacon, 1970, 249—260.

Stubblefield, R. L., "Antisocial personality and dyssocial behavior," in *The Child: His Psychological and Cultural Development*, Vol. II, A. M. Freedman and H. I. Kaplan, eds., New York: Atheneum, 1972, 172—179.

Vachon, B., "Hey man, what did you learn in reform school? Well, uh, like how to disconnect a burglar alarm," *Saturday Review*, September 16, 1972, 69—76.

Work, H. W., "Sexual deviations," in *The Child: His Psychological and Cultural Development*, Vol. II, A. M. Freedman and H. I. Kaplan, eds., New York: Atheneum, 1972, 185—192.

Young, L. *Out of Wedlock*, New York: McGraw-Hill, 1954.

Chapter 16

Boland, S. K., "Managing your instructional material dollar," *Teaching Exceptional Children*, 6, No. 3 (1974), 134—139.

Calovini, G., *The Principal Looks at Classes for the Physically Handicapped*, Arlington, Va.: Council for Exceptional Children, 1969.

Campbell, R. F., L. L. Cunningham, and R. F. McPhee, *The Organization and Control of American Schools*, Columbus, O.: Charles E. Merrill, 1965.

Christoplos, F., "Keeping exceptional children in regular classes," *Exceptional Children*, 39 (1973), 569–572.

Colella, H. V., and H. Foster, "BOCES: A delivery system for special education," *Phi Delta Kappan*, 55 (1974), 544–545.

Doyle, E. P., "Surprisingly, I really had a great day!" *Teaching Exceptional Children*, 6, No. 3 (1974), 150–152.

Duffey, J. B., and M. L. Fedner, "Educational diagnosis with instructional use," *Exceptional Children*, 44 (1978), 246–251.

Erdman, R. L., K. E. Wyatt, and H. W. Heller, *The Administration of Programs for Educable Retarded Children in Small School Systems*, Arlington, Va.: Council for Exceptional Children, 1970.

Ethical Standards of Psychologists, Washington: American Psychological Association, 1972.

Jackson, S. E., and G. R. Taylor, *School Organization for the Mentally Retarded*, Springfield, Ill.: Charles C Thomas, 1973.

Love, H. D., *Educating Exceptional Children in Regular Classrooms*, Springfield, Ill.: Charles C Thomas, 1972.

Marro, T. D., and J. W. Kohl, "Normative study of the administrative position in special education," *Exceptional Children*, 39 (1972), 5–13.

Meisgeier, C. H., and J. D. King, eds., *The Process of Special Education Administration*, Scranton, Pa.: International Textbook, 1970.

Melcher, J. W., "Some questions from a school administrator," *Exceptional Children*, 38 (1972), 547–551.

Morse, W. C., *Classroom Disturbance: The Principal's Dilemma*, Arlington, Va.: Council for Exceptional Children, 1971.

National Advisory Committee on the Handicapped, "The Individualized Education Program: Key to an Appropriate Education for the Handicapped Child," *1977 Annual Report*, Washington: Bureau of Education for the Handicapped, Office of Education (HEW), 1977.

Newman, K. S., "Administration tasks in special education," *Exceptional Children*, 36 (1970), 521–524.

Oakland, T., *Psychological and Educational Assessment of Minority Children*, New York: Brunner/Mazel, 1977.

Principal's Guide to Mainstreaming, Waterford, Conn.: Croft-NEI Publications, 1975.

Reynolds, M. C., and M. D. Davis, *Exceptional Children in Regular Classrooms*, University of Minnesota: Department of Audiovisual Extension, 1971.

Roe, W. H., and T. H. Drake, *The Principalship*, New York: Macmillan, 1974. (See especially pp. 199–209.)

Rubin, R. A., P. Krus, and B. Balow, "Factors in special class placement," *Exceptional Children*, 39 (1973), 525–532.

Scholl, G. T., *The Principal Works with the Visually Impaired*, Washington: Council for Exceptional Children, 1968.

Schultz, J. J., "Integration of emotionally disturbed students: The role of the director of special education," *Exceptional Children*, 40 (1973), 39–41.

Syphers, F. F., *Gifted and Talented Children: Practical Programming for Teachers and Principals*, Arlington, Va.: Council for Exceptional Children, 1972.

Theimer, R. K., and O. J. Rupiper, "Special education litigation and school psychology," *Journal of School Psychology*, 13 (1975), 324–334.

Chapter 17

Cook, J. J., "Accountability in special education," *Focus on Exceptional Children*, 3 (1972), 1–14.

Goldberg, I. I., and L. Lippman, "Plato had a word for it," *Exceptional Children*, 40 (1974), 325–334.

Gregory, S., *The Deaf Child and His Family*, New York: Halsted Press, 1976.

Heisler, V., *A Handicapped Child in the Family*, New York: Grune & Stratton, 1972.

MacMillan, D. L., "Issues and trends in special educaton," *MR/Mental Retardation*, 11, No. 2 (1973), 3–8.

Milofsky, C. D., "Why special education isn't special," *Harvard Educational Review*, 44 (1974), 437–458.

Ross, S. L., H. De Young, and J. S. Cohen, "Confrontation: Special education placement and the law," *Exceptional Children* (1971), 5–12.

Soeffing, M. Y., "BEH officials identify and discuss significant federal programs for the handicapped," *Exceptional Children*, 40 (1974), 437–442.

Turnbull, A. P., and H. R. Turnbull, III, *Parents Speak Out: Views from the Other Side of the Two-Way Mirror*, Columbus, O.: Charles E. Merrill, 1978.

U.S. Commission on Civil Rights, *A Better Chance to Learn: Bilingual-Bicultural Education*, Washington: Clearinghouse Publication, 51, 1975.

Appendix A

Birdwhistell, R. L., "Communicating on Purpose," keynote conference address, March 1963. (Mimeo)

———, "Communication: Group structure and process," *Psychiatric Quarterly* (Spring 1965), 37–45.

Dickinson, M. "Music as a tool in psychotherapy for children," *Music Therapy* (1957), 97–104.

Freud, A., *The Ego and the Mechanisms of Defense*, London: Hogarth Press, 1954.

Freud, S., *The Ego and the Id*, Vol. 19, London: Hogarth Press, 1929, 13–66.

Fultz, A. F., "Music therapy," *Psychiatric Opinion*, 3, No. 2 (1966), 32–35.

Gondor, E. I., *Art and Play Therapy*, New York: Doubleday, 1954. (Doubleday Papers in Psychology)

H'Doubler, M., *Dance—A Creative Art Experience*, New York: F. S. Crofts, 1940.

Howells, W., *The Heathens—Primitive Man and His Religions*, New York: W. W. Norton, 1948.

Kalish, B., "Body movement therapy for autistic children," paper presented at American Orthopsychiatric Association Workshop, Chicago, March 1968.

Kaslow, F., "Dance and movement therapies: A study in theory and applicability," unpublished doctoral dissertation, Bryn Mawr College, May 1969.

———, "A therapeutic creative arts unit for children with learning disabilities," *Academic Therapy Quarterly*, 7, No. 3 (1972), 297–306.

Langer, S. K., *Philosophy in a New Key: A Study in the Symbolism of Reason, Rite, and Art*, New York: Pelican Books, 1942.

Lewin, K., *A Dynamic Theory of Personality*, New York: McGraw-Hill, 1935.

Moreno, J. L., "Psychodrama and Group Psychotherapy," paper presented at American Psychiatric Association meeting, Chicago, May 1946.

———, *Theatre of Spontaneity*, New York: Beacon House, 1946.

Naumburg, M., "The nature and purpose of dynamically oriented art therapy," *Psychiatric Opinion*, 3, No. 2 (1966), 5–19.

Ruesch, J., *Therapeutic Communication*, New York: W. W. Norton, 1961.

Sachs, C., *World History of Dance*. New York: W. W. Norton, 1937.

Schilder, P., *The Image and Appearance of the Human Body*, New York: International Universities Press, 1950.

Shatin, L., G. Longmore, and W. Kotter, "A psychological study of the music therapist in rehabilitation," *Journal of General Psychology* (1964), 193–205.

Williams, G. H., and M. W. Wood, *Developmental Art Therapy*, Baltimore: University Park Press, 1977.

Appendix A

The Use of Creative Arts Therapy in Special Education, by Florence W. Kaslow[1]

Throughout the history of civilization a duality appears in the conception of man epitomized in dichotomous phrases such as soul-body, mind-body, psyche-soma, ego-id, and conscious-unconscious. Man seems to be divided within himself. The ego-orientation of the personality is manifested by the particular person *through his use of his body*. Current therapeutic efforts using the creative arts are geared to revitalizing and expanding the diminished role of the body, the corporal person, in the total living experience.

Current art therapy modalities are directed at working with the whole man as a means to rebuilding him into an integrated totality; that is, a person whose mind and body function as two interlocking, interdependent, and vital parts of the human organism. The body is conceived of as a primary target of therapeutic intervention (Kaslow, 1972, pp. 297–306). Dance-movement, music, art, and drama are the therapeutic media which will be explored here.

Overview of Rationale, Goals, and Techniques

The use of creative arts in therapy is predicated on concepts derived from several theoretical systems; mainly, psychoanalytic theory, ego psychology, Gestalt and holistic theories, and communication theory. A brief explanation of the most pertinent underlying assumptions is essential to an understanding of the value of these approaches.

The therapist using artistic media tries to help his student break through his superego constraints to recontact his unconscious impulses and desires and allow them to return to consciousness through nonverbal or symbolic verbal expression. He also attempts to engage in ego-supportive activities by building the student's self-concept through enabling him to achieve success and satisfaction

---

[1]Associate Professor, Dept. of Mental Health Sciences, Hahnemann Medical College and Hospital, Philadelphia, Pa.

in what he is attempting and by providing him an opportunity to participate in meaningful group activity.

Freud asserts that "the ego is first and foremost a body ego" (Freud, 1929, pp. 9–66). Therefore, a person's self-concept evolves from his body image, from how he views and experiences himself as subject and object and how he uses his body in interpersonal relations. During the early stages of ego development it is essential that the aggressive instincts be diverted outward. If they are turned inward against the self, the development of the body ego proceeds in a pathological direction. The skin, which is the exterior surface of the physical apparatus or body, serves as the receptor of sensations and of touch contact, and as such provides clues to the direction of ego development.

During infancy, a postural model evolves which provides the child with a picture of his body parts and their relationship to each other. More important than others in orienting a person to external reality, these are the parts which bring the individual into tangible contact with the outer world—like the soles of the feet standing rooted to the ground or hands which can touch and hold objects. Thus in movement therapy, some exercises are geared to holding and passing objects, touching parts of oneself or the surroundings, and planting feet squarely on the ground to heighten one's sense of reality.

Contact with the external world, the non-self, is imperative for the formation of the postural model which is the foundation of the body image (Schilder, 1950) and one's self-concept. Schilder defines body image as the picture of his body that a person forms in his own mind. The perpetual alternation of body position means that the body image is everchanging; it is a dynamic schema. Particularly in movement and art therapies, the student experiences his body image and physical self as he moves in space, stretches and touches parts of his anatomy, does exhilarating exercises, or as he draws pictures which reflect how he views himself. Through these media he can improve his body appearance and body image and bring his subjective ideas into consonance with how he appears to others.

Often the student participating in a movement, drama, art, or music session will regress to an infantile level of functioning and communicate his inner turmoil through the use of symbolism in art—primitive sounds in music, childish gestures, angry expressive movements, or dramatic reenactment of traumatic events in his life. He can communicate through these nonverbal channels the thoughts and feelings that he is unable or unwilling to relate in words and thus shed light on the nature of his difficulties to himself and his teachers or therapists. The ventilation in and of itself may have a cathartic and freeing effect.

The premise that people need narcissistic gratification is taken from the analysts. Thus the student "achieves" when he creates something that truly and uniquely belongs to him and expresses his innermost longing or tortures. If, in addition, he produces a picture that tangibly displays the fruits of his labor, his pleasure is heightened. Or, if he participates in a dramatic presentation or a music group, he experiences the joys of contributing to a shared endeavor and to being the recipient of applause and recognition—intangibles that are rarely bestowed on children with learning disabilities, language handicaps, or mental retardation.

The constructs of the ego and its mechanisms of defense undergird these treatment modalities (A. Freud, 1954). For example, regressive behavior can be dealt with by the educator-therapist; thus the student can function in the creative arts session at a level on which he is comfortable until he is ready to spontaneously move to the next higher developmental level. From this he can derive a sense of being accepted for what he is and of being "successful" because there is no external standard to be met and no competition inherent in the activity. Ideas and feelings which have been denied or negated as too dangerous can be brought back into consciousness as the therapist works with the meaning of what is impulsively expressed in the creations. For instance, in a movement session children may rock as if in a cradle, may simulate a temper tantrum, or be encouraged to do a dance-drama sequence exhibiting defiant or hostile attitudes and gestures.

In the life space (Lewin, 1935) of the child afflicted with a learning disability or mental retardation or one who is socially and culturally different, his family, home environment, peer group, and the school figure prominently. By utilizing one or several of the creative art media with him therapeutically, something new and vitally different is introduced into his life space. The impact of such freeing experiences that permit maximum self-expression and ventilation of pent-up feelings in a form that is less frightening than talking can be tremendous.

Communication is a central ingredient in *all* psychological healing approaches. Emotional, social, and learning disorders are held to be visible only in the patient's expressive behavior; the nonverbal cues he emits are used diagnostically. Because it is the person-to-person element which is common to all psychotherapies, the special ingredient responsible for client improvement is *the personal contact the therapist establishes* with his students (Ruesch, 1961).

Interpersonal communication is characterized by an expressive action on the part of one or more persons, the conscious or unconscious perception of this expressive action by others, and the observation that the expressive action was perceived. In therapeutic communication the intention of the teacher-therapist is to foster change in the system and manner of communicating. The therapist guides the communication in such a way that the patient is exposed to situations and message exchanges that will lead to more gratifying social relations.

In nonverbal interaction a message is sent and received through body motion communication. For instance, feedback occurs when the therapist responds in movement, music, or an art form. Messages are transmitted, perceived, and evaluated without resorting to words. The movement therapist attempts to enable the patient to communicate fully and accurately through expressive body behavior. It is possible to use words to obscure or distort thoughts and feelings; it is hard for the body to act deceptively because much of its functioning takes place on an involuntary level of unpremeditated behavior. Body actions are less susceptible to censorship and conscious efforts to shade meanings. Nonverbal communications from student to therapist have a greater likelihood of honestly expressing subjective reality. If the therapist's artistic responses are not genuine, the student is apt to sense this more readily than he would verbal deceptions. Face-to-face communication is heightened when therapist and student not only look at each other but also move, paint, sing, or act together. In the doing, they may hold hands or touch in some other manner (Kaslow, 1969, pp. 126—127).

The teacher or therapist must recognize that he is continuously interacting and communicating when he is with others. The fact that someone says very little does not mean he is not sending messages; the body in social living is constantly conveying messages and data. Only when the clinician or teacher becomes aware of what he is reacting to and what his message about that reaction is can he carry out his full professional responsibility and "communicate on purpose" (Birdwhistell, 1963, p. 30).

Many persons with physical handicaps, learning disabilities, emotional disorders, and social maladjustments suffer from confusion about body image, body boundaries, and identity. The creative arts, particularly movement and art, can help a person clarify his body boundaries, his separateness from others, and improve his body image and sense of self-worth. Since the earliest communication in one's life span takes place on the primitive nonverbal level of body behavior, nonverbal approaches have therapeutic value in dealing with body ego and body image disturbances.

To summarize, the various creative arts are used therapeutically to: awaken and revitalize the body; afford opportunity for physical expression of feelings and impulses; foster nonverbal communication of repressed desires and affects and lead toward improved verbal communication; reestablish a sense of trust in oneself and others; aid in resocialization and group participation; and provide an outlet for discharge of tension and hostility. Different techniques should be utilized selectively according to such factors as the students' interests, age, attention span, preference for working alone or in a group, and space available. No one approach constitutes a panacea for all those needing therapeutic help.

Historical Perspective

Dance has been called the "mother of the arts" (Sachs, 1937, p. 3). The creator and the thing created, the artist and the work of art are one and the same. Since his beginning, man has vividly recreated the world he perceived in his dances and his dramatic presentations. Because the only instrument or equipment a person needs in order to dance or act is his own bodily self, he is always prepared and can break into rhythmic dance movements or spontaneous setting improvisation impulsively or at the behest of a group. Herein lies the secret of the exciting potential of these artistic channels of communication and expression.

Primitive man danced to mark all important events in his own and the tribe's life cycle. Dancing allowed joint participation and encouraged comradeship. It provided an acceptable avenue for man to express his fears, hopes, and attempts to control his universe by imitating those forces in nature that he thereby hoped to tame or conquer. Dance has traditionally had such therapeutic purposes (Howells, 1948, p. 137) as exorcising evil spirits and allowing release from the routine by transporting the dance to the realm of fantasy and creative play. Dance was also used for magic and religious purposes. The most favored formation has always been the circle, as it was believed that the *mana* or power of the fire or chief, in the center of the ring, flowed outward to those in the perimeter and was passed around by those holding hands.

Many early magical dances began as pantomime rituals and might have been the forerunners of today's dance dramas. Make-up and costumes were worn to lend excitement, dramatize the dance, and provide an avenue for expression of the belief in the world of "make believe." Primitive man thought that if he imitated the spirit or animal in a very exact fashion he could gain control over or better communicate with the feared object.

Originally, music was created to enhance dance. Dance and music both spring from the same internal sources, the impulse to move and to respond to the natural rhythm of the universe. Therefore, they have an essential unity and are part of the univeral heritage of mankind. The style of music and type of melody reflect the ethos of the tribe just as do the dances (Sachs, 1937, p. 188). Gradually it was realized that music offered a way of communicating and expressing in its own right, and it developed as a separate form although it is still often used in combination with dance and drama.

Dance as a therapeutic tool has had a long, illustrious history. The role of dance within each culture is contingent upon the prevailing concept of the value of the body. Dance has held an exalted position and been endowed with magical powers; it has been officially banned whenever the significance of the body has been devalued as it was during the Middle Ages. But throughout man's lifetime, dance has flourished in some form because, through his moving body, man can express joy and sorrow, hope and fear, love and hate, and can regenerate his physical and psychical being.

The therapeutic, magical, and religious significance of the arts gradually diminished, and the creative media were employed primarily for personal pleasure or entertainment. It is only in the past few decades that the arts have again sprung forward as therapeutic techniques.

Therapeutic Dance

In 1968, I developed a diagnostic and treatment classification system, based on extensive observation and research, to determine what types of movement approaches are suitable to different client or student groups. The system includes the following items: diagnostic group or problem, characteristic postures and movement patterns, goals of movement therapy, treatment procedures and techniques (Kaslow, 1969, pp. 394–399). To illustrate its descriptive and treatment usage with one group of children, let us consider the autistic child. He characteristically exhibits mismatched movements of upper and lower portions of the body; there is little change in the energy or shape of his movements; he moves in an impulsive and infantile manner; he has a narrow range of movements and directional paths; and his activity is hyperkinetic and not goal oriented. Knowledge of these movement patterns helps the therapist to diagnose autism.

These are a few of the goals and appropriate treatment techniques of movement therapy with the autistic child. (1) Reach the child on his primitive sensory motor level through sensory stimulation. This can be done by using music for auditory stimulation, by dancing barefoot or touching the child for tactile stimulation, and by using movements geared to heighten kinesthetic perception. (2) Form an emotional relationship by spending a great deal of time with the child and moving in the child's pattern, functioning as an unthreatening, undemanding person. (3) Help the child build a body image by moving in such a way as to become the child's body double, blending with him so he can borrow the therapist's movements and ego but disentangling self from the child's ego when this is warranted (Kalish, 1968). (4) Integrate isolated body parts by naming and touching parts of the child's and therapist's bodies and showing what they are connected to; doing locomotor activities that use the entire body and explore dimensions of outer space; and investigating the body and its moving parts.

Other Media as Therapy

Like dance, drama, music, and art are utilized as diagnostic and treatment tools. Each is employed mainly as an adjunct to individual or group therapy or the more typical classroom learning situation. In some instances, the creative art modalities are used as treatment techniques in their own right.

Little appears in the literature on art therapy prior to the 1940s. Psychoanalytic concepts of defense mechanisms, particularly those of repression, projection, identification, sublimation, and condensation, are inherent in art therapy (A. Freud, 1954). "The techniques of art therapy are based on the knowledge that every individual . . . has a latent capacity to project his inner conflicts into visual form" (Naumburg, 1966, p. 5). Since the unconscious speaks in images, the symbolic communication value of a person's art work can be enormous. The student may be encouraged to discover for himself the meaning of his production through free association and by becoming aware of the mood or circumstances that prevailed at the time of its creation. The child may begin to relate positively to the art therapist when he becomes aware that the therapist accepts whatever he expresses. Eventually the child may feel free to release forbidden impulses and thoughts and may be helped to recognize that his artistic productions mirror his inner life.

Expressive therapies lead to verbalization as art forms expand a person's power of expression in both verbal and nonverbal idioms. "Those who are originally blocked in speech often begin to verbalize in order to explain their art productions" (Naumburg, 1966, p. 5). Art therapy helps release deeply buried material and thus reduces overall treatment time. As a person's art expression "improves," he becomes increasingly aware that by endeavoring to understand the meaning of his symbolic works, he participates actively in his own growth process. This strengthens his ego and decreases his dependence on the therapist.

Children's artwork abounds in clues to their inner needs and perspective. In art the child can have great freedom to explore and express himself. The therapist can enter into the art work and, by overtly sharing an activity with the child, open possibilities for a child-adult relationship that differs from those the youngster has previously experienced.

The significance of various body features in drawings has been established. For instance, aggressive youngsters draw themselves with big, dangling arms and long fingers. Helpless, withdrawing children often do not draw hands, either because they have not experienced anyone's helping hand or because hands are "guilty things" (Gondor, 1954). Emphasis on a particular body part may point to anxiety about that part or its function. Psychotic tendencies are apparent in certain bizarre drawings. (Similar principles apply in relation to movement; the psychotic individual moves in a disconnected, bizarre manner because that is how he experiences his body.)

Artists gain control of their world by creating it anew as they see it or wish it to be. For children with learning disabilities, who so often need to feel they can be instrumental in shaping their own lives, expressive therapies offer an opportunity to establish such control.

Psychodrama, perhaps the oldest of modern therapeutic art forms, was evolved by J. L. Moreno in 1923. It is often used in conjunction with movement therapy, and the two approaches rest on some similar psychological principles. "Drama is a transliteration of a Greek word which means *action* or a thing done." Psychodrama is "the science which explores the 'truth' by dramatic methods" (Moreno, 1946). Drama therapy and role-playing techniques are offshoots of psychodrama which perhaps are better adapted for use with school-age children. Psychodrama is the "umbrella term" used in this discussion to denote the various dramatic approaches.

Psychodrama rediscovered and dealt with the idea of mental catharsis. Moreno believes the common principle producing catharsis is spontaneity. That which is most startling and spectacular to see and feel on the stage "appears to the participants . . . as a process familiar to them . . . as their own selves." The individual aids in his own diagnosis by acting out his core conflicts in the presentation. In the therapeutic theater of spontaneity, resolution of conflicts can occur through the reliving of important events with help in viewing them objectively and with coping with them more adequately coming from the therapist and "auxiliary egos" (Moreno, 1946).

As a modern rehabilitation technique, music therapy received great impetus following World War II. Like dance therapy, it is utilized with children of all ages in a variety of treatment settings (Shatin, Longmore, and Kotter, 1964, p. 193). Music, a social art, is easily shared in the company of others. When the player or singer is one of a group of people blending his sounds with the sounds made by others, he not only shares the music with a listener, he also contributes to the process of creating music. Music offers a channel for communicating at a time when verbal interchange is difficult for a person who feels emotionally isolated. An ancient doctrine, still rather universally held, is that *"music is an emotional catharsis, that its essence is self-expression."* Music's primary function is to work off subjective feelings and "restore personal balance" (Langer, 1942, pp. 173–175).

Music therapy has a direct relationship to dance therapy. Dickinson states that "without music therapy there would be no dance therapy, for whether we work with piano, records, . . . voices, or drums, it's music." In attempting to work with emotionally disturbed boys ranging from 7 to 15 years of age, Dickinson found that they did not respond favorably to the idea of dancing. However, she was able to capture their interest when she began playing a sharp staccato rhythm on Chinese drums. She promised that at the end of the dance session each boy could have a turn with the drums. By asking a boy who seemed to be an indigenous leader to be first for follow-the-leader, she was able to motivate all to join in the exercises and then to go beyond the game and learn some extensions, contractions, releases, and falls (Dickinson, 1957, p. 97 ff.). Her young patients also listened to mood pieces and then improvised movement to the music. Both percussive beat and mood setting records were used as stimuli to foster the desire to move. Half of the group moved while the other half accompanied on instruments; thus they partook of both experiences and outlets.

Six of the rehabilitation aims of music therapy are also aims of art therapy, psychodrama, and dance therapy. The following goals are representative of a broader compendium:

1. To aid in diagnosis and treatment planning
2. To establish and cultivate socialization
3. To promote self-confidence
4. To control hyperactivity
5. To foster the development of skills
6. To speed the transition from nonverbal to verbal codification systems (Fultz, 1966, pp. 34–35)

Summary

In each of the art media, the student is afforded an opportunity for creative expression of self and of his inner world of experience. Feelings can be ventilated without damage to significant others. The expressive channels share the characteristic of fostering deep and total involvement of the subject as the instrument of doing something. Because he must "do something," the child takes an active part in his own learning. The freedom and flexibility afforded by these media are inducements to releasing tensions; the use of structure and specific directions help the children experience and accept external reality.

The expressive media are usually viewed as adjunctive therapies. Nonverbal communication frequently serves as a stimulus to more meaningful verbal communication. The child may spontaneously speak to explain his art, dance, music, or dramatic creation because he has invested himself in it and cares that it is understood. The art modalities, which cut through to the inner man more rapidly than verbalization does, are particularly useful with hard to reach and inarticulate students. The process of creating forces one to explore his inner self in search of truth and conduces to the development of insight. A creation which is an honest expression of inner reality has a ring of authenticity.

It is important that a greater variety of modes for reaching uncommunicative and unresponsive children with learning disabilities, retardation, social or linguistic dysfunctioning, and emotional disorders be developed, adapted for, and incorporated into educational practice. It has been shown that the creative art therapies improve body-image and motor coordination, release tension, and reintegrate the body with the mind by fusing thought and feeling into an action form, and contribute to a more positive self-image and sense of self-worth (Kaslow, 1972). As such, they should add a new and exciting dimension to the ancillary tools available to the profession for enabling students to think of themselves as worthwhile human beings who are capable of and free to learn more effectively.

Appendix B

Visual Aids for Special Education

Education of Exceptional Children—General

Accidents of Development   Harper & Row   (slide-tape)

> Presents the genetic factors in congenital defects and hormonal factors in environmentally caused defects in children, as well as other relevant aspects of developmental abnormalities.

Cast No Shadow   Professional Arts, Inc.   27 min.
Box 8484
Universal City, Calif. 91608

> Presents the positive benefits of a planned recreation program for people of all ages in a variety of diagnostic categories. It is particularly useful for preservice programs to familiarize learners with types of handicaps and possible therapeutic activities.

Even Love Is Not Enough . . . Children with Handicaps   Parents' Magazine
Films with the Frank Porter Graham Child Development Center

> A series of four filmstrip/record/cassette sets, one each on behavioral and emotional disabilities, physical disabilities, intellectual disabilities, and educational and language disabilities. Appropriate for parents, preservice and in service teachers.

He Comes from Another Room   NIMH Film Collection   28 min. color

> The film focuses on the process of mainstreaming as two boys are integrated from a special class to regular classes. The roles of school staff and ancillary personnel are demonstrated.

The Madison School Plan   Santa Monica School District   21 min.
Dr. Frank E. Taylor, Dir. of Special Services
Santa Monica S.D., 1723 Foust St., Santa Monica, Calif. 90401

> Describes the exploratory program in the Santa Monica Unified School District in which the major goal is to prepare exceptional children to spend as much time as possible in regular classrooms. Although the film leaves several questions unan-

swered, it does demonstrate movement from the readiness-to-learn program of the Learning Center (resource room) to integration in regular classes.

Stress: Parents with a Handicapped Child   McGraw-Hill Films   30 min.

In this film, five families discuss the problems involved in raising handicapped children. Useful for both preservice and inservice teacher education to increase understanding of the total life of the exceptional child.

View from Another World   Kansas Center   11 min., color

Set in the future, this film raises fundamental questions about the care and treatment of the mentally retarded and developmentally disturbed. Attention is focused on a proposed "normalization" project.

Developmental Theory

Children Growing Up   BBC-TV   4 films, 26 min. each
Time-Life Films, 43 W. 16th St., New York, N.Y. 10011

This series for teachers presents the physical and emotional development of young children, with emphasis on the role of family relationships.

The Precious Years   ABC Media Concepts   25 min.

Focusing on the years from birth to age 6, the film visits the Erikson Institute for Early Education, which was founded on the teachings of Erikson and Piaget. The programs of other child-care centers are also shown, with special attention paid to the problems of the development of the black child's self-concept.

The Springs of Learning   BBC-TV   6 films, 30 min. each

This series emphasizes the child's needs during his early critical period of intellectual, emotional, and physical growth. Differences in rate of growth are demonstrated, and methods of dealing with these differences are suggested.

Gifted and Creative

Creativity: The Professional Approach   Michigan State U.   30 min.

A discussion of creativity and the conditions that affect it, such as inner qualities, social environment, and external atmosphere.

The Golden Key   Creative Education Foundation   25 min.
c/o State Univ. College at Buffalo, Buffalo, N.Y.

This is a 45-slide color presentation with accompanying script that highlights the principles and procedures of creative problem-solving.

Understanding the Gifted   Churchill Films   33 min.

Four common traits of the gifted are demonstrated by students: abstraction-generalization abilities, diverse and complex interests, the urge to create, and a well-defined sense of ethics and values.

Wishes, Lies, and Dreams   Association-Stirling   28 min.

Poet Kenneth Koch teaches poetry writing and appreciation to fourth and fifth graders. The free-wheeling and exciting method should stimulate faculty to think about new ways of teaching.

Mentally Retarded

Beyond the Shadows   U.S. Dept. of Health, Education and Welfare   26 min.

Mental retardation is a community problem and concern, a situation clearly demonstrated in this film prepared by the HEW Children's Bureau.

Color Her Sunshine   Indiana University   21 min.

This film tells the story of Mary, a Down's syndrome adult. Emphasis is on her functioning at home, in a sheltered workshop, and in recreational activities.

Danny and Nicky   McGraw-Hill   56 min.

The film compares the care and training of two Down's syndrome boys, one living at home and attending a special neighborhood school, and the other in a large institution for the retarded. Many aspects of training and staff methods are shown.

Educable Mentally Handicapped   NET (Indiana Univ.)   29 min.

This film shows the learning, social, and emotional characteristics of educable mentally retarded children. A sequence of unit teaching, particularly useful for prospective teachers, is included.

Give Them a Chance   Calif. Dept. of Mental Hygiene   12 min.

The film shows classroom activities for elementary age educable retarded children (mental age 3 to 9). Shown are reading, arithmetic, art, music, and other class activities.

Inductive Teaching for the Mentally Retarded   Univ. of Iowa   30 min.

Explores the relevance of a new approach to teaching mentally retarded children at different stages of development how to think.

Just for the Fun of It   AIMS   19 min.

AIMS Instructional Media Services, P.O. Box 1010, Hollywood, Calif. 90028

This is a demonstration film showing physical education activities for trainable mentally retarded pupils, including the developmental and functional rationale underlying these activities.

Mental Retardation: Parts I and II   Univ. of Wisconsin   60 min.

An excellent film dealing with trends in the training, education, and rehabilitation of mildly and moderately retarded children. Sheltered workshops, special education services and facilities, and adjustment services are seen.

Non-SLIP   Kansas Center   25 min., color

This film focuses on a language initiation program that attempts to teach communications skills to nonverbal mentally retarded persons.

One Child in a Hundred   BBC-TV   20 min.

This film discussion attends to many questions related to mental retardation: goals, teaching techniques, home care versus residential placement, and adjustments that the family must make.

Personal Adjustment Training in a Sheltered Workshop   Indiana Univ.   28 min.

The theories, practices, and techniques used by sheltered workshops in providing therapy for troubled and handicapped people.

To Solve a Human Puzzle   Nat'l. Assoc. for Retarded Children   18 min.

Parents talk about their own experiences with their retarded children.

Tuesday's Child   Nat'l. Assoc. for Retarded Children   14 min.

A semidocumentary film that serves as an introduction to the problem of mental retardation in daily life.

Learning Disabilities

A Walk in Another Pair of Shoes   18.5 min. (filmstrip or slide-tape)   CANHC Film Distributors, P.O. Box 604 Main Office, Los Angeles, Calif. 90053

The presentation is aimed primarily at students, but is also useful for parents, and is designed to reduce the teasing of learning disabled children. Understanding is increased by showing a pre-teener in a variety of settings and demonstrating areas of difficulty and strength.

The Puzzle Children   Public Broadcasting System   50 min.

A television special on children's learning problems, with emphasis on the variety of learning disabilities and the help available for learning disabled children.

Why Billy Can't Learn   Calif. Assoc. for Children with Learning Disabilities PSU-PCR   28 min.

This film presents the learning and subsequent emotional difficulties of the child with learning disabilities. The variety of disabilities is discussed, as well as some of the approaches to remediation that have been undertaken in the schools.

Orthopedically Handicapped

Nancy Goes to School   Univ. of Iowa   30 min.

The film shows an average day at the University of Iowa's School for Handicapped Children. Included are occupational, physical, play, and speech therapy sessions, as well as children learning motor and self-help skills.

The Promises of Play   Bradley Wright Films   22 min.
309 N. Duane Ave., San Gabriel, Calif. 91775

A physical education program for the orthopedically handicapped is the basis for achieving positive growth, according to this film. Activities designed under an

ESEA Title VI project to increase the child's involvement with his peers and others are shown in what has been called "a happy film."

Rainbow Clubhouse   N.Y. Philanthropic League   c. 30 min.
150 West 85th Street, New York, N.Y. 10024

This film, narrated by Garry Moore, shows the varied activities carried on in a recreation program at the Rainbow Clubhouse and at Camp Carola, a residential camp for orthopedically handicapped children.

Hearing Handicapped

Can You Hear Me?   International Film Bureau   26 min.
332 S. Michigan Ave., Chicago, Ill. 60604

Demonstrates the difficulties of teaching a deaf child to speak. Both mother and child are shown in a learning program at the John Tracy Clinic (Los Angeles).

Lisa! Pay Attention   Bono Film Service   21 min.
1042 Wisconsin Ave. N.W., Washington, D.C. 20007

This film focuses on the behavioral characteristics of the hearing deficient. Aimed at the classroom teacher, it suggests the need for a comprehensive hearing evaluation in cases that might be misinterpreted as emotionally disturbed, retarded, or slow learner.

Principles of Parent-Child Programs for the Pre-School Hearing Impaired   PSU-PCR   28 min.

Parent and child involvement in an intensive multidisciplinary training program for young hearing impaired children.

The Search: Diagnosis and Treatment of the Hearing Handicapped   McGraw-Hill
26 min.

One of a series of TV films which shows the diagnostic evaluation of a 2-year-old boy and the training sessions that followed.

Visually Impaired

Blindness . . . It's No Big Deal   Stevenfeldt Educational Films   16 min.
4080 23rd St. San Francisco, Calif. 94114

Blind students in public elementary and secondary schools demonstrate how well they can learn, move about, and interact with sighted peers. There is no formal narration as the students speak for themselves.

Eyes of a Child   BBC-TV   30 min.

The film reports on the techniques and methods used in teaching blind children academic subjects and a relatively normal daily life.

I Have an Egg   McGraw-Hill   14 min.

> The problems of teaching young blind children are introduced by showing how a class of young children learns what an egg is by touching it in its various forms—raw, hardboiled, and as a newborn chick.

School Day: A Study of a Visually Handicapped Child   New York University 24 min.

> Presents the supportive efforts by family, school, and community that enable a blind child to develop her innate abilities.

Multiply Handicapped

Children of the Silent Night   CAMPF   28 min.

> Demonstrates methods used at the Perkins School for the Blind to teach deaf-blind children.

The Legacy of Anne Sullivan   Campbell Films   30 min.
Academy Road, Saxtons River, Vt. 05154

> Documents Anne Sullivan's pioneering work with deaf-blind children and also shows today's efforts with deaf-blind children and adults.

Wheels   Kansas Center   13 min., color

> Illustrates a wheelchair modification program that enables multiply handicapped children to be mobile at the Kansas Neurological Institute. The custom design for each chair has prosthetic and therapeutic purposes for its young patient.

Oral Communications Disorders

Articulation Disorders   Harper & Row   22 min.

> Individuals of different ages demonstrate a variety of articulation disorders. (With instructor's guide; for college and graduate level)

Forty Sounds of English   i/t/a   40 min.

> Pitman's Initial Teaching Alphabet is introduced with its in-class uses, among which are teaching English as a second language.

Language Disorders   Harper & Row   22 min.

> Individuals of different ages exhibit various types of language disorders. (With instructor's guide; college and graduate)

Stuttering   Harper & Row   22 min.

> Characteristic stuttering behaviors are seen in individuals of different ages. (With instructor's guide; college and graduate level)

Voice and Resonance Disorders   Harper & Row   22 min.

The types and varieties of voice and resonance disorders are demonstrated by individuals of different ages. (With instructor's guide; college and graduate level)

Learning Disadvantaged

A Chance at the Beginning   Anti-Defamation League   29 min.

The use of preschool training and the development of methods for interrupting the poverty-poor learning-poverty cycle are demonstrated in this film of a program in New York's Harlem.

Children at Risk   Franklin Inst. Research Labs.   1972   30 min.
Center for Pre-school Services, FIRL, 20th and Cherry Sts., Philadelphia, Pa. 19103

The film shows a demonstration program in Philadelphia that seeks to identify young children with potential learning problems. Special classes are shown in which new methods are used to correct specific disabilities before the children reach school age.

Day Care Today   Polymorph Films   27 min.

Three different types of day care centers are shown: a community-oriented infant care center, a factory center for employees' children, and a university teacher training center. In different ways, each provides good child care and interesting learning environments.

Growth Failure and Maternal Deprivation   McGraw-Hill   28 min.

This film stresses the important role of maternal stimulation in promoting normal physical and mental growth in babies. Techniques for remedying the effects of maternal deprivation are suggested and shown.

Operation Head Start   Bailey Films (PCR)   16 min.

A well-done film about children in a Head Start program in California and their home and school experiences.

Culturally Different

Brothers and Teachers   New York University   13 min.

This film presents an experimental tutoring program for educationally disadvantaged boys, operated on Saturday mornings and utilizing a "buddy" system.

Children Without   Natl. Education Assoc.   28 min.

The problems of children in economically depressed and emotionally rejecting homes are exemplified by focusing on one child's home and school life. This film can be correlated effectively with Young's comments in *Wednesday's Children*.

How's School, Enrique?   AIMS   18 min.

The purpose of this film is to increase sensitivity to cultural differences. Its focal example is the contrast between the Mexican-American environment and the typical junior high school program.

Strangers in Their Own Land: The Blacks   ABC Media Concepts   12 min.

Demonstrating that being culturally different is far from being culturally deprived, this film is "an exuberant collage of the unprecedented burst of creativity taking place in urban black ghettos today."

Strangers in Their Own Land: The Puerto Ricans   ABC Media Concepts   14 min.

The film focuses on the Puerto Rican Family Institute, the main goal of which is to help families stay together despite the great differences between the living conditions of their native land and those they find in New York City.

To All the World's Children   ABC Media Concepts   12 min.

Looking at the world of Navajo children in Arizona, the film examines the problems created by poverty, lack of education, and extremely low self-esteem and questions the effects of these factors on the Indian children.

Emotionally Disturbed

Aggressive Child   McGraw-Hill Films   28 min.

The film shows an intelligent but disruptive 6-year-old boy whose behavior stimulates authorities to suggest the need for psychiatric help to his parents.

Battered Child   A-V Center, Indiana University   58 min.

This film, a documentary prepared at the University of Colorado, presents a discussion of the causes and effects of child abuse.

The Broken Bridge   BBC-TV   35 min.

A documentary film study of the methods of Irene Kassoria to restore communication between autistic children and the outside world. The film shows actual therapy sessions over a 6-month period.

Cry Help!   NBC   83 min.

Three mentally disturbed teenagers are the subjects of this film. It documents their participation in a variety of currently used activities designed to help them regain their emotional stability and ability to function in society.

Just Different from Other Children   Kansas Center   20 min., color

The film contains general information about autism and also focuses on one of the most successful autism treatment programs in the country.

The Neglected   International Film Bureau   30 min.

The film deals with neglected children, their families, and child neglect or abuse. Suggestions are made for effective intervention by child protective agencies.

Randy's Up—Randy's Down   Kansas Center   21½ min., color

> Shows Randy, an institutionalized self-abusive child, the attempts to control his behavior by contingent shock therapy, and the moods and attitudes of those who work with him.

Socially Maladjusted

This Child Is Rated X   NBC   52 min.

> An NBC special report on juvenile justice in America, centering on the children who face the courts, detention facilities, and training schools. Both the innocent child, whose only crime is being a child, and the guilty child, who has committed a crime, are shown to suffer the unhappy consequences of existing programs.

Film Distributors[1]

Addresses are given in the film list for several distributors. The major distributors of educational films, however, are International Film Bureau, McGraw-Hill Films, New York University (Audio-Visual Services, Washington Square, New York, N.Y., 10003), and the Psychological Cinema Register (Pennsylvania State University, University Park, Pa. 16802). An excellent source of information is the Educational Film Library Association (17 West 60th St., New York, N.Y. 10023). Also see the Kansas Center for Mental Retardation and Human Development (The University of Kansas, Kansas University Affiliated Facility, 223 Haworth, Lawrence, Kansas 66045).

The television networks (ABC, CBS, NBC, and PBS) also produce a number of fine documentaries about exceptional children, and can be contacted at their offices in New York. Time-Life Films, as noted in the film list, is distributor for films produced by the British Broadcasting Corporation.

---

[1]There are an increasing number of audio tapes available. There are many sources, but the Council for Exceptional Children has produced a number of tapes, and convention addresses frequently also are available (National Education Association, American Educational Research Association, Educational Testing Service, and so on).

Appendix C

Agencies and Resource Centers

Nongovernmental Agencies

Alexander Graham Bell Assoc. for the Deaf, 1537 35th St., N.W., Washington, D.C. 20007

American Assoc. for the Gifted, 15 Gramercy Park, New York, N.Y. 10003

American Assoc. of Instructors of the Blind, 711 Fourteenth St., NW, Washington, D.C. 20005

American Assoc. on Mental Deficiency, 5201 Connecticut Ave., NW, Washington, D.C. 20015

American Foundation for the Blind, 15 West 16th St., New York, N.Y. 10011

American Speech and Hearing Assoc., 9030 Old Georgetown Road, Bethesda, Md. 20014

Assoc. for Children with Learning Disabilities, 2200 Brownsville Road, Pittsburgh, Pa. 15210

Black Child Development Institute, 1028 Connecticut Ave., NW, Suite 514, Washington, D.C. 20036

Council for Exceptional Children, 1920 Association Drive, Reston, Va.

Joseph P. Kennedy, Jr. Foundation, 719 Thirteenth St., NW, Washington, D.C. 20009 (mental retardation)

National Assoc. for Mental Health, 10 Columbus Circle, New York, N.Y. 10019

National Assoc. for Retarded Citizens, 420 Lexington Avenue, New York, N.Y. 10017

National Assoc. of Social Workers, 1346 Connecticut Ave., NW, Washington, D.C. 20036

National Catholic Education Assoc., Special Education Dept., 1785 Massachusetts Ave., NW, Washington, D.C. 20036

National Education Assoc. 1200 16th St., N.W., Washington, D.C. 20036

National Society for Crippled Children and Adults, 2023 West Ogden Ave., Chicago, Ill. 60612

National Society for the Prevention of Blindness, 79 Madison Ave., New York, N.Y. 10016

United Cerebral Palsy Associations, Inc., 66 E. 34th St., New York, N.Y. 10016

Governmental Agencies

Department of Health, Education, and Welfare:

Advisory Committees
National Advisory Committee on Education of the Deaf, 330 Independence Ave., S.W., Washington, D.C. 20201

President's Committee on Mental Retardation, South Building, Room 5064, Washington, D.C. 20201

Secretary's Committee on Mental Retardation, 330 Independence Ave., S.W., Washington, D.C. 20201

Office of Education
Bureau of Education for the Handicapped, Regional Office Building—GSA, 7th and D Sts., S.W., Washington, D.C. 20202

Public Health Service
National Institute of Child Health and Human Development, 9000 Rockville Pike, Bethesda, Md. 20014

National Institute of Mental Health, 5454 Wisconsin Ave., Chevy Chase, Md. 20015

National Institute of Neurological Diseases and Blindness, 9000 Rockville Pike, Bethesda, Md. 20014

Social and Rehabilitation Services, Rehabilitation Services Administration, 330 Independence Ave., S.W., Washington, D.C. 20201

Children's Bureau, 330 Independence Ave., S.W., Washington D.C. 20201

Medical Services Administration, 330 Independence Ave., S.W., Washington, D.C. 20201

Department of Labor
President's Committee on Employment of the Handicapped, Constitution Ave. and 14th St., N.W., Washington, D.C. 20210

Library of Congress
Division for the Blind and Physically Handicapped, 1291 Taylor Street, N.W., Washington, D.C. 20011

Office of Economic Opportunity, 1200 19th St., N.W., Washington, D.C. 20036

Special Resource Centers

National Center on Educational Media and Materials for the Handicapped
Ohio State University, Columbus, Ohio 43210

Circulates descriptions of books, audio- and videotapes, films, filmstrips, and other materials for teachers, teacher training, and parents.

National Regional Resource Centers (ESEA, Title VI)

A planned network of cooperating Regional Resource Centers that provides diagnostic and prescriptive services for referred students, training and supervision of teachers and aides working in self-contained classrooms and resource centers, and a comprehensive reference service for special educators (publications, instructional materials, research searches). Several Regional Centers are already operating in various states.

Regional Education Laboratories

The Regional Educational Laboratories are partially supported by funds from the Office of Education, U.S. Department of Health, Education, and Welfare. They investigate educational problems indigenous to their regions, develop educational materials designed to meet these problems, and publish the results of their research.

Special Education Information Center

SEIC helps parents locate services for their handicapped children. The project is sponsored by the Bureau of Education for the Handicapped, Office of Education, HEW, under 1968 amendments to the Elementary and Secondary Education Act of 1965.

Exotech Systems, Inc.
1828 L Street, N.W.
Washington, D.C. 20036

Educational Resources Information Center (ERIC)

ERIC is a national information system designed and supported by the U.S. Office of Education to provide ready access to results of exemplary programs, research and development efforts, and related information that can be used to develop more effective educational programs. There is a network of clearinghouses, each of which is responsible for a particular educational field. Current significant information is monitored, acquired, evaluated, abstracted, indexed, and listed in ERIC reference publications. Each clearinghouse produces a number of publications for reference. These services are available to school administrators, teachers, researchers, information specialists, professional organizations, and graduate and undergraduate students. The ERIC clearinghouses most relevant to exceptional children are:

Director of ERIC Clearinghouse for Disadvantaged
Teachers College, Columbia University
New York, N.Y. 11027

Director of ERIC Clearinghouse on Early Childhood Education
University of Illinois
Urbana, Ill. 61801

Director of ERIC Clearinghouse on Exceptional Children
Council for Exceptional Children
Reston, Va. 22091

Director of ERIC Clearinghouse on Teaching of English
National Council of Teachers of English
Urbana, Ill. 61801

Council for Educational Development and Research, Inc.

The CEDAR information office publishes a variety of materials related to education, including the current programs, projects, and products of eleven educational laboratories and nine university-based research and development centers.

CEDAR Information Office
775 Lincoln Tower
1860 Lincoln Street
Denver, Col. 80203

Deaf-Blind Centers

The ten regional centers are required to provide comprehensive diagnostic and evaluation services, education adjustment and orientation programs using all relevant professional services, and consultation for parents, teachers, and others who play a direct role in the lives of deaf-blind children. The locations and service areas for the centers are:

Regional Center for Deaf-Blind Children
c/o Alabama Institute for Deaf and Blind
Box 268
Talladega, Ala. 35160
(Alabama, Tennessee, Georgia, Florida, Kentucky, Mississippi)

New England Regional Center for Deaf-Blind Children
c/o Perkins School for the Blind
175 N. Beacon Street
Watertown, Mass. 02172
(Massachusetts, Maine, New Hampshire, Vermont, Rhode
Island, Connecticut)

Regional Center for Deaf-Blind Children
430 State Office Building
Denver, Col. 80203
(Colorado, Utah, Kansas, Nebraska, New Mexico, Wyoming)

Regional Center for Deaf-Blind Children
c/o Michigan State School for the Blind
715 Willow St.
Lansing, Mich. 48906
(Michigan, Wisconsin, Illinois, Indiana, Ohio)

Regional Center for Deaf-Blind Children
c/o New Institute for the Education of the Blind
999 Pelham Parkway
The Bronx, N.Y. 10469
(New York, New Jersey, Pennsylvania, Delaware)

Regional Center for Deaf-Blind Children
c/o North Carolina Dept. of Public Instruction
Education Building
Raleigh, N.C. 27602
(North Carolina, South Carolina, Virginia, West Virginia,
Maryland, District of Columbia)

Regional Center for Deaf-Blind Children
1966 Inwood Road
Dallas, Texas 75235
(Texas, Arkansas, Louisiana, Oklahoma)

Regional Center for Deaf-Blind Children
c/o Washington State School for the Blind
P.O. Box 1865
Vancouver, Wash. 98663
(Washington, Oregon, Alaska, Idaho, Montana)

Regional Center for Deaf-Blind Children
c/o State Dept. of Education
721 Capitol Mall
Sacramento, Calif. 95814
(California, Nevada, Arizona, Hawaii)

Regional Center for Deaf-Blind Children
c/o Minnesota State Dept. of Public Welfare
Centennial Building
St. Paul, Minn. 55101
(Minnesota, Iowa, Missouri, North Dakota, South Dakota)

Appendix D

Individual Education Programs (Sample IEPs)

As noted several times in this book, PL 94-142, the Education for All Handicapped Children Act, requires that individual education programs, or IEPs, be developed for all handicapped children. In Pennsylvania, this is extended to include IEPs for gifted and talented children as well.

The sample IEPs that are reprinted in this appendix are for gifted children. "Anne Spears" is a fictitious third grader, and her IEP is a composite of those developed for several third-grade children. David Woodman is a real fifth grader whose parents and teacher have generously given permission to use his IEP for 1978−79. The names of the school district and the director of special education have been changed, however.

Note that in each of the short-term instructional activities, there is more than one evaluator. In some cases, it is the student and the teacher; in others, the peers of the gifted child and the teacher. Also, in both IEPS, the participants in the planning conference included the student as well as parent(s) and professionals.

The format of IEPs is the same for all exceptional children—present status, long-term and short-term instructional goals, evaluation of activities designed to meet these goals, and a commitment to review of the IEP a year in the future. The activities and goals vary, as can be seen in this appendix, for children within categories and between categories of exceptionality. This emphasis on the *individual* rather than the exceptionality has long been sought.

INDIVIDUALIZED EDUCATION PROGRAM (IEP)

SCHOOL DISTRICT OF RESIDENCE: UPPER ASHLEY

Student's
Name: Anne Spears

Birthdate: 4/26/69

Participants in IEP Development
& Writing:

Name	Title

Mrs. Jacqueline Warren—Director of
                Special Education
Mr. Michael Rothstein—TEC Teacher

Mr. and Mrs. Spears—Parents

Anne Spears—Student

Current Assignment: Round Meadow
                        Third Grade

Date Written: 3/10/78

Date of Annual Review: 3/10/79

Operating Agent: Upper Ashley Sch. Dist.

Person responsible for Implementation
 of Program: Jacqueline Warren

Date of IEP Planning Meeting: 3/3/78

PRIMARY ASSIGNMENT AND STATEMENT OF INTEGRATION	DATE OF INITIATION	EXPECTED DURATION OF SERVICES
Regular education	3/78	Ongoing
Gifted—Participation in the gifted		
program (TEC) with integration in		
regular education for all remaining		
areas of instruction.		

RELATED SERVICES:	DATE OF INITIATION	EXPECTED DURATION OF SERVICES
Physical education	3/78	Ongoing
Bus transportation	3/78	Ongoing

SPECIAL MEDIA OR MATERIALS:

Copies to:
 — Teacher (Original)
 — Parent
 — Operating Agent
 — District of Residence

203

STUDENT NAME ___Anne Spears___

DATE IEP WRITTEN ___3/3/78___

PRESENT EDUCATION LEVELS

Anne's intellectual functioning and classroom performance indicate that she is eligible for and could benefit from participation in The Enrichment Class (TEC) Program in the areas of Language Arts, Fine Arts, Science, and Social Science.

Information from Anne's parents also suggests that she would benefit from inclusion in such a program.

Anne's interests include reading, art, dramatics, and story telling.

INSTRUCTIONAL AREAS & ANNUAL GOALS	SHORT TERM OBJECTIVES & EVALUATION PROCEDURES (INCLUDE TERMINAL BEHAVIOR, CONDITIONS, AND CRITERIA)
General: Student will expand her ability to use library efficiently.	1. Student will be able to write a resource survey card when working on or designing a project, citing information from books, and/or periodicals to teacher and librarian satisfaction. 2. Given a specific reference, student will be able to locate materials via the card catalogue to teacher and librarian satisfaction.

INSTRUCTIONAL AREAS & ANNUAL GOALS	SHORT TERM OBJECTIVES & EVALUATION PROCEDURES (INCLUDE TERMINAL BEHAVIOR, CONDITIONS, AND CRITERIA)
Language Arts: Student will explore folktales from countries of cultural origin.	1. Student will experience no less than five (5) folktales from countries of ancestral origin. 2. Using techniques of interviews and library skills, student will research specific aspects of cultural background to satisfaction of self and teacher. 3. Student will research customs of areas of cultural background as they relate to folktales to satisfaction of self and teacher. 4. Student will trace customs of her cultural background from past to present to the satisfaction of self and teacher. 5. Student will rewrite a folktale of her choosing, updating it to present day cultural level for presentation to her class.

INSTRUCTIONAL AREAS & ANNUAL GOALS	SHORT TERM OBJECTIVES & EVALUATION PROCEDURES (INCLUDE TERMINAL BEHAVIOR, CONDITIONS, AND CRITERIA)
Fine Arts: Student will explore folk songs as expression of her cultural heritage.	1. Student will have experience with no less than ten (10) folk songs from countries of her ancestral origin and be able to relate each to its country to her and teacher satisfaction. 2. Student will be able to compare and contrast cultural aspects of American folk songs with those of her ancestral background to student and teacher satisfaction. 3. Using techniques of interview, active listening, and library research, student will be able to explain the part folk music of her ancestors played in the development of American folk music.

STUDENT NAME___Anne Spears_____

DATE IEP WRITTEN_____3/3/78_____

INSTRUCTIONAL AREAS & ANNUAL GOALS	SHORT TERM OBJECTIVES & EVALUATION PROCEDURES (INCLUDE TERMINAL BEHAVIOR, CONDITIONS, AND CRITERIA)
Science: Student will explore principles of weather as determinants of culture.	1. Student will be able to interpret specific bodies of weather data and extrapolate information relating to effects of culture to her and teacher satisfaction. 2. Student will be able to compare and contrast modern techniques of weather data collecting with past folklore pertaining to weather to her and teacher satisfaction. 3. Student will be able to translate modern weather data into original folklore type stories for presentation to her peers. 4. Student will collect weather data from two different geographic regions and be able to hypothesize as to comparative effects on cultures to her and teacher satisfaction. 5. Working with a peer group, student will research, design, and construct a functioning weather station to her and peer satisfaction. 6. Using small test experiences within her school, student will compare differences in behaviors during a variety of weather conditions, i.e., rainy day/sunny day and present her data to class as part of group project to her and peer satisfaction. 7. Working within a peer group, student will develop and carry out a project studying the effects of weather on school children and possibly adults to satisfaction of self, teacher, and peers.

STUDENT NAME   Anne Spears

DATE IEP WRITTEN   3/3/78

INSTRUCTIONAL AREAS & ANNUAL GOALS	SHORT TERM OBJECTIVES & EVALUATION PROCEDURES (INCLUDE TERMINAL BEHAVIOR, CONDITIONS, AND CRITERIA)
Social Science: Student will expand her appreciation of music of foreign cultures.	1. Student will have experience with no less than two (2) of each of the following: folk songs, children's songs, and classical compositions from no less than five (5) foreign cultures to satisfaction of self and teacher. 2. Student will explore musical instruments native to specific cultures and design a presentation to self and peer satisfaction. 3. With the help of peers, teacher and outside resource people, student will attempt to construct a folk type musical instrument to her and teacher satisfaction. 4. When presented with folk song, children's song or classical composition experienced in number one of this page, student will be able to identify title and country of national origin with 80% accuracy.

INDIVIDUALIZED EDUCATION PROGRAM (IEP)

SCHOOL DISTRICT OF RESIDENCE: UPPER ASHLEY

Student's
Name: David Woodman

Current Assignment: Woodlawn
                          Fifth Grade

Birthdate: 8/30/67

Date Written: 4/26/78

Participants in IEP Development
  & Writing:

Date of Annual Review   4/26/79

Operating Agent: Upper Ashley School
                  District

Name	Title
Jacqueline Warren—Director of Special Education	
Michael Rothstein—TEC Teacher	

Person responsible for Implementation
  of Program: Jacqueline Warren

Mrs. Lou Woodman—Mother

Date of IEP Planning Meeting: 3/10/78

David Woodman—Student

PRIMARY ASSIGNMENT AND STATEMENT OF INTEGRATION	DATE OF INITIATION	EXPECTED DURATION OF SERVICES
Regular Education	4/78	Ongoing
Gifted—Participation in the gifted program (TEC) with integration in regular education for all remaining areas of instruction.		

RELATED SERVICES:	DATE OF INITIATION	EXPECTED DURATION OF SERVICES
Physical education	4/78	Ongoing
Bus transportation	4/78	Ongoing

SPECIAL MEDIA OR MATERIALS: _____

Copies to:
  — Teacher (Original)
  — Parent
  — Operating Agent
  — District of Residence

STUDENT NAME _____David Woodman_____

DATE IEP WRITTEN ___4/26/78_____

PRESENT EDUCATION LEVELS

David's intellectual functioning and classroom performance
indicate that he is eligible and could benefit from participation in
The Enrichment Class (TEC) Program in the areas of Language Arts, Fine
Arts, Science, and Social Science.

Information from David's parents also suggests that he would benefit
from inclusion in such a program.

David's interests include reading, art, dramatics, and sports.

STUDENT NAME ___David Woodman___

DATE IEP WRITTEN ___4/26/78___

INSTRUCTIONAL AREAS & ANNUAL GOALS	SHORT TERM OBJECTIVES & EVALUATION PROCEDURES (INCLUDE TERMINAL BEHAVIOR, CONDITIONS, AND CRITERIA)
Language Arts: 1. Student will explore the field of debate as it relates to his areas of interest.	1. When given a specific topic, student will be able to find, interpret, and organize printed materials in order to present a debate, pro or con, to the satisfaction of peers and teacher. 2. Using information from his studies of science and/or social science, student will be able to build an argument to influence his classmates toward his viewpoint, to his and peer satisfaction.
2. Student will expand his abilities to use photography as a means of expressing his ideas.	1. Using a 35mm reflex camera, student will develop a photo essay as part of his ecology project (see Science) to his and peer satisfaction. 2. Using the movie camera, student will create film essay related to one or more of the areas of the TEC program to his and peer satisfaction.

STUDENT NAME ___David Woodman___

DATE IEP WRITTEN ___4/26/78___

INSTRUCTIONAL AREAS & ANNUAL GOALS	SHORT TERM OBJECTIVES & EVALUATION PROCEDURES (INCLUDE TERMINAL BEHAVIOR, CONDITIONS, AND CRITERIA)
Fine and Performing Arts: 1. David will extend his appreciation of the artist as a social commentator.	1. Using the facilities of the Philadelphia Museum of Art and slides belonging to the TEC program, David will look at the work of American and European artists who most closely reflect the events of their time to the satisfaction of his teacher. 2. Given a representative group of paintings, David will be able to differentiate Realism, Expressionism, and Abstraction to his and teacher satisfaction. 3. After reading representative works of William Shakespeare, David will explore the following question to his and teacher satisfaction: Why did this specific author's work survive centuries when the work of his contemporaries did not? 4. Working with Romeo and Juliet and West Side Story, David will compare and contrast the cultural conflicts to the satisfaction of his teacher.

INSTRUCTIONAL AREAS & ANNUAL GOALS	SHORT TERM OBJECTIVES & EVALUATION PROCEDURES (INCLUDE TERMINAL BEHAVIOR, CONDITIONS, AND CRITERIA)
Social Science: 1. David will expand his awareness of local political systems.	1. Using his ecology project (Science), David will study the impact of local government on his environment and design an effectiveness rating scale to his and teacher satisfaction. 2. David will design a questionnaire for a public opinion poll in order to assess community concern for the ecology problem he has selected. Evaluation to be made by peers and teacher. 3. David will compare and contrast political effectiveness of other communities in dealing with this problem with that of his own to his and teacher satisfaction.

STUDENT NAME   David Woodman

DATE IEP WRITTEN   4/26/78

INSTRUCTIONAL AREAS & ANNUAL GOALS	SHORT TERM OBJECTIVES & EVALUATION PROCEDURES (INCLUDE TERMINAL BEHAVIOR, CONDITIONS, AND CRITERIA)
Science: 1. David will extend his knowledge of solutions for environmental problems.	1. David will make a community survey of problems affecting local ecology with the aid of resource people from the Pennypack Watershed Association to his and teacher satisfaction. 2. David will be able to identify, define and research a specific local ecological problem, assessing possible solutions to his and teacher satisfaction. 3. David will formulate a theoretical model for his ecology project reflecting known principles and observations based on standard sources to the satisfaction of teacher. 4. David will use this model to evaluate the relationship between one or more hypotheses and observational evidence. Success will be measured by criteria on checklist designed by teacher and student. 5. David will use this theoretical model to deduce new hypotheses and to propose a plan for testing same. Performance will be assessed by student/teacher rating scale.
2. David will increase his knowledge of astronomy.	1. Working with a group of his peers, David will attempt to construct a telescope and be able to explain the principles of its functioning to his and peer group satisfaction. 2. Given a map of the heavens, David will be able to locate and identify each of the planets in our solar system to his and teacher satisfaction. 3. Using the telescope and/or the naked eye, David will be able to locate no less than six (6) constellations.

Appendix E   Literature and Exceptionality

The following short stories and books are a sample of biographical and fictional readings in which the exceptional individual is a leading character.

Personality Development

Hughes, Richard: *A High Wind in Jamaica*

Williams, William Carlos: "The Insane" (from *The Farmer's Daughter*)

Gifted and Creative

Curie, Eve: *Madame Curie*

McConnell, James: "Learning Theory" (from *Imagination*)

Mentally Retarded

Buck, Pearl S.: *The Child Who Never Grew*

Keyes, Daniel: "Flowers for Algernon"

Nichols, Peter: *Joe Egg*

Spencer, Elizabeth: *The Light in the Piazza*

Steinbeck, John: *Johnny Bear*

Orthopedically Handicapped

Berg, Margaret: *Wednesday's Child*

Killalea, Marie: *Karen*

O'Connor, F.: *Good Country People*

Sheed, Wilfred: *People Will Always Be Kind*

Hearing Impaired

Fields, Rachel: *And Now Tomorrow*

McCullers, Carson: *The Heart Is a Lonely Hunter*

Visually Handicapped

Chevigny, Hector: *My Eyes Have a Cold Nose*

Husing, Ted: *My Eyes Are in My Heart*

Multiply Handicapped

Monsarrat, Nicholas: *The Story of Ester Costello*

Peare, Catherine Owens: *The Helen Keller Story*

Speech and Language Impaired

Caldwell, Erskine: *Tobacco Road*

Huxley, Aldous: *Eyeless in Gaza*

Culturally Different

Gambino, Richard: *Vendetta*

Haley, Arthur: *Roots*

Hall, Edward T.: *The Silent Language*

Kingston, Maxine Hong: *The Woman Warrior*

Wheeler, Thomas C. (ed.): *The Immigrant Experience*

Emotionally Disturbed

Aiken, Conrad: *Silent Snow, Secret Snow*

Braithwaite, E. R.: *To Sir With Love*

Cather, Willa: "Paul's Case"

Craig, Eleanor: *P.S. Your Not Listening*

Daudet, Alphonese: "The Arlesian Girl" (from *Lettres de Mon Moulin*)

Greenberg, Joanne: *I Never Promised You a Rose Garden*

Stevenson, Robert Louis: "The Strange Case of Dr. Jekyll and Mr. Hyde"

Rubin, Theodore: *David and Lisa*

Appendix F   Glossary

Most of the terminology of special education is defined in context throughout the book. Included in this glossary are additional terms with which you should be familiar.

Acute condition   a condition which comes on suddenly (as from an injury, or pain from an illness or other ailment) and which is usually temporary or limited in duration.

Aphasia   a condition in which the ability to speak is lost or impaired.

Chronic condition   a condition which is persistent over an extended period of time (e.g., cerebral palsy, deafness) with little expectation of cure.

Cleft palate   a fissure or opening in the roof (palate) of the mouth that is present at birth (congenital).

Endogenous   genetic factors that affect development (e.g., a genetic mutation).

Exogenous   acquired or nongenetic factors that affect development (e.g., illness, injury, deprivation) either prenatally, perinatally, or postnatally.

Itinerant teacher   usually a specialist (e.g., speech, remedial reading, art) who is assigned to work with students in more than one school location.

Language bifurcation   refers to inadequate command of two or more languages (e.g., English and Chinese).

Mainstreaming   refers to placing exceptional children in regular classes (either part-time or full-time).

Muscular dystrophy   a progressively degenerative disease in which there is increasing weakness and atrophy of the skeletal muscles.

Osteomyelitis   a disease characterized by an inflammation of bone.

Perinatal   refers to events occurring at birth or very shortly thereafter.

Phenylketonuria (PKU)   an inherited error in metabolism in which there is a deficiency in phenylalanine hydroxylase (an amino acid).

Prenatal   refers to events occurring before birth (i.e., during pregnancy).

Resource rooms   central locations in schools that are equipped with special learning materials used to help exceptional children acquire or develop specific skills.

Retrolental fibroplasia (RLF)   a disease of the retina of the eye that results in blindness.

Sibling   brother or sister.

Spina bifida   a defective closure in the spinal column.

Index

Abilities, emphasis on, viii, 6, 9, 15, 65
Abstractions and the learning disabled, 32
Academic performance and skills, 116, 117
Accents, foreign or regional, 75
Acoustic puzzles, 55
Acoustically handicapped. *See* Hearing
    impaired
Adjustments, personal, 41, 50–51, 61–62
Administration of special education, 39,
    126–134
  recommendations for, 133–134
  See also Principal, building
Adolescence, 8, 11
Adolescents
  blind, 61–62
  emotionally disturbed, 112
  and English language instruction, 80
  retarded, 28, 30
Advanced-placement programs, 19
Affective instruction, 119
Aid to Dependent Children, 95
Alaskan children, 94
Amblyopia (lazy eye), 57
Ameliorative preschool program, 91–92
American Indians, 77, 84, 97, 98
American Printing House for the Blind, 60
Amplification equipment, 75
Anastasi, A., 77
Anoxia, 23
Apartment without walls, 26
Aphasia, 65, 67, 73
Appalachians, 77, 84, 97
Arithmetic, 26–27, 82
Art, 27, 35, 46, 55, 60, 67, 83, 102
  therapy, 105, 180, 184–185. *See also*
  Creative arts therapy
Arthritis, 41
Articulation disorders, 73–74
Asian-Americans, 97
Auditorially handicapped. *See* Hearing
    impaired
Auditory perception defects, 32
Auditory training, 35, 59
Audiologists, 129

Audiometric tests, 51
Audiovisual aids, 27, 54–55
Authoritarian teacher, 121
Authority figures, 80, 101, 138
Autism, 50–51, 139
  and arts therapy, 110–111, 184
  causes of, 107
  defined, 107
  infantile, 23
Autonomy, 8, 9

Battered children, 109
Behavior. *See* Home behavior; Limits on
    behavior
Behavior modification
  with the emotionally disturbed, 112–113
  with the language handicapped, 81–82
  with the learning disabled, 36
  with the retarded, 26
  with the socially maladjusted, 118–119,
    120, 121, 122
Bereiter-Engelmann approach, 92
Bilingual education, 78, 101, 140–141
Bilingual teachers, 103
Bilingualism, 77, 79, 80, 82–83
Blacks, 97, 98
Blind, the, v, 57, 66
  aids for, 40
  attitudes toward, 61, 62
  curriculum for, 59–60
  diabetic, 59
  emotional problems of, 58, 64
  infant, 59
  preschool activities for, 59
  self-esteem of, 64
  See also Deaf-blind
Blindness, definitions and causes of, 57, 58
BOCES, New York State, 139
Body image, 180, 181, 182, 184, 187
Body language, 52
Braille, 59, 60, 61, 63
Brain damage, 23, 31
  minimal, 31, 32, 33, 138
Brooklyn Botanical Garden, 60

Buddy system, 82
Budget preparation, special education, 126, 129
Bureau for Education and Training of the Handicapped, 39
Bureau of the Handicapped, 34, 72

Calovini, G., 132, 133
Camp programs, 52, 60−61
Canada, bilingualism in, 80
Cardiac conditions, 41
Caretakers, 9
    training of, 93
Catharsis through art, 180, 185−186
Caution, excessive, 57
Center for Multiple Handicapped Children, New York City, 68
Center for Preschool Services in Special Education, Franklin Institute, 91
Cerebral palsy, 41, 65, 66, 67, 73, 75
Cerebral disfunction, minimal, 31
Certification. *See* Special education teacher, preparation of
Charnofsky, S., 97, 98
Child development, 1, 8, 68, 84−85, 89, 90, 94
    programs, 90
Child Development Associate Consortium, 93
Child-rearing practices, 93
Children, rights of, 116, 118
Children's Hospital, Los Angeles, 108
Chinese, 77, 78
Civil Rights Act (1964), 131
Civil Rights Commission, 140
Class assignment. *See* Placement
Class size, 2−3
Classroom management, 131−132
Classroom teacher. *See* Teacher, classroom
Cleft palate, 73, 75
Clubfoot, 41
Clumsiness, 32
College for gifted, 18−19
Colorado, 138−139
Colorblindness, 67
Columbia Institution for the Deaf, 52
Communication
    for the hearing impaired, 50, 51, 52−55, 67, 73
    for the language handicapped, 71, 77, 79
    nonverbal, 181−182, 186, 187
    oral, difficulty with, 3, 34, 71, 72, 73
    in-school and out-of-school, 80
    theory, 179
    therapeutic, 181−182, 184−185
Community
    integrated preschool program, 92
    resource agencies, 95
    study of, 101
    workers, 122

Compensatory education, 88−89, 90, 91−93, 94
Competence
    capacity, 92, 93
    sense of 7, 8, 9, 10, 11, 58, 82, 98, 101, 110
Computational skills, 50
Condensation, 184
Conference of Executives of American Schools for the Deaf, 49
Conflict, developmental, 8. *See also* Child development
Conflict resolution, 185−186
Congenital conditions, 41, 65
Congress, 52, 66
Conroy, P., 93−94
Contracts, study, 36, 112, 122
Coopersmith, Stanley, 7, 8
Cordova, F. A., 77
Correctional institutions, 117−118
Correspondence courses, 122
Council for Exceptional Children, viii
Counseling, 112−120
Counselors, school, 129, 130, 132
Creative, the, 7, 13, 15−16, 17−18, 20−21
    identification of, 15−16
    parental attitudes toward placement of, 138
    teaching, 22
Creative arts therapy, 179−187
    goals of, 186
Creative Problem-Solving Institute, 21
Creativity, 20−21
    tests, 16
Creoles, 77
Crisis room, 119
Crisis teacher, 119, 121
Cubans, 77, 97
Cued speech, 53
Cuisenaire rods, 35
Culturally different, the, vi, 87, 97−103
    educational needs of, 97, 98−99, 99−100
    language handicaps of, 77, 79
    parents, 138
    peer evaluation, 16
    self-esteem of, 7, 87
Curriculum
    cultural pluralism in, 101−102
    design, 126, 129−130
    traditional, 97, 100, 118−119
Curvature of the spine, 41
Cutaneous cues, 52

Dance, 182−183
    therapy, 183−184, 186
Day care, 94−95
    workers, 93
Deaf, the, 3, 49
    and color blindness, 67
    schools for, v, 51, 52

Deaf, the (cont.)
  teaching, 56
  translators for, 40
  See also Hearing impaired
Deaf-blind, the, 3, 65, 66, 67, 68, 130
Deafness, definition, of, 49
Debating team and stuttering, 74
Decibel impacts, 50
Defense mechanisms and art therapy, 181, 184
Delinquency, 115, 116, 123
Desensitization, 111
Developmental norms, 13, 138. *See also*
    Child development
Diana v. California State Board of Education
    (1970), 131
Dickinson, M., 186
Direct verbal preschool program, 91–92
District of Columbia, teacher requirements in,
    5
Double vision, 57
Drake, T. H., 132
Drama therapy, 180, 184, 185–186
Drop-out rate, 102–103
Drug addicts, 116, 122
Drugs
  for emotionally disturbed, 111
  prenatal effects of, 23, 65
Due process for gifted, 139
Durrell Analysis of Reading Difficulties, 36
Dyslexia, 31

Easter Seal Society, 39
Economic disadvantage, 97, 130
Educable mentally retarded, 23, 24–25, 26,
    27, 28, 66
Education. *See* Public education for excep-
    tional children; Special education
Education Amendments (1974), Special
    Projects Act, 18
Education for All Handicapped Children Act
    (1975), vii, 3–4, 5, 25, 36, 40, 131,
    133, 139–140, 202
Ego development, 180
Ego psychology, 179
Einstein, A., 18
Electronic devices for the blind, 59, 60, 61
Elementary and Secondary Education Act, 18
Emergency exits, 46
Emergency School Aid Act (1973), 20, 78
Emory University parent-child development
    program, 89
Emotional disturbance
  diagnosis and causes of, 106
  prevention of, 91
Emotionally troubled, the, 106–114, 139
  arts therapy for, 186, 187
  behavior and personality of, 8, 9–10, 11,
    105, 106–108
  contracts with, 112

Emotionally disturbed, the (cont.)
  curriculum presentation for, 110–111
  population of, 3
  problem reduction and prevention, 109, 112
  special classes for, 110, 112
  teacher preparation for, 113, 123
Endogenous causes of retardation, 23
Energy level, low, 41
English as a second language, 84
English, standard
  learning, 81–82, 82–84
  teaching, 80–82
English instruction, 79, 140–141. *See also*
    Non-English-speaking children
Enrichment programs, 18, 19, 84
Environment, least restrictive, 3, 36, 126, 131
Environmental privation, 59
Environmental stimulation. *See* Stimulation,
    environmental
Erikson, Erik, 7, 8, 9–11, 94, 107
Eskimos, 97
European immigrants, 97
Exceptional children
  emotional adjustment of, 11
  family of, 135–137
  population of, 1, 2, 3
    ages of, 3
Exogenous causes of retardation, 23
Experience chart, 83, 101
Experiential disadvantage, 88–90, 91
Expulsion, 118
Extortion, 119, 120
Eye, hygiene of, 64
Eye-hand coordination, 10, 32, 35, 52
Eye irritation, chronic, 57

Family of exceptional child, 135–137
  rejection of, 78–79
  and special placement, 130, 139
Family rights, 109
Federal Detention Center, Washington, D.C.,
    122
Federal funds, 40, 91
  for the deaf and hearing impaired, 51, 52
  for the learning disabled, 34, 35
  for teacher preparation, 4–5
Federal legislation. *See* Legislation, federal
Field trips, 55, 60, 91, 101–102, 119
Films, 54, 75, 102
Finger-spelling, 52
Fire drills, 46, 63
Flash cards, 83
Flexibility
  in classes, 21–22
  in programming, 18
Florida, teacher of gifted requirements in, 17
Fluency problems, 72
Foster grandparent programs, 93

Franklin Institute, Philadelphia, 20
    Center for Preschool Services, 91
    Research Laboratories, 43, 45
French-Canadians, 77, 97
Freud, S., 180
Frustration
    constructive handling of, 111
    low tolerance of, 32

Gallaudet College, Washington, D.C., 51, 52
Gangs, 115
    leader of, 115–116
Gates-McKillop Reading Diagnostic Test, 36
Genetic intellectual differences, 88. *See also*
    Heredity and intelligence
Geographic isolation, 88, 93–94, 97
George Peabody College for Teachers and
    working with the deaf-blind, 68
Gestalt theory, 179
Gestures, 52
Get Set program, 78, 91
Gifted, the, 4, 13, 15–22, 139
    identification of, 15–16, 102
    IEPs for, 202–215
    placement of, 20, 130, 138
    problems of, 9, 11, 21
    public education for, 15, 139
    teacher preparation for, 17, 22
Glasser, W., 112
Golden Gate Park arboretum, San Francisco, 60
Grandparents, 135, 137
Griggs et al. v. Duke Power Company (1971), 131
Grooming, personal, 62
Group therapy for socially maladjusted, 118
    techniques, 121, 123
Guilford, J. P., 16

Half-way houses, juvenile, 118
Ham and citizens' band radios, 47
Hard of hearing, 3, 49
Harvard Pre-School Project, 90
Head Start program, 88, 91
Hearing aids
    group, 54
    vest, 54–55
Hearing impaired, the, 49–56
    and communication skills, 49, 52–56, 67
    diagnosis of, 51
    educational categories of, 49
    emotional well-being of, 52
    self-concept of, 8
    See also Deaf; Hard of hearing
Hearing loss
    causes of, 49
    and speech, 72, 73, 75

Hearing specialists, 34. *See also* Audiologists
Hearing tests, postnatal, 51
Heber, Rick, 89–90
Heredity and intelligence, 89–90
High school
    art or music, 20
    in correctional facility, 122
    magnet, 20
    technical, 20
Higher education, 51
    early entrance by gifted, 19
    minority students in, 98
    teacher preparation, 4–5
Higher Horizons Program, New York City
    schools, 102
Home behavior, 119, 138
Home economics, 83–84, 110
    teacher, 113
Homebound instruction, 25, 47, 140
Homeroom assignment, 19, 28
Homogeneous grouping, 19–20
Hospitalization, 41, 47
Hostility, 106
Hygiene, personal, 27
Hyperactivity, 31, 32, 186
Hyperdistractibility, 32
Hypersensitivity, 32

Identification, 184
Identity crisis, 8, 11
Idioglossia (twin speech), 79
Illinois, University of, preschool project, 91–92
Impulsiveness, 32
Inattention, abnormal, 57
Individualized education program (IEP), 37, 129
    development of, 5, 129–130, 131
    defined, 4
    format of, 202
    samples of, 202–215
Industrial arts, 46, 83–84, 110
Industry vs. inferiority, 8, 10
Infancy
    importance of routine in, 9
    development of self-concept in, 8
    educational programs in, 89–90
Infant day care, 90
Infantile autism. *See* Autism, infantile
Infections, 57
Initiative vs. guilt, 8, 9
Inservice training, 4, 113, 129
Institutionalized children, 88, 93
Instructional materials, 64
    selection, 128, 129, 132
Instructional techniques, 35–36, 52–55, 74–75, 80, 81–84, 131–132

Integration into regular classes, 3—4, 36—37, 39, 43, 51, 55, 63, 66, 75, 82—84, 111. *See also* Mainstreaming
Intelligence, distribution of in population, 13—14
Intelligence quotient (IQ), 13—14
 of the blind, 58
 of gifted, 15
 of the hearing impaired, 50
 and learning disability, 32
 of mentally retarded, 23
 of retarded mothers and their children, 89—90
 and socioeconomic class, 99
Intelligence tests, 13, 15—16, 50. *See also* Minority children, testing of;
Intervention, 89, 90, 109, 117
 projects, 94—95
 See also Preschool intervention
Isolation, social, 97. *See also* Geographic isolation
Israel and education of children, 90
Itinerant special education teachers, 39, 63, 126, 132. *See also* Special education teachers

Jacobsen, L., 100
Jensen, A. R., 88
John Tracy Clinic, 51
Johns Hopkins University clinic, 51
Johns Hopkins University study of gifted, 19
Juvenile institutions, 121—123

Kansas, teacher of gifted, requirements in, 17
Kansas, University of, infant day-care center, 90
Kaslow, Florence W., vii, 179—187
Keller, Helen, 65
Kendall Demonstration School, 52
Kennedy, President John F., 24
Key Math Diagnostic Arithmetic Test, 36
Kindergarten children, group screening of, 32
Kinesthetic cues, 52
Kobrick, J. W., 97
Korean adoptions, 140
Krannert Art Museum, University of Illinois, 60

Language, 100, 103, 140
 bifurcation, 77, 78
 development, 35, 58, 91
 foreign, 75
 instruction, 78, 101, 140—141
 native, 80, 101, 140—141
 See also English

Language handicapped, the, 71, 77—85
 curriculum for, 80—84
 defined, 77
 families of, 79
 psychological conflicts for, 79, 80
 self-esteem of, 77, 82, 83
 See also Non-English-speaking children
Language Master, 54, 74, 75
Larry P. v. Riles (1972), 131
Lau v. Nichols (1974), 101, 140
Law. *See* Street law
Law and the socially maladjusted, 105, 116, 121
Learning
 ability, enhancing, 91
 active, through arts, 187
 cubicles, 36
 environment, group, 93
 frustrations in, 118
 and ineffective communication, 71
Learning disabled, the, 13, 31—37
 and art therapy, 185, 187
 class placement of, 34—35, 36, 66, 130
 curriculum for, 35—36
 emotional problems of, 32, 34
 identification of, 31—32, 36
 perceptual and expressive problems of, 10, 11, 32, 36
 population, 3, 31, 34
 regional centers for, 34
 teacher certification, 37
Learning disadvantaged, the, 34, 88—95
Least restrictive environment. *See* Environment, least restrictive
Legg-Perthes disease, 41
Legislation, 71, 139
 federal, 3—5, 24, 39, 40, 54
 See also State
Library privileges, 47, 111
Library skills, 18
Lighthouse for the Blind, 39
Limbs, shortened, 41
Limits on behavior, 119, 121
Limps, 41
Lip reading, 52, 53, 54
Louisiana, teacher of gifted requirements in, 17
Lovaas, I., 107
Luxembourg, hearing tests in, 51
Lyon, Harold, 22

Madison Plan, 28, 110
Mainstreaming, vi, 3—5, 5, 28, 50, 66. *See also* Integration into regular classes
 mandating, 4
Mandating special education, vi, 140—141
March of Dimes, 39

Massachusetts, mandating of language instruction in, 78
Mathematics, 5, 110, 118
Mathematically and Scientifically Precocious
Youth, Study of, 19
Maturation and learning disability, 34
McCandless, Boyd, 89
McDonald Comprehensive Elementary School,
4, 43
Michigan State University and preparation for
teachers of deaf-blind, 68
Mental health
personnel, 110, 121
referral, 118
Mental retardation
causes of, 23
and cerebral palsy, 65
and environmental deprivation, 59
and learning disability, 34
mild, 66
prevention of, 24
signs of, 51
and speech development, 72
Mentally retarded, the, 10, 23–30, 139
in adolescence, 11, 28, 30
arts therapy with, 187
classifying, 10, 13, 130
curriculum for, 26–27
defined, 13, 23
number of, 3
preschool for, 25, 66
programs for, v, 24, 139
public education for, 25–26, 66, 139
teaching, 26, 30
See also Educable mentally retarded;
Profoundly retarded; Trainable mentally
retarded
Mexican-Americans, 77, 97
Migrant workers, children of, 97, 101, 102
Military personnel, injuries of, 39, 41
Minority group children
motivation of, 101–102
options for, 98–99
self-esteem of, 98, 101–102
successful models for, 102
testing of, 130–131
Mirrors, 75
Mobility training, 64
Montessori program, 92
Moreno, J. L., 185–186
Mothers
child development classes for, 89, 94–95
enjoyment of children, 90
improving practices and attitudes of, 94–95
retarded, 89–90
See also Unwed mothers
Motor coordination, 32, 35, 49, 75, 187
Motor development, delayed, 58
Movement therapy, 180, 181–182, 183–184

Multiple sclerosis, 41
Multiply handicapped, the, 65–68
blind, 66
curriculum for, 67–68
number of, 3, 65
psychological disturbance in, 65
technology benefiting, 67
Muscular atrophy, 41
Muscular dystrophy, 41
Museum of Natural History, New York, 20
Music, 27, 35, 55, 67, 75, 83, 102
origins of, 183
therapy, 110–111, 180, 184, 186

Narcissistic gratification, 180–181
National Advisory Committee on Handicapped
Children, 39
National Association for Retarded Citizens, 30
National Center for Law and the Deaf, 52
National Program on Early Childhood
Education, 90
National/State Leadership Training Institute for
the Gifted and Talented, 22
National Technical Institute for the Deaf,
Rochester Institute of Technology, 51
National Theater of the Deaf, 54
Negativism, 32, 106
Neighbors of the exceptional child, 135, 137
Neurological defects and testing, 31
New Hampshire, child abuse reporting in, 109
New York, "600" schools in, 120. See also
BOCES; Higher Horizons Program
New York Hospital Medical Center and the
handicapped, 68
Non-English-speaking children, 71, 99–100,
101, 140
Nordoff, P., 110–111
Normality as a goal, 108–109
North Carolina programs for the gifted, 17
Northern Arizona University language-
handicapped program, 84
Northwest Regional Educational Laboratory,
94
Number concepts for learning disabled, 35
Nutrition and retardation, 23

Occupational
counseling, 30, 122
goals, 42, 51–52, 58–59, 73, 80
therapists, 105
training, 59
See also Vocational rehabilitation, state
Open classroom, 112
Optacon, 59
Opthalmologists, 33–34, 129
Optometrists, 33–34
Orthogenic disciplinary schools, 120
Orthopedically handicapped, the, 10, 41–48
group participation of, 46

Orthopedically handicapped, the (cont.)
number of, 41
opportunities of, 42
in preschool, 42
in public schools, 4, 42–43, 46–47, 66
self-concept of, 8
teaching, 47–48
transportation for, 42
Orthopedists, 129
Osteomyelitis, 41
Overprotection of the blind, 58, 59
Overhead projector, 55

Page-turner, automatic, 46
Paralysis, 41
Paraprofessionals, training of, 30, 68
Parent-child development program, 89
Parent-child relationship, 51, 59
Parent effectiveness, 94, 106
training programs, 90
Parent groups, v, 138–139
Parental abuse, 106, 107, 109
Parental neglect, 8, 108
Parents
active cooperation of, 41, 51, 64, 73, 85,
107, 111–112, 136
administrator contacts with, 128, 131, 132,
133
and child's self-concept, 6, 8
counseling of, 17, 59, 66
and homogeneous grouping, 19
and IEPs, 5, 129
reaction of to exceptionality, 135–136, 137
of regular students, 133
and special placement, 135, 137–138, 140
and standard English, 78–79
teacher perception of, 137, 138
See also Mothers
Parole officer, 122
Parnes, S. J., 16
Partially sighted, the, 63–64, 66
Peabody Language Development Kit, 75
Peabody Picture Vocabulary Kit, 84
Peer evaluation, 16
Peer-group pressure, 115, 116, 117
Pennsylvania
and gifted programs, 17
IEP requirement, 202
physical planning for exceptional children,
4, 26, 43
right to education for mentally retarded, 139
teacher requirements in, 5
See also Philadelphia
Pennsylvania Association for Retarded
Children, 25, 138
Pennsylvania State University clinic and
parents of hearing impaired, 51
Perceptual disabilities, 32, 139

Perceptual-motor disturbances, 31
Perinatal damage, 23, 39
Perkins School for the Blind, 68
Perseveration, 32, 138
Personality development, 1, 7–11, 17, 94
Personality and inability to communicate, 72
Phenylketonuria (PKU), 24
Philadelphia
orthogenic disciplinary schools, 120
retarded programs, 28
use of home economics and physical
education teachers, 113–114
Phonic Ear apparatus, 54
Phonics inventories, 36
Phonograph equipment, 59, 75
Physical education, 27, 35, 36, 46, 55,
60–61, 83, 102
teachers, 113
Physical facilities, 3, 4, 25–26, 63–64
modifications in, 40, 42–43, 46, 53, 54, 66
Physical therapy, 39
Physically handicapped, the, 3, 39–68, 139
frustration of, 9, 10
modifying environment of, 39. See also
Physical facilities
state vocational rehabilitation for, 39
teacher adjustments to, 48
Piaget, Jean, 8–9
PL 94-142. See Education for All Handicapped
Children Act
Placement
class, 47, 120–121
decisions, 112, 130–131
grade, retarded, 116
regular class, 117, 118–119, 126, 130
school, 110
special class, 130–131, 135, 137–138
parents understanding of, 133, 135,
137–138, 140
See also Student selection
Poliomyelitis, 41, 42
Postnatal injury, 23, 39, 65
Postnatal meningitis, 49
Posture defects, 41
Poverty, teacher perception of, 100
Power
capacity for, 92
feeling of, 7, 11, 116, 117
Powerlessness of cultural minority families,
97, 98
Prematurity, 49
Prenatal damage, 23, 39
Preparation-for-motherhood classes, 120, 121
Preschool intervention programs, 91–92
Preschool learning experiences, 91, 93
President's Panel on Mental Retardation, 24
Preventive programs, 89, 90, 94. See also
Intervention
Primary years, 9

Principal, building, 132
    functions vis-à-vis special education
        program, 126, 129, 130, 132–133
    interaction with parents, 131, 137
    personnel responsibilities, 128, 129,
        132–133
Private special schools, 35, 139–140
Probation officers, 105, 121
Problem solving, 52
Profoundly retarded, 24
Programmed materials, 122
Progress in special education, 97, 135, 137
Projection, 184
Psychiatrists, 105, 129, 130
Psychoanalytic theory, 179, 184
Psychodrama, 185–186
Psychologists, 105, 118, 121, 122, 129,
    130–131, 132
Psychotherapy, 34, 35, 73, 74, 111, 118, 122
Public education for exceptional children,
    v–vi, 3–4, 90, 138–139
Public facilities and the handicapped, 42, 43,
    44
Public welfare programs, 3
Puerto Ricans, 77, 97
Puppets, 75

Racial integration, 99
Readers, 26, 94, 101
Reading, 34, 68, 83, 110, 117
    devices, 59
    problems, 31, 32
    remedial, 118
    specialist, 130
Recreation programs, 48, 138
Regional synonyms, 80–81
Regression, 180, 181
Regular students and the retarded, 28
Rehabilitation programs in correctional institu-
    tions, 122–123. See also Vocational
    rehabilitation, state
Reinforcement, 26
    techniques, 121, 122
    See also Behavior modification
Remedial help in crisis rooms, 119
Remedial techniques and materials, 123
Repression, 184
Research, 131–132, 138
Residential placement, 65
Resource person, 133
    bilingual, 82, 83
    parent as, 139
Resource rooms, 5, 28, 36, 63, 126
Resource teachers, 48, 63, 132
Rest periods, 43, 46
Retrolental fibroplasia (RLF), 57
Rh factor, 49, 65
Right-left discrimination, 32

Right to education, 2–3, 65, 71, 138,
    139–140
Risley, T. R., 90
Robins, C., 110–111
Roe, W. H., 132
Role diffusion, 11
Role-playing, 185
Ronald Bruce Nipon Association, 28
Rosenthal, R., 74, 100
Rubella, 23, 49, 57, 65
Runaways, 116
Rural lifestyle, 97
Rural South, 77
Russia and education of children, 90

Safety instruction, 27, 55, 63–64
San Francisco, Chinese in, 78
San Francisco State University and working
    with the deaf-blind, 68
Sanday, Dr. Peggy, 99
Scandinavia, 89, 93
Scheduling, 133
Schilder, P., 180
Schizophrenia, 106
Scholarships, 20, 139
Scholl, G. T., 132, 133
School board, 128, 129
School district support for private education,
    35
School performance, 32, 33
School personnel, supervision and evaluation
    of, 133
School phobia, 108, 111
Schools. See Physical facilities
Schools, private. See Private special schools
Schwartz, L. L., 97
Science, 18
Scouting, 60
Seattle, technology for the multiply handi-
    capped in, 67
Selective attention, 31
Self-advancement, 97
Self-concept, 6, 7, 32, 51, 74, 79–80, 93,
    179–180
Self-consciousness, 41
Self-control, 8–9, 107
Self-esteem, 7–11, 93, 108, 187
Sensorimotor development, v, 59
Sensory impairments, 65
"Sesame Street," 26, 28
Sex education, 28, 30
Shaping, 82
Sheltered workshops, 24
Shoplifting, 115
Siblings of exceptional child, 135, 136–137
Sign language, 40, 52, 53, 54
Significance to others, 7, 8, 11, 117
Skinner, B. F., 26

Skipping, 18, 19
Smithsonian Institution, 20
Social relations, 19, 52, 59, 71, 72, 75, 79
Social skills, 17, 36, 55–56, 60, 117
Social studies, 27, 83
Social workers, 105, 110, 111, 121, 122, 129
Socialization, 26, 27, 91, 186
Socially maladjusted, the, 115–123
  self-esteem of, 11, 116, 117, 119
  and society, 105, 116, 117, 119–120
  special classes for, 117, 120–121
    instructional techniques in, 118–119,
     120–121
  structure of, 120
Socioeconomic class, 99
Socioeconomic mobility, 79
Spanish-Americans, 98
Spanish culture, 83–84
Spanish language, 81
Spatial orientation, 60, 63
Special education
  administration of, 126, 128–129, 130, 131,
    132–134
  classes, v–vi, 65, 110, 120
    acceptance of, 132–133
    integration of, 133–134
  defined, 2
  programs, 11, 132, 133, 139
  right to, 140
  schools, 5
Special education coordinator, responsibilities
  of, 129, 130, 131
  in instructional matters, 132, 133, 134
  in a line position, 126, 127, 128, 131, 132
  in a staff position, 126, 127, 128, 131, 132,
    134
  students and personnel, 128, 129, 131–133
Special education teachers, 5–6, 105, 139
  and coordination with regular classes, 63,
    132–133
  innovation and research efforts of, 128,
    131–132
  interaction with school personnel, 132–133,
    133–134
  personal qualities of, 21–22, 30, 48, 56,
    68, 85, 123
  and placement decision, 130
  preparation of, 3, 5–6, 17, 22, 37, 47–48,
    52, 56, 64, 68, 84–85, 103, 113–114,
    123
  selection and evaluation of, 126, 128–129
  selection of materials by, 132
  teaching conditions of, 2
Speech
  development of, 32, 58, 71, 72
  disorders, organic, 73, 75
  and the hearing impaired, 49, 50, 51, 52,
    53
  and the orthopedically handicapped, 66

Speech impaired, the, 3, 72–76
  emotional problems of, 73, 75
  instructional aids for, 75, 76
Speech impairment, 10, 71
  anxiety as a cause, 72, 74, 79
  types of, 72
Speech therapy, 71
  for the learning disabled, 35
  for the neglected child, 108
  preparation in, 56, 76
  in the professional team, 85, 129
  for the speech impaired, 73–75
Spina bifida, 41
Spontaneity in drama therapy, 185–186
*Standards for Educational and Psychological
  Tests* (1972), 131
Stanford-Binet intelligence test, Hayes version,
  58
State
  duty of to assess handicapped needs, 5
  education department requirements, 5–6.
    See also Name of state
  funds for special education, 3, 17
  laws on exceptional children, 2–3, 139,
    140
  schools, 3
  subsidies for private special schools, 35,
    139
  See also Vocational rehabilitation, state
Stimulation
  developmental, 42
  environmental, 35, 36, 89–90
  experiences, 90, 91, 92–93
  inadequate, 88
  sensory, 184
  See also Environmental deprivation
Street law, 52
Student
  performance, 100
  selection, 126, 130–131, 133, 137
  supervision, 133
  tutors, 82–83
Stuttering, 71, 72–73, 74, 79
Subcultures in the curriculum, 84
Sublimation, 184
Sullivan, H. S., 74
Superintendent of schools, 128, 129
Surgery, 73, 75
Sweden and education of children, 90
Swimming for the handicapped, 46

Tactual stimulation, 59
Talking Books, 60
Tape recorders, 46, 54, 59, 75
Teacher
  accountability, 128
  aides, 35
  attitudes and consciousness of, 15, 98,
    100–101, 103

Teacher (cont.)
  classroom, 129, 131—132
    regular, 28, 39, 132—133
  homeroom, 137
  importance of task, 6, 11, 119
  preparation of for mainstreaming, 4
  self-concept of, 21
  See also Special education teachers
Teacher Corps, 84
Teacher-to-pupil ratio, 35, 91, 113
Teaching. See Instructional techniques
Teaching, quality of in early levels, 34
Teaching English as a Second Language
    (TESL) programs, 84
Teams, professional, 111—112, 122
  and development of IEPs, 5, 129—130
  and the emotionally disturbed, 105,
    111—112
  identification of learning disabled, 31
  student selection and placement, 133
  teaching the language handicapped, 85
  working with the handicapped, 46, 47
Technical programs for the deaf, 51, 52. See
    also High school, technical
Telephone communication for the hearing
    impaired, 55
Telephones, public, 43, 45
Testing, 81
  educational, 5, 130—131
  psychological, 130—131
  See also Intelligence tests
Thalidomide, 65
Thinness, 41
Time-out room, 112—113, 121
Timidity, 107
Torrance, E. P., 16
Touch, learning by, 60
Toxemia of pregnancy, 23
Traditional preschool program, Illinois project,
    91—92
Trainable mentally retarded
  parents of, 24
  in the schools, 4, 24, 26, 27, 66, 130
  teenage, 27—28
Transportation, public, 43
Transportation, school, 42
Tremors, 41
Truancy, 116, 118

Trust vs. distrust, 8
Tuberculosis, 41
Tumors, 57
Turnbull, A. P., 137
Turnbull, H. R., 137
Typewriters, 46, 63

Unconscious, the, and art, 179
University Museum, University of Pennsyl-
    vania, 60
Unwed mothers, 116, 119, 120, 121
  education of, 89, 120, 121
Urban areas, 97
  and the language handicapped, 77, 84
Urban youth, teaching of, 23, 118—119
U.S. Office of Education (USOE), 2, 22, 39,
    65

Verbotonal method of speech, 53—54
Vietnamese adoptions, 140
Virtue, sense of, 7, 11
Vision impairment, symptoms and causes of,
    57
VISTA, 84
Visual
  cues, 52
  discrimination, 35
  perception difficulties, 31—32
Visually impaired, the, 3, 57—64. See also
    Blind; Partially sighted
Vocal disorders, 71, 73
Vocational rehabilitation, state, 39, 52
Vocational Rehabilitation Act (1973), 4—5, 40
Voice, use of, 74—75
Volunteers, training of, 60

Watts, Jean Carew, 90
Wechsler Preschool and Primary Scale of
    Intelligence (WPPSI), 78
Western Maryland College and teaching the
    deaf, 56
Wheelchair, elevating, 43, 45
White, B. L., 90
Wisconsin, University of, at Milwaukee,
    Infant Education Center, 89—90
Work-study programs, 28
Writing, teaching of, 52